Tempered Strength

Tempered Strength

Studies in the Nature and Scope of Prudential Leadership

Edited by
Ethan Fishman

LEXINGTON BOOKS
Lanham • Boulder • New York • Oxford

LEXINGTON BOOKS

Published in the United States of America
by Lexington Books
A Member of the Rowman & Littlefield Publishing Group
4720 Boston Way, Lanham, Maryland 20706

PO Box 317
Oxford
OX2 9RU, UK

British Library Cataloguing in Publication Information Available

Library of Congress Cataloging-in-Publication Data

Tempered strength : studies in the nature and scope of prudential leadership /
edited by Ethan Fishman.
   p. cm.
Includes index.
ISBN 0-7391-0402-0—ISBN 0-7391-0403-9
1. Leadership. 2. Prudence. I. Fishman, Ethan M.

BF637.L4 T43 2002
158'.4—dc21   2002004880

Printed in the United States of America

♾ᵀᴹ The paper used in this publication meets the minimum requirements of
American National Standard for Information Sciences—Permanence of Paper
for Printed Library Materials, ANSI/NISO Z39.48-1992.

Dedicated to the memory of John H. Hallowell (1913–1991)

Contents

Foreword

Francis Fukuyama

Of the many consequences of the terrorist attacks of September 11, 2001, on the United States, one positive one has been to underline some important truths: first, that politics is an art and not a science, and second, that leadership matters.

During the preceding Clinton boom years, the United States at times seemed to be on autopilot. Prosperous at home and secure abroad, leadership consisted of managing fiscal deficits and fine-tuning policies over which there was substantial partisan consensus. Bill Clinton's personal moral failings were condemned by many and marked by almost everyone, but a large number of Americans also felt that they did not matter to the health and welfare of the broader society. Judgment, constancy, moral purpose, a willingness to make difficult and often unpopular decisions—all of these may have been lacking in national leadership, but they were not sorely missed.

September 11 proved once again that politics is an art by being completely surprising and unprecedented. While specialists had warned about terrorism for years, no one had imagined that a group of people training in one of the most backward countries in the world could turn the emblems of modernity—skyscrapers and airliners—against the society that created them in such an effective way. All of the careful public policy calculations that had dominated the preceding period were now thrown out the window, with the realization that world politics had entered a new and more dangerous era. It was, moreover, an era that did not have many obvious historical models for statesmen to follow.

The attacks underlined the importance of leadership in obvious ways as well. To credibly stand up in front of the nation, condemn the attackers, and promise that the victims would be vindicated became a far more important job than any of the small, technical decisions that characterize routine policymaking. To understand the nature of the threat, mobilize the military, build a political coalition, protect the country, and all the while maintain political support at home quickly became a task of bewildering complexity, one requiring not just judgment and decisiveness, but also a sense of when to rely on oneself and when to delegate authority to others. We do not know at this writing whether America's present leadership will acquit itself well or poorly; but it is abundantly clear that the quality of that leadership will matter crucially to the nation and the world in the coming years.

It is in this context that the current volume on prudential leadership is important. As several of the authors point out, the older tradition of political science begun by Plato and Aristotle understood that a science could not admit of more precision than its underlying subject allowed. Unlike modern political science, which strives to replicate the accuracy and certainty of the natural sciences, classical political philosophy recognized that there were some issues that could not be codified into universal laws or optimized according to a mathematical algorithm. What was instead needed, as the present volume makes clear, was both leadership and moral vision, but also leadership that could exercise prudential judgment in balancing the underlying moral vision with what was possible or achievable in the real world of politics. In this realm there are no right or even clear answers. Yet we can see, by looking backwards in history (as this book does) at specific instances of leadership, the ways in which the exercise of prudential judgment has made all the difference to the fate of nations.

Tempered Strength provides us with a theoretical guide to the role of prudential leadership in the history of political philosophy, as well as practical guidance with regard to the exercise of such leadership (or at times, its lack) from ancient times to the present. The authors present a wide range of perspectives on leadership, and show how personal character, for better or worse, mattered to individual politicians from Frederick Douglass to Bill Clinton. Meditating on the nature and scope of prudential leadership as this volume does should be at the core of any serious study of politics in the future.

1

Introduction: What Is Prudential Leadership?

Ethan Fishman

Americans have endured a very low caliber of political leadership in recent decades. From Vietnam to Desert Storm we have been asked to fight and die in wars the purposes of which remain elusive to this day. We have witnessed a president who first was permitted to resign from office in order to avoid impeachment and then was pardoned to escape further prosecution. We have been taught that a healthy economy requires our national government to tax less and spend more. We have seen another chief executive lie under oath, barely survive the impeachment process, and abscond with the White House silverware. We have participated in a botched presidential election. And here in Alabama we have watched a succession of governors preside over the dismantlement of a public school system that stood on pretty shaky ground to begin with.

Compounding the problem is an apparent tendency on the part of many Americans to accept out of frustration a radical dumbing down of their political expectations. It will be recalled that, in the depths of Monicagate and the Starr investigation, Bill Clinton was able to receive close to a 70 percent public approval rating. Is there a realistic antidote available to our present-day cynical attitude toward politics? The authors whose essays are included in this volume answer with a resounding "Yes!" We find in the philosophy of *phronesis* or prudence, developed over the last two and a half millenia by several great Western thinkers including Aristotle, St. Thomas Aquinas, and Edmund Burke, the alternative standard of leadership for which

Americans may be searching. We are attracted to this prudential alternative precisely because it is home grown—that is, indigenous to Western culture—and because, in seeking to avoid the extremes of moral cynicism and idealism, it establishes a balanced standard that is both reasonable in nature and practical in scope.

What is prudential leadership?[1] In the third century B.C. Aristotle examined the traits of successful political leaders and determined that their achievements were based primarily on the exercise of *phronesis*, the term he coined to describe a leader's ability to "calculate well for the attainment of a particular end of a fine sort,"[2] i.e., translating morally preferable ideals into politically feasible policies. The model for Aristotle's *phronimos* or prudent leader is Pericles, the great Athenian lawgiver. Pericles, Aristotle writes, possessed "the power of seeing what is good for [himself] and for humanity."[3]

Aristotle observes that political leaders such as Pericles retain certain distinctive characteristics that permit them to reconcile moral principles with the practice of politics without jeopardizing the integrity of their ideals. According to Aristotle, these characteristics include: the desire to articulate and support noble ideals that serve the public interest by calling upon society to treat all of its citizens with fairness, decency, and justice; the capacity to delineate a particular society's public interest by envisioning its present needs in the context of both its past successes and failures and future hopes and fears; the talent to propose laws and policies that accurately reflect their vision while dealing effectively with existing political issues; and the skill to devise methods to overcome obstacles to the realization of proposed reforms that are consistent with their ends.

At the heart of Aristotle's theory of prudent leadership lie certain assumptions about reality and human nature. Aristotle assumes that reality consists primarily of transcendent immaterial ideals and, to a lesser extent, of transitory representations of these ideals. He also believes that humans are qualitatively different from other beings. "It is the peculiarity of man, in comparison with the rest of the animal world," Aristotle writes, "that he alone possesses a perception of good and evil, of the just and unjust, and of other similar qualities."[4] For Aristotle, therefore, human existence represents a dramatic struggle between our immortal souls, which inspire us to nobility, and our bodily instincts that conspire for instant gratification of selfish aims.

If Aristotle grants us the capacity for moral choice, he must allow for the possibility of immoral behavior. His view of human nature, in other words, takes seriously both our capacity for justice and potential for evil. Reinhold Niebuhr neatly captures that view when he locates the human condition as "standing in the paradoxical situation of freedom and finiteness."[5] Like Niebuhr, Aristotle believes each time we congratulate ourselves for a job well done and come to the conclusion that we are essentially good, we fall prey to the sin of pride. Each time we question our motives and consider ourselves to be essentially evil, our ability to reach such a judgment "would seem to negate [its] context."[6]

Indeed, it is because Aristotle entertains no illusions about the ability of the flesh to undermine even the most basic standards of decency that he stresses the importance of ideals in his views of reality and human nature as well as in his theory of prudence. As imperfect creatures, he teaches, we must strive for moral perfection through rational control of our animal passions if we want to gain at least some measure of justice and fulfillment in our lives. "Rather ought we," he writes, "so far as in us lies, to put on immortality and to live in conformity with the highest thing within us."[7]

Consistent with these views Aristotle develops a definition of political justice that relies upon a reconciliation of individual rights, "doing what one likes" as he writes,[8] with moral responsibility, choosing to follow the universal laws of common decency. On the one hand, Aristotle maintains, citizens must be permitted to enjoy enough autonomy to exercise the gift of free will that makes us human. At the same time, citizens must be held accountable for the effects their freely willed choices have on others. When citizens are denied sufficient autonomy, he concludes, a society is created that is inhospitable to human beings. When freedom outweighs responsiblity, political justice begins to disintegrate and becomes replaced by what Aristotle depicts as "licentiousness."[9]

Aristotle explains the rationale for his theory of prudence in Book VI of his *Nicomachean Ethics*. There he distinguishes between the theoretical and practical forms of reason and the intellectual and moral virtues or talents that each form of reason employs. Theoretical reason and the intellectual talents, he argues, apply to such subjects as metaphysics and mathematics that are learned in abstract for their own sake and yield universal truths that humans cannot alter.

Practical reason and the moral talents, on the other hand, apply to subjects such as ethics and politics that yield truths which hold true in only a majority of cases and involve knowledge of the noblest human motives for the sake of noble action. The task of practical reason and the moral talents, according to Aristotle, is to take the first principles discovered by the intellect and integrate them with life experiences.

During the course of his analysis Aristotle sees fit to compare the theoretical reason of two of his contemporaries, Thales and Anaxagoras, to the prudence of Pericles. While admitting that Thales and Anaxagoras are "deep" and "exceptional" thinkers, Aristotle argues that their thought "lacks common sense" and "is useless" for politics because "it is not the good of humanity that they explore." Since, to Aristotle, the primary purpose of prudence is to "concern itself with human affairs," he describes it as the architectonic moral talent that takes precedence over all others.[10] As Ronald Beiner explains:

> *Phronesis* is not one virtue among others, but is the master virtue that encompasses and orders the various individual virtues. Virtue is the exercise of ethical knowledge as elicited by particular situations of action, and to act on the basis of this knowedge as a matter of course is to possess *phronesis*. Without *phronesis* one cannot properly be said to possess any of the virtues, and to possess *phronesis* is, conversely, to possess all the virtues, for *phronesis* is knowledge of which virtue is appropriate in particular circumstances, and the ability to act on that knowledge. *Phronesis* is a comprehensive moral capacity because it involves seeing particular situations in their true light in interaction with a general grasp of what it is to be a complete human being, and to live a proper human life.[11]

For Aristotle, consequently, the unique value of prudence for politics is its ability to explain how to realize abstract ends through concrete means available to human beings so that we may do the right thing to the right person at the right time "for the right motive and in the right way."[12] In order to meet the standards of prudence, he argues, political leaders are required to do their very best to create policies that prevent the subversion of moral ideals even under the direst circumstances. Prudent leaders aim high but accept less when their efforts inevitably fall short of the mark. They never give up hope for a better world even as they respect the obstacles to such hope. They expect, in sum, neither too much nor too little from the politics they practice.

For these reasons, the prudent political leaders Aristotle describes are neither cultural relativists nor ideologues. Since his theory of prudence posits the existence of universal ideals, it repudiates claims made by relativists that all values are culturally biased. Since the function of prudence is to reconcile transitory political issues with transcendent political standards, moreover, it rejects ideological thinking for advancing one doctrinaire solution such as socialism, capitalism, or feminism to every problem regardless of the circumstances. From the perspective of Aristotle's theory of prudence, indeed, relativists, who discount forever, and ideologues, who neglect today, appear to have engineered simplified, one-dimensional versions of politics based on reductionist views of reality and human nature.

What also differentiates prudent leaders from cultural relativists and ideologues is their attempt to apply to politics the same balance between the intangible and the tangible that they perceive in the universe. Prudent political leaders thus stress the immutable and the transcendent, but not to the exclusion of the imminent and the transitory. They accent forever but still pay close attention to today. They look first to the universal but are not blind to particulars. They stress the forest but do not neglect the trees. They view human behavior with a compassion that does not preclude toughness. And they are not prepared to excuse human pettiness even as they understand its underlying source.

In their effort to reconcile material circumstances with universal ideals, prudent leaders are first obliged to determine what specific ideals should be applied to what specific situations. "Since, in practical life, there are always multiple ends to pursue [e.g., security and freedom, inclusiveness and excellence, etc.]," Richard Ruderman explains, "*phronesis* should determine, at any given time, which end to pursue [in light of the resources, not the least the moral resources, required to pursue it]." For Ruderman, therefore, "the beginning of prudence is the recognition that conflict [of principle as well as interest] is a permanent part of political life."[13]

The methods prudent leaders can utilize to best serve the public interest of a given society at any given time are clarified by Aristotle's discussion of plutocratic regimes in Book V of his *Politics*. He is unable to justify rule of the rich because he realizes that the ability to govern well is not directly related to the acquisition of material possessions. He nevertheless recognizes that knowledge of plutocracy's inherent unreasonableness alone is inadequate to reform well-established plutocratic states. He thus devises a strategy, exploiting the greed underlying all plutocracies, to convince plutocrats that the preservation of their rule requires them to share power with those poorer citizens who, unlike themselves, possess genuine political leadership capabilities. In this fashion Aristotle combines his theory of good government, that citizens should perform tasks for which they are best suited, with the practice of unjust regimes and mediates the political realities of selfishness and incompetence with his values of justice and reason.

A common misconception about prudence is that it represents a type of cunning. Cunning implies great skill in discovering the most efficient way to achieve an end whose morality is never seriously questioned. Even Nazi SS men can be cunning. Prudent political leaders, however, cannot divorce themselves from moral principles. They must dedicate themselves to serve the public interest and are required to choose means that are commensurate with that goal. Otherwise, as W. D. Ross observes, their behavior becomes "mere clever roguery."[14]

Of course, Aristotle does not prohibit political leaders from having recourse to clever schemes and ploys as long as their use abides by scrupulous guidelines. At Aristotle's insistence: they must be a means of last resort; they must serve just ends; and leaders must never become smug or complacent about employing them. Under these circumstances, and within these strict parameters, schemes and ploys in the hands of prudent leaders represent examples of tempered strength or what Niebuhr refers to as "love and power in tension."[15]

Nor is prudence the equivalent of compromise. When political leaders act prudently, they are able to reconcile immutable abstract ideals with variable concrete circumstances. But while these reconciliations bear some resemblance to compromise, they are made for the express purpose of serving a higher end, namely the public interest, not for the sake of compromise itself. As Eugene Garver points out, "prudence is not simply the middle ground between two extremes."[16]

Since, to Aristotle, politics is characterized by freely willed decisions and constantly changing circumstances, it can never be an exact science. While he teaches that the goal of *phronesis* is to discover the mean between policy extremes, consequently, Aristotle also counsels that attempts by leaders to pinpoint the precise location of the mean will always be futile because it asks more of politics than it can possibly "admit."[17] As Walter Lippmann observes: "We must not think of the mean as being a fixed point between the extremes. When we do that, we are allowing ourselves to suppose that the mean is the point at which a kind of bargain is struck between 50 per cent of excess and 50 per cent of deficiency. But that is not the true mean. Courage is not half cowardice and half rashness. Temperance is not half self-indulgence and complete abstinence. The true mean is at the tension of push and pull, of attraction and resistance among the extremes."[18]

According to Francis Canavan, prudent leaders consider ideals to be necessary but insufficient for politics.[19] They judge ideals to be necessary because they provide infallible standards of justice towards which fallible human beings who tend to be unjust can strive. They judge ideals to be insufficient because ideals are unable to adjust themselves to the constantly changing complex demands and challenges of everyday life. From this perspective, prudent leaders emerge as authentic realists in their quest to reconcile the theory and practice of politics, abstract ideals with concrete situations, the productive and destructive impulses of human beings, the present with the past and future, facts and values, and rights with responsibilities.

Aristotle furthermore upholds personal moral character as a prerequisite for political prudence. Human beings, he argues, cannot be expected to provide prudent leadership, that is, virtuous leadership, unless they are already virtuous themselves. "Virtuous actions are not done in a virtuous—a just or temperate—way merely because *they* have the appropriate quality," he writes. "The *doer* must be in a certain frame of mind when he does them."[20] Since Aristotle is quite aware of human pride, greed, and selfishness, however, he cannot require prudent leaders to be wholly without sin—only that they honestly strive to act with as much common decency as possible. The standard of virtue by which he evaluates leaders, consequently, applies to lifetime behavior patterns, not to isolated acts of human weakness that may have been performed while in or out of office.

As Joseph Dunne observes, "Aristotelian *phronesis*, more than simply directing us to the love of good action, is already the fruit of a life devoted to the love of good action."[21] Given the recent controversies involving presidential politics in the United States, this may very well be Aristotle's most controversial position on leadership. To former President Clinton as well as to many Americans, personal

moral character has nothing whatsoever to do with political per-
formance. To Aristotle, however, it is possible to be virtuous and fail
as a political leader, but impossible to succeed at political leadership
without the type of personal virtue to which people become habituated over the course of their lives. He writes:

> If a man possesses the two qualifications of capacity and loyalty to the
> consitution, is there any need for him to have the third qualification of
> goodness, and will not the first two, by themselves, secure the public
> interest? We may answer this question by asking another. May not men
> who possess these first two qualifications be unable to command their
> passions? And is it not true that men who have no command of their
> passions will fail to serve their own interest—even though they possess
> self-knowledge and self-loyalty—and will equally fail to serve the pub-
> lic interest (even though they possess a knowledge of public affairs and
> public loyalty)?[22]

An Aristotelian *phronimos*, or expert practitioner of political prudence, is a member of that group of persons Aristotle classifies as
"great-souled men" for whom personal virtue "is a *sine qua non*."[23] For
Aristotle personal virtue is defined as the ability to practice moderation
in the fulfillment of our animal passions by not losing sight of the higher
human purposes the passions are intended to serve; that is, by not permitting them to become ends in themselves. "The man who is passion's
slave" is immoderate and thus unjust, he writes.[24] Aristotle clearly is not
a prude. He teaches that the food we consume might as well be deli-
cious as long as we remember that we eat to live, not live to eat. The
sex we have should be exciting as long as we understand that sexual
relations are an intimate expression of love, not a cheap form of pleasure. Similarly, the quest for political power can be commendable as
long as we use power primarily to serve others, not only ourselves.

Because prudence involves the most precarious of political skills,
the ability to convert morally preferable ideals into politically feasible
policies, there is a significant element of uncertainty in its achievement. According to James Bill, "the practice of prudence is often fragile and fleeting. No statesman practices it to perfection. All leaders
have weaknesses and make mistakes. They can easily lose sight of
their moral goals; moral vision can slip into moralism and polemi-
cism; the means can become ends in themselves; and the temptation
to vanity is ever present. The statesman's knowledge and under-

standing may be imbalanced and imperfect and, if unwilling to admit this, the leader may not recruit the necessary expertise."[25]

Bill here refers to internal factors that mitigate against practicing prudence successfully. But there are external impediments as well, including some very powerful groups with selfish interests they long to satisfy and enormously intricate national and international forces that may or may not be amenable to change. "The certitude of prudence," St. Thomas Aquinas notes, "cannot be so great as completely to remove all anxiety."[26] Because of these obstacles, Aristotle concludes that there is an element of what Martha Nussbaum identifies as "moral luck" inherent in *phronesis*.[27]

Aristotle's conclusion that prudence is not a purely intellectual activity leads him to observe that harnessing "moral luck" in the service of the public interest also requires of leaders a complex blend of practical experience in government and what Ronald Beiner refers to in Chapter 7 as a "knack" for political judgment. Of course by this standard Aristotle himself probably would have been an imprudent leader. "Just because a philosopher can tell us the *conditions* for *phronesis* does not mean that we should expect the philosopher also to *exercise phronesis*," Beiner writes. "Theorists who devote their life to reflecting on what is *general* are notoriously unreliable when it comes to apprehending *particulars*, which is precisely the skill or aptitude that we associate with practical wisdom. Judgment, as opposed to the application of 'principles' or 'theories,' is a 'knack,' inextricably bound to the concrete particulars that are pledged."

Aristotle thus cannot guarantee that any combination of realistic values and rational planning always will result in prudent policies. As he well knew, even Pericles ultimately was defeated by conditions and events beyond his control. Having decided in favor of a defensive strategy instead of a direct attack against the superior Spartan army that was besieging Athens during the Peloponnesian War in 429 B.C., Pericles nevertheless was unable to combat a deadly plague that engulfed the city and killed a third of its inhabitants, including Pericles himself. On the basis of Pericles' own experiences, Aristotle cautions leaders that those who hold public office have a responsibility to serve the public interest that is neither excused nor relieved when their best efforts come to naught.

A note of caution: the concept of prudence seems to have undergone a radical redefinition in recent American parlance. In contrast to the dynamic, visionary quality of classical *phronesis*, today prudence is frequently used to signify "caution, a special regard for one's personal interests, and a pragmatic approach to life."[28] This tendency to confuse *phronesis* with the rather passive defense of moral principles found in what Aristotle means by *prudentia* or pragmatism was illustrated during the presidency of George Bush, Sr. While in office Bush habitually borrowed the phrase "Wouldn't be prudent!" to justify policies that often did little more than employ the trimmer's practice of "splitting the difference" between competing points of view.[29] As Francis Fukuyama notes in his Foreward, it remains to be seen whether the current occupant of the Oval Office will adopt his father's penchant for pragmatic presidential leadership.

Scholars such as Harvey Mansfield Jr. trace this new way of thinking about prudence back to the political thought of Niccolo Machiavelli in the sixteenth century A.D. Mansfield points out that Aristotelian prudence enables leaders to utilize reason, cunning, cleverness, and a sense of common decency to combine "private interest with the common good by governing the virtues for the sake of both."[30] According to Mansfield, however, "Machiavelli's prudence is nothing but cunning, and his principality or republic (each of which is a mixture of both), when prudently understood, inspires its princes or citizens to abandon all loyalties impartially, save the one to themselves."[31] By Mansfield's estimation, it is Machiavellian prudence, in a toned-down version domesticated for use in American politics by Thomas Hobbes, John Locke, and Charles de Montesquieu, that has been systematized in the United States.

What, then, is prudential leadership, as the term was originally conceived by Aristotle almost 2500 years ago? Erwin Hargrove observes that it is the rare capacity to "keep in mind not only the absolute best, but the best in the historical context."[32] Norman Dahl describes it as "the virtue of reason in its practical employment."[33] Harry Jaffa characterizes it as a leadership strategy meant to "guide political men, who need to know what is right here and now, but to guide them in the light of what is just everywhere and always."[34] To St. Thomas Aquinas, it attempts to see that "the highest things come alive in human action."[35] To Edmund Burke, it enables leaders to operate on the one plane that politics will admit: "on the more or less, the earlier or the later, and on a balance of advantage and inconvenience, of good and evil."[36] For Michael Oakeshott, it is the recognition of "what action permitted by (a leader's moral beliefs) should, in the circumstances, be performed."[37] In Aristotle's own words, prudence "makes good shots at some attainable advantage."[38]

The following essays develop these themes. Section I studies the evolution of the theory of *phronesis* in the history of Western political philosophy. Gary D. Glenn discovers in Xenophon's studies of Socrates and Cyrus a fascinating treatise on the meaning of prudence that requires leaders to: resist the temptation common to philosophers of relying exclusively on abstract ideas; abandon the desire for gaining absolute certainty about the future; question the assertion that the philosophic life is undeniably superior to the life of politics; and practice self-control and moderation in the consideration of complex issues. On the basis of his analysis of the ontology, ethics, and politics of St. Thomas Aquinas, and over the objections of scholars such as Leo Strauss, Kenneth L. Deutsch finds Christianity's teachings on humility to be quite consistent with classical Greek and Roman principles of prudent and magnanimous statesmanship. Peter J. Stanlis expands on the thesis he proposed in 1958 with his influential *Edmund Burke and the Natural Law* that many modern commentators have misinterpreted Burke's conception of political prudence by equating Burkean prudence with utilitarian expediency and disconnecting it completely from normative ideals.

Carnes Lord observes that when contemporary Western democracies suffer political failure, it frequently is due to their inability to provide leaders with an appreciation of the intellectual components of Aristotelian political science with its emphasis on *phronesis* or practical judgment. According to Lord, we seem to have traded in the complicated balancing act associated with prudential leadership for a one dimensional form of legalism in which it is expected that political issues can be resolved by simply referring to certain articles and sections of the law. In the "Postscript" to his critically acclaimed 1983 volume, *Political Judgment*, Ronald Beiner draws upon Aristotelian and Kantian sources to argue that the vitality of democratic societies depends upon a comprehension of political prudence by leaders as well as by the voters who elect them. Since Beiner agrees with Lord that contemporary Western culture is neglecting to teach the value of prudence to either of these groups, he is concerned about the future of democracy.

Section II demonstrates how the theory of *phronesis* can be applied to practical political issues. Richard S. Ruderman employs the inspiring life story of Frederick Douglass to help make the point that a realistic view of human nature and an insistence on personal responsibility in freedom are crucial elements in the formulation of prudent political judgments. Joseph R. Fornieri interprets the leadership role Abraham Lincoln played in authorizing the Emancipation Proclamation as a model of prudential decision-making. He identifies Lincoln's purposes as a prudent alternative to the Civil War Democrats, who felt the Proclamation went too far in defending equality and black freedom, and the Radical Republicans, who felt it didn't go far enough. Wynne Walker Moskop assesses the puzzling political career of Bill Clinton and finds that the serious problems Clinton experienced as president are directly attributable to his inability to reconcile the philosophical ideals and technical information that comprise Aristotelian prudence. Finally, George Anastaplo explains why he considers the U.S. Supreme Court's decision in the 2000 presidential election controversy to be an imprudent one and why he feels that, under those extraordinary circumstances, the most prudent solution to the ballot counting problem in Florida would have been to draw lots for the winner.

In the course of completing this volume, international terrorists violently attacked the United States, destroyed the World Trade Center in New York City as well as portions of the Pentagon in Washington, D.C., and murdered an estimated 4,000 innocent victims. These cowardly acts underscore the fact that the increasing globilization of politics will continue to place unprecedented strains on American government. Twenty-first century technological developments in weaponry, transportation, and communication will require our leaders to confront, often at lightning fast speeds, very dangerous enemies and baffling policy questions with frightful implications for our country and the world. Is it possible that a 2,500-year-old strategy can deal more effectively with these never before known pressures than the pragmatic "split the difference" style that currently masquerades for prudential leadership in the United States? Our purpose is to persuade readers that *phronesis* involves the very skills leaders will require to get the job done.

This volume is dedicated to the memory of my academic mentor on the subject of *phronesis*, John H. Hallowell. Professor Hallowell was a legendary teacher, a distinguished scholar, and a loyal friend. I also am grateful to my colleague, Sam Fisher, for his gracious intellectual and technical support of my research.

NOTES

1. Portions of this introduction have previously appeared in *The Prudential Presidency: An Aristotelian Approach to Presidential Leadership*, by Ethan Fishman, published by Praeger in 2001. Copyright © 2001 by Praeger. Reprinted by permission.

2. Aristotle, *The Ethics*, trans. J. A. K. Thomson (Baltimore: Penguin Books, 1966), 176.

3. Aristotle, *The Ethics*, 177.

4. Aristotle, *The Politics*, trans. Ernest Barker (New York: Oxford University Press, 1962), 6.

5. Reinhold Niebuhr, *The Nature and Destiny of Man*, vol. 1 (New York: Charles Scribner's Sons, 1941), 192.

6. Niebuhr, *The Nature and Destiny of Man*, 2.

7. Aristotle, *The Ethics*, 305.

8. Aristotle, *The Politics*, 234.

9. Aristotle, *The Politics*, 233.

10. Aristotle, *The Ethics*, 180.

11. Ronald Beiner, *Political Judgment* (London: Methuen, 1983), 73. All emphases in this Introduction are the author's own.

12. Aristotle, *The Ethics*, 65.

13. Richard Ruderman, "Aristotle and the Recovery of Political Judgment," *American Political Science Review* 91, no. 2 (1997): 416.

14. W. D. Ross, *Aristotle* (New York: Meridian Books, 1960), 214.

15. Kenneth Thompson, "The Political Philosophy of Reinhold Niebuhr," in *Reinhold Niebuhr: His Religious, Social, and Political Thought*, ed. Charles Kegley and Robert Bretall (New York: Macmillan, 1956), 169.

16. Eugene Garver, *Machiavelli and the History of Prudence* (Madison: University of Wisconsin Press, 1987), 19.

17. Aristotle, *The Ethics*, 28.

18. Walter Lippmann, *The Public Philosophy* (New York: New American Library, 1963), 112–13.

19. Francis Canavan, *The Political Ideas of Edmund Burke* (Durham, N.C.: Duke University Press, 1960), 25.

20. Aristotle, *The Ethics*, 61.

21. Joseph Dunne, *Back to the Rough Ground: 'Phronesis' and 'Techne' in Modern Philosophy and in Aristotle* (Notre Dame: University of Notre Dame Press, 1993), 310.

22. Aristotle, *The Politics*, 231.

23. Aristotle, *The Ethics*, 123.

24. Aristotle, *The Ethics*, 310.

25. James Bill, *George Ball: Behind the Scenes in U.S. Foreign Policy* (New Haven: Yale University Press, 1997), 228.

26. Aquinas quoted in Josef Pieper, *The Four Cardinal Virtues* (New York: Harcourt, Brace and World, 1959), 18.

27. Martha Nussbaum, *The Fragility of Goodness: Luck and Ethics in Greek Tragedy and Philosophy* (Cambridge: Cambridge University Press, 1994), xiv.

28. Bill, *George Ball*, 203.

29. Louis Koenig, *The Chief Executive* (New York: Harcourt, Brace, 1996), 298. As Kenneth L. Deutsch will explain in chapter 3, there also is a Latin term *prudentia* that Aquinas uses to mean prudence and is synonymous with *phronesis*. But the ancient Greek term *prudentia* is closer to what contemporary Americans mean by pragmatism because of its deemphasis on moral principles.

30. Harvey Mansfield Jr., *Taming the Prince* (Baltimore: Johns Hopkins University Press, 1993), 209.

31. Mansfield, *Taming the Prince*, 280.

32. Erwin Hargrove, *The President as Leader: Appealing to the Better Angels of Our Nature* (Lawrence: University Press of Kansas, 1998), 7.

33. Norman Dahl, *Practical Reason, Aristotle and the Weakness of the Will* (Minneapolis: University of Minnesota Press, 1984), 107.

34. Harry Jaffa, *Crisis of the House Divided* (Chicago: University of Chicago Press, 1982), 1.

35. Clarke Cochran, "Aquinas, Prudence and Health Care Policy," in *Public Policy and the Public Good*, ed. Ethan Fishman (Westport, Conn.: Greenwood Press, 1991), 52.

36. Burke quoted in Canavan, *The Political Ideas of Edmund Burke*, 14.

37. Michael Oakeshott, "Learning and Teaching," in *The Concept of Education*, ed. R. S. Peters (London: Routledge and Kegan Paul, 1967), 168.

38. Aristotle, *The Ethics*, 66.

I

THE NATURE OF PRUDENCE

2

Prudence in Xenophon's *Memorabilia* and *Cyropaedia*

Gary D. Glenn

INTRODUCTION: PRUDENCE AND CERTAINTY

When attempting to learn what prudence is, as Xenophon under-stands it in these two books, we encounter two difficulties. First, early in *Memorabilia* Book 1 he implicitly admits that Socrates imprudently taught Critias and Alcibiades dialectic before he taught them modera-tion (1.2.17). Yet in the last paragraph of *Memorabilia*, when Xenophon sums up Socrates' virtues, one of them is said to be that he was "so prudent as not to make mistakes in deciding what was better and worse" (4.8.11).[1] What are we to make of this? Perhaps Socrates' seeming imprudence in teaching these future tyrants can be defended on his ground that to know with certainty is beyond human prudence so one must consult the gods.[2] Since part of prudence is knowing that one cannot know the future with certainty, Socrates could not have known with certainty that they would become tyrants. However, Socrates did not consult the gods before teaching Critias and Alcibi-ades.

Secondly, this partial severing of prudence from certainty about fu-ture consequences might also excuse Cyrus from responsibility for both needlessly overthrowing the old, reasonably decent and stable Persian regime and then for failing to do the most obvious thing nec-essary to preserve the resulting empire after his death, namely prop-erly educating his sons to be the future rulers. In order to understand Xenophon's teaching on prudence, we need to know whether the

Socrates of *Memorabilia*, and Cyrus, either teach or exemplify prudence or whether the books rather than the principal figures do so.

Prudence is mentioned explicitly both near the beginning and at the end of *Memorabilia*. It is first mentioned explicitly at 1.2.10. There Xenophon in his own name says it is something in which one must "train" oneself. Those who thus acquire it thereby become "competent to teach the citizens what is advantageous" in a way that makes them "least likely to become violent." Prudence here utilizes "persuasion" to foster "friendship" in contradistinction to "violence" which fosters "hatred." What is advantageous is presumably an object of prudence rather than of *theoria* because the advantageous belongs to "things whose outcomes were not clear" as distinguished from "necessary things" to which logic (in its mode) and theory (in its object) presumably belong (1.1.6).[3] This is supported by the fact that *theoria* occurs only once in *Memorabilia* (4.8.2) whereas *phronesis* occurs eleven times and *phronemos* twelve times. *Memorabilia* would seem to be more about what is the advantageous than about what is the good or the true.

Prudence is last mentioned in *Memorabilia's* last paragraph. Xenophon concludes Socrates was "so prudent as not to make mistakes in deciding what was better and worse, nor to need another in addition, but to be self-sufficient in his judgment of these matters." In addition, and apparently as part of his prudence, he was "competent also to say and to define such things in speech; . . . to test others and to refute them when they made mistakes, and to turn them toward virtue and gentlemanliness (nobility and goodness)" (4.8.11).

But again at the beginning Xenophon says: "He advised [his friends] regarding the necessary things that they also act as he held best. But concerning things whose outcomes were not clear, he sent them to seek divination about whether they should be done" (1.1.6). Prudence is necessary in order to distinguish acting better from acting worse; but part of prudence is knowing that merely human knowledge is insufficient for knowing the outcomes of some kinds of things. These outcomes are known only to the gods.

That unclear outcomes belong to a class distinct from "necessary things" seems to mean that such outcomes, while foreseeable to some extent, are not humanly foreseeable to the extent of certainty, presumably because there might exist circumstances that no human wisdom could foresee. In that sense we are unable to know what will come to pass as a result of our actions although we are somehow able to know what we cannot know. This knowledge of the limits of what human knowing seems to be is part of prudence. But it also seems to be part of prudence to know what is "necessary" in order to act "better" rather than "worse" in the circumstances in which we have to act, even though we lack certain knowledge of the outcome. "Better" and "worse" are independent of the certainty of their outcomes, as far as their prudence is concerned.

But how is it possible to know how to do the right thing in the circumstances without some knowledge of the future? Can we live according to reason understood as the capacity for forethought, without assuming we can somehow (however uncertainly) know what will come to pass tomorrow? Presumably not. But the prudent man knows from experience how easy it is to be mistaken about what tomorrow will bring. Prudence is necessary as a corrective to these short-term expectations.

Prudence would seem to be a kind of capacity for forethought. Forethought enables us to be "moderate rather than rash" and is the opposite of "senseless and reckless" (1.4.9). Forethought sends us to the dentist, even at the cost of some pain, because it tells us that this present pain will be good for us "in the long run." If we lacked such forethought, our desires would incline us to seek present pleasures and avoid present pains because desires simply seek pleasure and avoid pain. Forethought enables us to act so that future outcomes are desirable. But prudence knows that it cannot guarantee future outcomes. Prudence cannot know with certainty whether there will be a "long run" for us. In that sense, we know that we cannot know the future. In that way prudence participates in the limits of knowing. But it is prudence that enables us to know that, if there is to be a long run for us, it is prudent to accept present dental pain for the sake of a better future. In that way, prudence is a kind of knowledge of what is necessary for a better life and thus participates in certainty. Prudence thus is in-between the certain and the uncertain.

In particular, our bodies cannot distinguish the good pain, which enhances future health, from the bad pain, which does not. That distinction is made by reason acting on memory. That memory may be either our own or that of other witnesses whom we regard as reliable. Prudence assumes that bodily health is advantageous on the basis of trusting those memories. But it does not know that such bodily health will be advantageous under all possible future circumstances, as Socrates shows Euthydemus (4.2.26–32).

Remembering past circumstances in which an apparent advantage was not a real advantage does at least two things. First, it reveals the limitations of prudence understood as mere memory. An adequate prudence requires reflection of a certain kind on the memory. Reflection on the memory of when what is advantageous in general turned out not to be in particular circumstances shows the insufficiency of mere memory, however firmly and reliably held, for sustaining a way of life against certain kinds of threats. Thus Burke, modernity's most explicit defender of a kind of prudence, which reminds of Xenophon: "From this source, history, much political wisdom can be leaned, that is may be learned as habit, not as precept."[4] Burke implies that mere historical memory cannot instruct about the exceptional or unprecedented cases. Hence, it cannot guide us either in anticipating or handling them well. In particular, it cannot alert the guardians of the city's memory to the coming into being of such situations. Again Burke: "Prudence in new cases can do nothing on grounds of retrospect."[5] But prudence, as distinguished from mere historical memory, can perhaps enable us to recognize the new situation as unprecedented.

PRUDENCE IN THE *CYROPAEDIA*

The *Cyropaedia* presents the young man Cyrus as such an unprecedented situation for Persia. Cyrus began his undermining and overthrow of the ancestral Persian regime the first time he addressed his army by saying that he could not understand what their ancestors (as well as implicitly they themselves) gained from their traditional, arduous self-discipline of the body and its desires (1.5.8ff). Nor could his listeners answer at the time thereby revealing the *telos* of the old regime to be unintelligible to them. An answer would have required a philosopher or a philosophical statesman (like a Burke). Long after it was too late to be of use to the Persians, an answer is suggested in *Cyropaedia* by the philosophical historian Xenophon. But that answer is never stated explicitly. Explicitly, *Cyropaedia* is the "history" of the enormous advantages to the Persians and their neighbors that resulted from the Persian peers abandoning their traditional "virtue for its own sake" for Cyrus's new "virtue for the sake of gain." Only in the last chapter of the last book, with the collapse of the new Persian empire after Cyrus's death, does it becomes evident to the discerning reader[6] what has been lost by the peers not knowing what their traditional discipline had gained for them. It enabled them to preserve their traditional way of life.[7]

Can a traditional way of life be defended against attack of an unprecedented kind? An entirely novel threat is, by definition, a threat for which no adequate defense is found in mere ancestral memory. However, there may be material in the ancestral memory from which a prudent guardian could fashion a defense. That would be akin to what Burke did, or tried to do, in mining the British Constitution. From that mining, Burke produced "prescription" to defend the ancestral British way of life—including the Constitution's prudence—against the French Revolution's novel attack of philosophic origin[8] on both that way of life and that prudence. Prudence understood as mere experience, mere historical memory, almost certainly cannot defend a traditional way of life against philosophic attack.

But "almost certainly cannot" is at best a prudent judgment, not a theoretical truth. "Almost" means it might have been possible to defend a merely traditional way of life against Cyrus's unprecedented attack. Such a defense would have required there to be someone in Persia whose wisdom was broader and deeper than the merely traditional. That someone would have understood that the traditional discipline supported the traditional simple, spartan, non-imperial, way of life and who could therefore foresee the undermining of that "way" by Cyrus's transformation of traditional virtue into mercenary virtue.[9] Defense of the traditional Persian regime would have required the presence in Persia of philosophy in some form, whether a Socrates or a Burke. But there was neither. Xenophon comes along after Cyrus's reforms have worked their way through the regime, too late to preserve the old regime. At most he could instruct the philosophers of the future.

Xenophon records that there had once been such a wise man in Persia. This comes to light in a conversation between Cyrus and his father while on their way to the Medean border as Cyrus goes to lead a Persian army to defend their Medean allies against Assyria. During that conversation, Cyrus's father instructs him in a "Machiavellian" way, namely, that "it was right to deceive friends even, provided it were for a good end, and to steal the possessions of a friend for a good purpose" (1.6.32). Cyrus recognizes that this violates the traditional Persian notions of right which he had been taught in the "schools of justice." "Why were we not taught these things before?" Cyrus asks, in puzzlement and/or indignation. His father answers that there was once a "teacher of the boys" who taught justice "in the very way" Cyrus now asks for. However, this teaching had turned out to be too dangerous in that the boys used it "to take unfair advantage of their friends." So such teaching was outlawed though he does not say what became of that teacher. At any rate, the Persians chose to simply teach the youth to tell the truth, not to deceive and not to take unfair advantage. By thus teaching them only to believe, accept, and obey traditional ideas of justice, rather than to think, they were protected against the danger occasioned by the philosopher. But they were made vulnerable to dangers unforeseen by their traditional, solid, decent but unintelligent idea of right. Thus while the Persians had learned from experience that philosophy is morally and politically dangerous to the traditional order, we learn from Xenophon that so is its absence.

Similarly, Xenophon records that there had once been a kind of Socrates in Armenia with whom Cyrus had hunted as a boy. Armenia was governed by a king. But when Cyrus defeated the Armenian, he discovered that the Armenian king had had the philosopher killed for "corrupting" the king's son and "alienating his affection" for his father (3.1.14 and 3.1.38–40).

The absence of philosophy meant that there was no guardian of the Persian memory capable of responding to Cyrus's unprecedented threat to the old Persian regime. That is, there was no one to explain how and why the old Persian ways were advantageous to the Persians. The actual guardians of those ways, the teachers in the schools of justice, were neither philosophers nor informed by philosophy. Their wisdom was merely historical. That kind of wisdom has certain advantages, as Burke observes: "This retrospective wisdom, and historical patriotism, are things of wonderful convenience, and serve admirably to reconcile the old quarrel between speculation and practice." But also great disadvantages: "Men are wise with but little reflection in the business of all times except their own."[10] Men "wise"[11] in this way are not prudent as either Xenophon or Burke understand prudence.

Persia's traditional regime preferred traditional means of defending and preserving itself because it had experience with how philosophy endangered their traditions. It sought refuge from philosophy by preserving itself in customary education derived from memory, especially that of "teachers" and "fathers." But the inadequacy of that education is revealed by the fact that neither they nor Cyrus understood what justified or necessitated their hard work and self-discipline. With no philosopher to render those things intelligible, Cyrus turned to transforming the old, stable, decent aristocracy into an empire. What was gained was wealth, power, and greatness. What was lost was the ability to pass on the old decent way of life to their children.

PRUDENCE IN *MEMORABILIA*: DOES XENOPHON DEPRECIATE THE PHILOSOPHIC LIFE?

It is not difficult to understand why neither kings nor merely traditional regimes welcome political philosophers.[12] And it is old news that fathers and even not so traditional regimes like Athens view Socratic philosophers as dangerous to their authority. Xenophon knew that Socrates had been made to appear to the city as corrupting the young men and teaching them to have contempt for their fathers (1.2.51ff). Similarly, Xenophon shows that not only democratic and not so traditional Athens but also aristocratic and traditional Persia, as well as kingly Armenia, do not tolerate philosophy.[13]

We have seen that, while Xenophon defends Socrates, he admits clearly enough, in fact goes out of his way to indicate, that Socrates was not guiltless in the matter of the future tyrants Critias and Alcibiades. Xenophon's response to the charge that he should have taught them moderation before he taught them dialectic, admits that this is true and says only "well all the teachers do it." This surpassingly weak defense implies that, if Socrates had properly educated them, these future tyrants would have been less politically dangerous and may even have been politically salutary. Xenophon here seems to claim greater prudence than he attributes to Socrates.

Nor is this Xenophon's only indication of his reservations about Socrates' prudence. Recall the contradiction between his virtual admission of Socrates' imprudence here and his later statement that Socrates was "so prudent as not to make mistakes in deciding what was better and worse, nor to need another in addition, but to be self-sufficient in his judgment of these matters" (4.8.11). This contradiction either must intensify one's awareness that Xenophon thought Socrates had been imprudent in at least one important case or else suggest that Xenophon might think Socrates intended to teach them better means of tyranny rather than to turn them from tyranny. In Xenophon's view, either Socrates was imprudent in inadvertently and thoughtlessly fostering tyranny or guilty of deliberately doing so. It is a nice question which would be the greater indictment of Socrates. In contrast, Xenophon's Simonidies tried to teach moderation, not dialectic, to *Hiero*.

Just as the Socrates of *Memorabilia* is not perfectly prudent, neither is his prudence (apparently) related to any eternal things such as the idea of the Good. This Socrates neither appealed to such high and universal beings, nor accounted for particular good qualities as manifestations of such strange beings as "ideas." In contrast, Plato seems to have thought that all the goods that we aim at cannot really be called good unless they are understood in terms of the "idea of the good."[14]

Nor does *Memorabilia* apparently either contain or suggest a comprehensive view of nature, and of humans' place in nature, in light of which one could give prudence a theoretical justification. Such a defense would presumably be needed to provide a theoretically adequate answer to the question "where does prudence fit within the whole of human life?" The absence of such an answer does not distinguish Xenophon from Plato or Aristotle. It is arguable that Aristotle thinks that prudence depends upon a natural teleology,[15] but that is more than Xenophon teaches. However, he once appeals to a divinely instituted teleology when his Socrates tries to make Euthydemus "moderate about gods" by showing him teleological evidence that "the gods attentively furnish human beings with what they need" (4.3). Whether a divinely instituted *telos* might provide a theoretical defense for prudence, I cannot say. But it is evidence that Xenophon might have regarded prudence as a gift or grace of the gods (like say *eros*), however much one might have to train oneself in its proper use, rather than regarding it as grounded in "the ideas" and as such accessible to anyone who could think.

Partly as a consequence of the absence of "ideas," Xenophon's Socrates, unlike Plato's, is not explicitly presented as advocating the philosophic life as simply superior to the life of politics. Neither, apparently, can one extract such a teaching from *Memorabilia*. Nor is Xenophon so modern that one can extract the opposite teaching. Rather he appears to be a Socratic who doubts the simple superiority of the philosophic way of life over other ways of "benefiting one's companions" such as through philosophically informed statesmanship or writing philosophically informed histories. Instead of an explicit or implicit teaching about the relative claims of the philosophic life compared to others, what one finds is a series of examples about how Socrates "benefited his companions." Moreover, this benefiting is said to have political consequences—namely, that Socrates "deserved honor from the city rather than death" (1.2.62). Yet he says this not in anger at injustice but in puzzlement: "I often wondered" how the Athenians convicted him (1.1.1, 1.1.20, 1.2.1, 1.2.64).

Xenophon's wondering does not seem to lead to knowledge of how the city could judge Socrates deserving of death. And Xenophon somehow knows that he does not understand. He may or may not know why he does not understand what he knows he does not understand. But among the possibilities is that there is nothing there to understand. That is, if Socrates was wrongly convicted, then Xenophon could never know how he was found guilty because strictly speaking there would be nothing there to know. One cannot properly know that which is not knowable. About nothingness, one can have only a kind of awareness. We know we have that awareness because we can articulate what non-being is not. This is what each Xenophontic refutation of a charge against Socrates articulates. When Xenophon is finished with all the charges, if each is refuted, what he has accomplished is to articulate his "wonder" at Socrates' even being indicted, let alone convicted. Knowing that he cannot understand is a claim to have Socratic knowledge: "I know that I know nothing." It is not quite a claim to know that Socrates was innocent though that innocence would be a reasonable opinion.[16] A reasonable opinion is not knowledge either in the sense of "knowledge of being" or of "metaphysics." Neither is it simple ignorance (lack of awareness). It is in between knowledge and simple ignorance, and participates in both. That seems to be what Xenophon's prudence is, though in order to describe it we have had to resort to theory.

Xenophon's prudence is the opposite of the anger at injustice characteristic of political men and political speech and also, apparently, of the modern political philosophers beginning with Machiavelli. Machiavelli is angry at Christianity and at France, maybe even at Italy, but Xenophon is not angry at Athens, as even the Platonic Socrates was not angry at Athens. The Platonic Thrasymachus, who represents Athens in the *Republic*, is angry. For both, Socrates' anger is more a political than a philosophic quality, however necessary anger may be to provoke philosophizing. Rather than being angry at Athens, Xenophon reacts to Socrates' death in a "philosophical" way by missing his presence and longing for him.[17] If longing for philosophic conversation is a sign of a philosopher, rather than a mere historian or rhetorician, the *Memorabilia* shows that Xenophon has that. His status as a philosopher is also suggested by his control or suppression of his anger in the face of provocation. Xenophon calls this self-control to our attention, though with characteristic indirection, by recording Socrates' once calling him a "fool" which would easily provoke to anger any ordinary military man (to say nothing of an historian) (1.3.13).

What seems to take the place of Plato's Socrates' defense of the philosophic life as simply superior to statesmanship is Xenophon's praise of Socrates as the best man he ever knew, for whom he still longs, and who did nothing but benefit his companions by turning them towards virtue. His Socrates seems to do nothing but fill others' need for wisdom about how to live. Because he seems to have such wisdom himself, Xenophon thinks Socrates is better or more complete than his companions. But does this necessarily mean that Xenophon thinks Socrates' philosophic way of life is superior to that of those like statesmen who might also benefit others? For the Platonic Socrates, philosophy is the highest way of life because contemplation of the eternal, unchanging ideas participates more fully in the eternal than does a life devoted to doing. But Xenophon praises Socrates not for his devotion to contemplation but for benefiting his companions—that is, for a life of doing rather than contemplating. It is as if Xenophon's Socrates might have thought that whether a life of contemplation is superior to a life of doing depends on the circumstances, in particular what one might contemplate as compared to what one might do. For example, one might *contemplate* false things and another might *do* good things. In such cases, might not the life of contemplation be inferior to a life of doing? For example, is it absolutely clear that today Plato's Socrates would say a life devoted to post-modern contemplation (the denial

of the ideas, of teleology, and of any apparent object of the intellect) is superior to a life of making human life better by doing justice in the manner of a Platonic statesman?

WHAT TO "LOOK AT" IF NOT
"THE IDEAS": XENOPHON'S SOCRATES
ALTERNATIVE TO PLATO'S SOCRATES

To what does Xenophon's Socrates point his companions, if not to
contemplation? Apparently, to self-control or moderation.

If the greatest benefit of being a companion of Xenophon's
Socrates is guidance about acting well, wisdom of a kind is needed for
clarity about what that is. Socrates, says Xenophon, never separated
wisdom (*sophia*) from moderation (3.9.4). Does this not look like a
severe criticism of Plato's Socrates? For that Socrates develops a perfectly just city which requires a thoroughgoing uprooting of the most
natural relationships, suppression of the most natural desires, and
complete abolition of the private. It is not implausible, if finally theoretically incorrect, to call this teaching "totalitarian."[18]

Plato's Socrates appears to separate wisdom from moderation by a
mad proposal for absolute communism. Strauss and Bloom read this
proposal as ironic and as intended to instill moderation in the souls of
those tempted to expect too much perfection from politics. Thus, the
apparent separation of wisdom from moderation is perhaps only a
strategy intended to ultimately unite them more strongly. Nevertheless, that separation, however provisional, and however philosophically persuasive the argument by which Strauss and Bloom justify it,
would look to the prudent Xenophon to be imprudent because to
think otherwise would be too politically dangerous. Taken literally, it
is immoderate in the extreme and there are always immoderate Critias
and Alcibiades types around who might take it literally. Moreover, in-
stilling moderation in citizens by immoderate means is vulnerable to
the Platonic Socrates' doubt that justice can be produced by injustice,
good by bad, etc.[19]

Accordingly, Xenophon presents his alternative to Plato's Socrates
as less inclined to theoria. The one time this word occurs in *Memorabilia* (4.8.2) it is Socrates that is visible, not the objects of philosophy.
However, "looking at" (*theaomai*)[20] occurs eight times. Yet even these

are negative. Four of the eight times are explicitly negative. It is "dangerous" (1.3.13) and "reckless" (4.3.14). The personification Vice "looked at herself" (2.1.22)—implying vanity—while the modest personification Virtue did not. Finally, Virtue describes Vice as having "never seen a good work of your own" (2.1.31).

The remaining four times all have to do with the Theodote episode (3.11) in which Socrates takes his companions to gaze upon a woman whose beauty reportedly "surpasses speech" (3.11.1). Why did he do this? Not, apparently, so they could all see an instance of "the idea of the beautiful" but rather to learn such self-control in the presence of such beauty that one can both still think and act in keeping with that thinking. This, at least, is what Socrates does while they gaze upon Theodote. He and she have an admittedly flirtatious dialogue regarding hunting friends. The lesson seems to be that when a philosopher or a gentleman encounters a beautiful woman they should engage her in philosophic discussion as a means of self-control.

The Theodote story is not only the most memorable and erotic in *Memorabilia* but also contains its most dense concentration of "looking at." The four instances are not negative on their face. Once Socrates speaks of "a sense of satisfaction in the spectator."[21] The remaining three simply refer to Socrates and his group looking at her (*theasomenous, etheasametha*). One even generates laughter in the reader ("and they looked on" *etheasanto* 3.11.2).

Yet these four actually imply the danger and even the inadvisability of "looking at" some things, in this case, at great or unrivaled beauty. This is suggested by the following. Earlier Socrates had warned Xenophon: "this creature that they call beautiful and in bloom is so much more terrible than spiders that, while spiders inject something when they touch, it (even when it does not touch, but if one just looks at it) injects even from quite far away something of the sort to drive one mad." Thus "I counsel you Xenophon, whenever you see some one beautiful, to flee without looking back" (1.3.11–13). Evidently, Xenophon's Socrates (unlike Plato's Socrates) does not regard fearlessly looking at all things as prudent. But what does one make of Xenophon's Socrates' prudence about this matter? For he first describes Xenophon as a "wretch" and a "fool" for not being aware of the danger of being enslaved by looking at beauty, and then he takes the group to see for themselves. The defense is insufficient that Socrates now has such self-control in these matters that it is no longer a danger to him. For what about the other young men who accompany him? Is this another instance of Xenophon's calling attention to Socrates' imprudence?

Still, Xenophon's Socrates taught his companions how to "look at" even dangerous things. So did Plato's Socrates, but for him looking at is more akin to, and for the sake of, contemplation rather than to action. For Xenophon's Socrates, it is more akin to self-control and moderation.

CONCLUSION

When students of the history of political philosophy think of what prudence is, they think first of Aristotle among the ancients and of Burke among the moderns. Prudence was discovered and justified by classical political science as a particular kind of reason in between theory and logic. Though it may utilize theory and logic, it is not reducible to them. Prudence thus understood fits Xenophon's understanding in general but not entirely. In addition, for Xenophon prudence is mostly limited to what benefits particular companions and regimes in particular circumstances and such benefit does not seem to depend on "the advantageous" or "the true" or "the just" simply. This downplaying of the ideas goes together with his implicit criticism of the other Socrates who teaches these "ideas" and with his reservations about the simple superiority of the contemplative life over that of benefiting one's friends and companions. Xenophon's love for Socrates, his longing for his presence, and his praise of how Socrates benefited his companions did not blind him to Socrates' imprudence. Thus, there is more to be learned about prudence in these books besides what Xenophon's Socrates and his Cyrus say and do. We also learn from Xenophon's delicately revealed judgment about what they say and do.

NOTES

1. The summary statement is actually a repetition presumably for emphasis. Just before this, Xenophon says, "he did not rush his companions to become skilled in speaking and in taking action, and in contriving, but he thought that moderation should come to be in them before these things. For he held that those who had these abilities without being moderate are more

unjust and more able to do mischief" (4.3.1). Xenophon may take advantage of his praise of Socrates' prudence in order to make the point that Socrates should have known better than to teach Critias and Alcibiades.

2. Socrates says we are "unable to know in advance what is advantageous for the future." Hence the need for divination (4.3.12).

3. Prudence has recently been described as a "mode of thinking that falls between scientific or technical rationalism (or historical determinism), on the one hand, and willful self assertion (or relativism) on the other." Richard S. Ruderman, "Aristotle and the Recovery of Political Judgment," *American Political Science Review* 91, no. 2 (June 1997): 410.

4. "Remarks on the Policy of the Allies with Respect to France" (1793), in *The Works of Edmund Burke* (Boston: Little, Brown, 1865-67), Vol. 4, 468.

5. "Thoughts on French Affairs," *Works*, Vol. 4, 349.

6. Though not to Walter Miller, editor and translator of the Loeb edition of *Cyropaedia* (Cambridge: Harvard University Press, 1960). At the end of Bk. 8, Ch. 7, 438–39, Miller describes Ch. 8 as "a later addition to Xenophon's work." He thinks it does not fit "the perfect unity of the work." So, although Ch. 8 is included in "all the manuscripts and editions" it is "recommended to close the book at this point and read no further."

7. This is formally the same reward for the faithful and observant Jew who adheres strictly to the arduous demands of the law. The reward for observing those demands is said to be the law itself.

8. "The present Revolution in France seems to me . . . to bear little resemblance or analogy to any of those which have been brought about in Europe, upon principles merely political. It is a Revolution of doctrine and theoretic dogma." "Thoughts on French Affairs" (1791), *Works*, Vol. 4, 318–19.

9. The transformation begins at 1.5.8.

10. "Thoughts on the Causes of the Present Discontents" (1770), *Works*, Vol. 1, 442.

11. "Wise" here seems clearly ironic.

12. Xenophon's *Hiero* is a seemingly Socratic dialogue between a poet and a tyrant. However, the poet seems to have subordinated himself and his recommendations to the tyrant's desires. It is doubtful that a Socratic philosopher would willingly do that and Simonides is apparently *Hiero*'s willing discussant.

13. In the *Hiero*, the tyrant explains that tyrants fear rather than admire "the wise, because they might contrive something." Ch. V.1., Leo Strauss, *On Tyranny*, ed. Victor Gourevitch and Michael S. Roth (New York: The Free Press), 12.

14. Aristotle denies this. *Nicomachean Ethics*, Book 1, Ch. 6, 1096a12ff. So does Xenophon's Socrates, who asserts that he knows only good things that are good for specific ends and that he knows no good things that are simply good (3.8.3 & 7). This evidence might suggest that the "idea" of the good may be Platonic rather than Socratic.

15. Roger D. Masters thinks that phronesis requires that we "embrace Aristotelian natural science." *The Nature of Politics* (New Haven: Yale University Press, 1989), 179–83.

16. The only time Xenophon asserts Socrates did not deserve death (1.2.62), he states that as "my opinion." Not to deserve death is not the same as being innocent of the chareges.

17. 4.8.11. But Xenophon prudently reminds us that not all longing is a sign of goodness for Critias and Alcibiades also, in a manner, "had yearned for Socrates" (1.2.16). Prudence first comes up explicitly just prior to this at 1.2.10.

18. Most famously by Karl Popper, *The Open Society and Its Enemies* (Princeton: Princeton University Press, 1962).

19. *The Republic* 335aff (Polemarchus).

20. *Theaomai* "can refer to the mind's contemplation, to the watching of a play, to the reviewing of troops." Wayne Ambler, trans. and annotator, *The Education of Cyrus* (Ithaca: Cornell University Press, 2001), 289, note 46.

21. *Theomenois* 3.10.8.

3

Thomas Aquinas on Magnanimous and Prudent Statesmanship

Kenneth L. Deutsch

The contemporary Western world has experienced very few statesmen. Some commentators have placed primary responsibility for this phenomenon on the influence of Christianity on our civilization. Leo Strauss mentions "the Christian mistrust of purely human virtue, for the sake of humiliating pride in its own virtues."[1] Christian moral teaching is seen to conflict with human excellence. Christianity, it has also been claimed, negates the heroic virtues of "magnanimity" or greatness of soul that are considered basic to statesmanship. Christian humility has restricted men and women of great ambitions. The critics of Christianity claim that revival of statesmanship would require a return to the Greek and Roman pagan virtues of magnanimity—the pursuit of great ambition that strives for fame and power, honor and glory, which will manifest itself in deeds surviving the vicissitudes of political life.[2] It is the purpose of this paper to demonstrate, through a discussion of Thomas Aquinas' political thought, that a Christian notion of the magnanimous and prudent statesman is conceivable and consistent with Christian ethics. Before exploring Thomas Aquinas' approach to magnanimous statesmanship in some detail, we shall compare the meaning that Aristotle, Cicero, and Augustine gave to the virtue of magnanimity as a feature of political leadership.

ARISTOTLE AND GREEK MAGNANIMITY

Aristotle was a true representative of the ancient Greek position which expressed a supreme disdain for servile subjection. The Greeks contrasted human grandeur (*megalopsychia*) with servile subjection. The Romans would later refer to this grandeur as "greatness of soul" (which Cicero translated as *magnanimitas*). For Aristotle this grandeur was based on an ethically good attitude toward life.

The Greek notion of human grandeur took two forms, both founded on the same basic attitude—the disdain for servile subjection. One form was active and consisted of political grandeur. This disposition sought to make great plans and use one's talents to carry them out. The world of material interests was held in contempt for a great cause. The other form was contemplative ethical grandeur. Here human greatness must be founded in ethical excellence. Socrates is the prototype of this approach in which the wise person transcends all the outward vicissitudes of political life through inner integrity, self-awareness, and self-respect. For the person of ethical grandeur, the political actor is a dangerous fool who must be kept down.[3]

The Aristotelian man of grandeur is a variation on the two Greek forms. Magnanimity is the crown of all the virtues because it presupposes excellence in all of them. It is the virtue that concerns itself with the right attitude towards the most important of all external goods: honor, or the recognition of one's own excellence. Since the truly great-souled man is pre-eminent in all the virtues, he deserves the highest honor. Any honor that he demands is only what is his due. Magnanimity is the only virtue that cannot lapse into vice. For Aristotle, no truly great-souled man can claim more honor than is his due. If he actually has the excellence of soul that deserves the highest recognition, failure to demand that recognition would be a mark of weakness, a sign of pusillanimity.

The magnanimous man does not set his heart on either political power or riches for themselves, but he esteems them for the honor that accrues to their possessor. He is conscious of the fact that, for the small-minded many, political power and/or wealth are more easily discernible than the virtue that is his true claim to respect. For Aristotle, the truly magnanimous man has contempt for his *merely* rich and powerful inferiors. That contempt is justified by the fact that he *is* superior, whereas that of the merely rich and powerful is not justified because they are only *apparently* superior. This magnanimous man should be a ruler. It is not the glory of the cause nor the help he might be to others that galvanizes him into political action but the fear of having his own reputation besmirched with the accusation of cowardice. In the absence of any extramundane immortality to look forward to, Aristotle affirmed the pagan Greek concern for the perdurance of his name and fame after death by the political and other deeds done while he still lived.

From the Christian perspective, Aristotle's magnanimous statesman is characterized by some self-centered qualities that are at the basis of statesmanship. Aristotle's magnanimous statemanship betrays the "bad side" of Aristotle's ethics.

CICERO AND ROMAN MAGNANIMITY

In the Roman ideal it was not the personal glory of the individual Roman that was important but rather the glory of the political community. Cicero's discussion of the magnanimous man may be taken as fairly typical expression of Roman thought on the matter. He actually composed a whole treatise on the subject of glory and "greatness of soul," but unfortunately it has been lost. He says enough about it in his *De Officiis*, however, to give us a sufficiently clear notion of his approach to magnanimous statesmanship.

Cicero, as much as Aristotle, takes it for granted that the great-souled man deserves the highest honor, but he does not make personal glory the end-all of life. Rather, he insists that self-interest is not the supreme good. There are times when one's own reputation has to be sacrificed to a higher good, to the good of the commonweal:

> It is our duty, then, to be more ready to endanger our own than the public welfare and to hazard the honor and glory more readily than other advantages.[4]

The basis of honor for Cicero, as for Aristotle, is pre-eminence in virtue or moral goodness. But, unlike Aristotle, Cicero emphasizes the virtues that are social in character rather than those qualities that focus attention on the excellence of the individual in himself. In discussing the marks of true fortitude he summarizes what for him are the two most important qualities of the truly great statesman:

> The soul that is altogether courageous and great is marked above all by two characteristics; one of these is indifference toward outward circumstances; for such a person cherishes the conviction that nothing but moral goodness and propriety deserves to be either admired or wished for or striven after, and that he ought not to be subject to any man or

any passion or any accident of fortune. The second characteristic is that, when the soul is disciplined in the way above mentioned, one should do deeds not only great and in the highest degree useful, but extremely arduous and fraught with danger both to life and to many things that make life worth living.[5]

What is to be especially noted is not only the emphasis on moral goodness but, even more significant, the insistence that the truly great-souled man does deeds that are beneficial to others even at the cost of great personal sacrifice. Magnanimous man does not find happiness preening himself on his own intellectual and moral superiority, but in a public career in which he can devote these virtues to the common-weal. His highest honor will be derived from such public service.

This exalted social-minded ideal of Cicero was, of course, not very often achieved by Romans in public life. The danger to the greatly gifted leader is that he become self-willed and tyrannical. As Cicero puts it, "The more notable a man is for his greatness of spirit, the more ambitious he is to be the foremost citizen, or, I should say rather, to be sole ruler. But when one begins to aspire to pre-eminence, it is difficult to preserve the spirit of fairness which is absolutely essential to justice."[6]

It is also important to note Cicero's persistent caution to those who hold public trusts to avoid arrogance and to be courteous and fore-bearing in all their dealings with the public:

> Neither must we listen to those who think that one should indulge in violent anger against one's political enemies and imagine that such is the attitude of a great-spirited, brave man. For nothing is more com-mendable, nothing more becoming in a pre-eminently great man than courtesy and forbearance. . . . If punishment or correction must be ad-ministered, it need not be insulting; it ought to have regard to the wel-fare of the state, not to the personal satisfaction of the man who ad-ministers the punishment or reproof.[7]

Cicero's approach to the magnanimous statesman places the greatest emphasis on the willingness of the statesman to sacrifice himself for the commonweal.

AUGUSTINE'S REACTION TO PAGAN HUMAN GRANDEUR

The teachings of Jesus emphasized that he was a king, but that his kingdom was not of this world. His kingdom was not a thing of political power but a reign in the souls of men who were meek and humble. To the Jews this would be a disappointment and a scandal—a "stumbling block." To the Greeks, his example of humility, charity, and universal forgiveness was mere foolishness. Jesus' claims to be divine and yet his refusal to accept the honors and acclaim demanded by even the mere earthly kings would have made Jesus, in pagan Greek eyes, a kind of apotheosis of the pusillanimous man. Jesus also emphasized that human beings had dignity as children of God and that this was the motive for loving and honoring each other. This emphasis on the great dignity and worth of every single human individual was seen by the Greek and Latin church fathers as a corrective both to the Roman aberration of the total subordination of the individual to the state and the Greek pursuit of personal glory.

Such high-minded pagan figures as Epictetus, Marcus Aurelius, and Celsus could only view Christian humility and martyrdom as weak and cowardly pettiness that expressed perverse disgust for human grandeur and distrust of the autonomous power of men. Celsus viewed Christian humility as not only a plagiarism of Plato, but claimed that the Christians had interpreted Plato incorrectly. For Plato's *tapeinos* or humble man must always bear witness to a "well-ordered" humility. According to Celsus the Christians did not preach this reasonable ordering: Christians, after all, allowed thieves and prostitutes to enter first what they called the kingdom of God.[8]

For Augustine and many of the early church fathers, humility or greatness of soul is an original Christian quality that was unknown among the pagans. Augustine was to express this general patristic conviction very clearly: To know your own humanity is true humility, for true humanity is God's creation that has been vitiated by human sin. Therefore knowing oneself in the light of God and sin should bring about humble obedience in faith—this should be called *magnanimitas*, human greatness. So over against pagan humanism and statesmanship, Augustine stressed the grandeur of God who has mercy on man in his insignificance. Members of the City of God may be recognized for their achievement, but they must transmit all the recognition they receive to the glory of God. True happiness cannot come to Christian statesmen from power, wealth, or adulation:

> But we say they are happy if they rule justly; if they are not lifted up amid the praises of those who pay them sublime honors, and the obsequiousness of those who salute them with an excessive humility, but

remember they are men . . . ; if they prefer to govern depraved desires
rather than any nation whatever; and if they do all these things not
through ardent desire of empty glory, but through love of eternal felic-
ity, not neglecting to offer to the true God, who is their God, for their
sins, the sacrifices of humility, contrition and prayer. Such Christian em-
perors, we say, are happy in the present time by hope and are destined
to be so in the enjoyment of the reality itself, when that which we wait
for shall have arrived.[9]

Augustine's notion of individual happiness takes a very limited
view of the whole sphere of earthly political pursuits. It is a view
that sees no possibility of a reconciliation between the pursuit of
temporal glory in the earthly city and the pursuit of eternal glory in
the City of God. There was no question of a synthesis between pagan grandeur and Christian humility. The relationship between
man's liberation of himself politically and salvation from God
would receive particular emphasis later with Thomas Aquinas. In
their recognition of God's true greatness, patristic and early me-
dieval theologians negated man's secular grandeur and were unable to accord to it a reasonable or proper place. Not until Thomas
Aquinas in the thirteenth century was an accommodation between
human grandeur and humility ventured. What Aquinas has to present is a creative tension between Aristotelian virtue and Christian
humility and revelation. As reliant as Aquinas is on Aristotle and
Augustine for the terms and the structure of his thought, the virtue
of magnanimous statesmanship as he defines it turns out to be
something quite different from the virtue as Aristotle and Augustine
define it.

AQUINAS AND MAGNANIMOUS MAN

Aquinas agrees with Aristotle that magnanimity is a virtue dealing
with the right-reasoned attitude toward honor; and he agrees, too,
that it is concerned with the great honors owing to a great man who
is pre-eminent in all the virtues. Aquinas, like Aristotle, writes of two
virtues dealing with honor—one nameless and dealing with the ordinary honors owing to ordinary men and another dealing with the
great honors owing to the men who are truly extraordinary. The latter is the virtue of magnanimity.

We must conclude that the proper matter of magnanimity is great honor, and that a magnanimous man tends to such things as are deserving of honors.[10]

The wording here is quite significant. It suggests that, for Aquinas, the magnanimous man should be more concerned with the great deeds that deserve honor than with the honor that accrues to them. The good deeds are the end of his endeavor; the honor is only the natural consequences of the end achieved.

Nature, claims Aquinas, is not a mere shadow of the supernatural but contains spiritual energies itself. The divine plan of creation cannot be understood without the human race whose existence gives earthly and heavenly meaning to it. Humanity is a partner of God in the building up of the world.

According to Aquinas, the act of creating is the unfolding of a multiplicity of existences. He notes that in *Genesis* it states that "God created man in his image, in the image of God he created him" (I:27). Whoever speaks of the "image of God" finds himself facing the inevitability of multiplicity. Since God cannot be sufficiently well represented by one finite creature, the diverse multiplication of human creatures provides a compensation for their individual deficiencies. Diverse human beings reflect the multiple beauty of God.

God has produced things in the human being in order to communicate his goodness to the created things and to represent his goodness in them. And because his goodness cannot be represented efficiently in one single creature, he created multiple and diverse things in such a way that whatever is lacking in one creature in representing the divine goodness may be made up for by another. Thus the goodness which in God is simple and unique is found in countless and differentiated creatures. Consequently it is the entire universe which shares perfectly the goodness of God and represents it more than any one creature by itself.[11]

This interrelatedness among human beings is a sacred ordering of creation in which humanity has a sacred vocation—the humanization of nature. Through the realization of the "image of God" in the world, human persons with specific talents build up the world. Human beings are not totally wretched. Man is responsible for his good actions as well as his evil deeds. As a humble creature, man knows that his powers are gifts of God. Aquinas does not present a drama of God's grandeur as contrasted with puny man. The drama is shifted to man; it is concerned with the tension between human grandeur and human limitations. Magnanimity, for Aquinas, is a virtue of human social and political hope, to be realized through one's own human strength and good deeds; honor must be viewed as the natural consequence of good deeds and not merely as an end in itself.

Man has his own worth not only thanks to God's worth but also "as an inalienable human worth which is peculiarly his own."[12] In an important text, a commentary of *Job*, man is viewed as the ultimate subject. Here Aquinas defends Job's argument with God:

> Thus it seems as though a discussion between man and God is unthinkable because of the eminence with which God transcends man. But in that case we must remember that the truth is not different depending on who speaks it; therefore one who speaks the truth can never be put in the wrong, *no matter who he is speaking with*.[13]

From the very outset of his discussion of magnanimity, Aquinas is careful to reconcile it with humility. There is no necessary conflict between humility and magnanimity; they are, rather, necessary concomitants in a great man who looks at himself—his talents—truthfully:

> There is in man something great which he possesses through the gift of God; and something defective which accrues to him through the weakness of nature. Accordingly magnanimity makes a man deem himself worthy of great things in consideration of the gifts he holds from God: Thus if his soul is endowed with great virtue, magnanimity makes him tend to perfect works of virtue; and the same is to be said of the use of any other good, such as science or external fortune. On the other hand, humility makes a man think of his own deficiency, and magnanimity makes him despise others in so far as they fall away from God's gifts. Yet humility makes us honor others and esteem them better than ourselves, in so far as we see some of God's gifts in them.[14]

Any great gift, such as effective rulership over insufficient human beings, must engender in their possessor not the desire for great honor but rather the desire to do great things on behalf of the community of insufficient persons and in the glorification of God. Aquinas claims that this is what Jesus was advocating when He said: "So let your light shine before men, that they may see your good works and glorify [not you but] your Father who is in Heaven" (Matt. 5:16). Aquinas defines the meaning of magnanimous man in such a way that Aristotle's and Augustine's positions are appropriated, altered, and transformed.

AQUINAS AND MAGNANIMOUS STATESMANSHIP

The desire of magnanimous man to do great things for God and his neighbor, to realize to their fullest the gifts God has given him, is consonant with a recognition that in himself and left to himself he has many weaknesses and sinful tendencies. This double condition or tension within himself, of strength and weakness, also affects his attitude toward his fellow man and the nature of politics. The desire for social and political honor can be irrational in three ways:

> First, when a man desires recognition of an excellence which he has not; this is to desire more than his share of honor. Secondly, when a man desires honor for himself without referring it to God. Thirdly, when a man's appetite rests in honor itself, without referring it to the profit of others.[15]

The first aberration is that of the excess of mediocre man—the desire for political honor or responsibility for excellence that he actually does not possess. The last two aberrations the magnanimous man may be guilty of. His honored status may tempt him to forget his created status and his obligation to employ those gifts for other insufficient human beings. The political ruler must be motivated by a concern for the political good and not for personal ambition alone. These two limitations on a great man's attitude toward honor demonstrate the importance of the Christian virtues of humility and charity as clear norms for judging the rationality of a true statesman's attitude toward the great honors that *are* his due.

As an infinitely perfect being, God has no need for honor or glory. God did not create the world in order to receive the recognition, the honor, and the glory of human beings. God created in order to communicate and manifest His perfection to someone outside Himself. Rational creatures, seeing the excellence of God manifested in His creatures, do acknowledge it, do honor and glorify God; but that was not the motive for which God created. Magnanimous statesmen should be like God. Their chief concern should be great deeds and should acknowledge them in others. But the glory and the honor must not be the sole motive of the talented magnanimous statesmen, who administer or create a polity for the common good, any more than glory was the motive for God in creating.[16] Men in high positions of public trust cannot be indifferent about their reputations; but they should secure their reputations by performing the duties of their positions in such a way as to *merit* honor and glory.

Like Aristotle, Thomas Aquinas admits that a great man may, out of ignorance of his own abilities or from fear of failure, become guilty of pusillanimity by not doing the great things of which he is actually capable. The repeated cautions that Aquinas gives to men about their attitude toward honor suggests to him that the far more dangerous aberration from magnanimity is by excess rather than by defect. This position reflects his view of both the need for prudent rulership or statesmanship and the need for limits placed on that honorable political task.

Aquinas' approach to the qualities of excellence in rulership and the limited nature of the political task is best discerned in his partial rejection of both the pagan and patristic notions of magnanimity. His standard of magnanimous statesmanship clearly rejects the arrogance of political power. Although it is anachronistic to declare Aquinas to be a precursor of "Whiggery," it shall be shown that he, like Cicero, considered rulership to be a public trust that must not devolve into tyranny. As Aquinas put it:

> First it is necessary that the man who is raised up to be king by those whom it concerns should be of such condition that it is impossible that he should become a tyrant. . . . Then, once the king is established, the government of the kingdom must be so arranged that the opportunity to tyrannize is removed. At the same time his power should be so tempered that he cannot easily fall into tyranny.[17]

For Aquinas, civil society was regarded as an integral part of the divine order and, like the whole, as being diversified in degrees. Relations between human beings, as well as between the faculties of the individual human being, reflected the cosmic law by which the higher entity ruled the lower. Thus,

> the [power of] reason rules the irascible and concupiscible powers by a political rule, such as that by which free men are ruled, who in some respect have a free will of their own.[18]

A man's bodily power was subject to the "sensitive powers" and both were ruled by the intellect or reason. (In a similar way, in civil society the proper "order among men" was for those who possessed talents in understanding and administration to rule those who were less intelligent but strong in body.) For Aquinas, the power of the magnanimous statesman is never concerned with purely "despotic" methods, but it is better understood in terms of "political" rule. The above analogy claims that the rule of reason within the individual is likewise a "political" rule: each of these lower powers contains within itself a certain freedom of its own, a certain inner power of resistance, and it is the role of prudence and charity to "overcome" this resistance, although never in such a way as to repress the power itself. Likewise the magnanimous statesman is able to distinguish real from apparent greatness.

Prudence as "practical wisdom" found in the magnanimous statesmen rarely "overpowers" the activities of others in civil society in the manner of political manipulation, but rather channels these activities into a prudent mode of response for the common good. A magnanimous ruler, therefore, is not a dictator, even a benevolent one. Rather, he appeals to the citizens in terms of their own nature by trying to do what is just. Civil society is in disorder when a person is in authority "not because of the eminence of his understanding," but because he has usurped the government by "bodily strength" or has been appointed to rule "on the basis of sensual affection." Such a situation is like that in which an individual intellect merely followed the lead of the sensual faculty.

MORAL PRUDENCE AND THE MAGNANIMOUS STATESMAN

The meaning and centrality of prudence in Aquinas' political philosophy is found in the analogy of the Divine Providence in which God is the prudential Person *par excellence*. Man is at his best as man when, both as rational creature and as created being made in the image of God, he acts according to the measure of practical wisdom that comes to the person, whether by a kind of human or divine inspiration, or by human industry, or by a combination of these elements. Man can learn from prudence not only self-governance, but the management of the affairs of the state as well. For Aquinas prudence is the master virtue that controls all the rest. Taken as a moral virtue that

properly directs man to his final end, prudence presupposes not only
a knowledge of the end as well as the means that lead to it, but the
"rectitude of the appetite" (or will) insofar as it conformed to the end.
Aquinas clearly distinguishes "prudence" in the sense of "cleverness"
(*astutia*) from "moral prudence" (*prudentia*) which is a virtue of practical reasoning. Thomas Gilby characterizes Aquinas' view of moral
prudence as:

> a good habit or settled quality, of the practical reason giving an active
> bent toward right doing as an individual act; it ranges from our pon-
> dering over what should be done through our judgment of what we
> should choose to do, and is completed in that being made an effective
> command.[19]

A magnanimous and prudent person is one who makes his decisions in the full light of the moral law as best he can know it through
the light of his reason and in consultation with others who are wise.
For Aquinas, being prudent means not only knowing the moral law,
but knowing also how to apply it in particular material circumstances
and in a way that fully respects the right order of means to ends. In
effect, for Aquinas, political prudence requires that (a) the ends of
one's actions be morally right, and that (b) the means be morally
suited to those same ends. An obvious case in point would include
"national security" as a legitimate moral end, but not all means can
justify its pursuit. For Aquinas, the common good must be aligned
with the virtue of *prudentia* whereby public disorder, scandal, and
crime are regulated. It is of great importance that *prudentia* be present in the highest degree in the rulers of a state. A magnanimous and
prudent statesman is one who (1) assiduously investigates alternative
courses of conduct together with the means for accomplishing a
moral end; (2) who, beyond the initial process of policy inquiry and
investigation, knows how to make practical judgments as to what
needs to be done; and most crucially, having made this judgment (3)
commands through his will that a given course of political action be
omitted or performed. Such a ruler also needs a good memory
whereby he can draw from the storehouse of his past experience; cir-
cumspection, which involves close attention to the attendant circumstances of a moral decision; and foresight, whereby he can reasonably project into the future certain consequences of a given line
of action.[20]

Most importantly, the magnanimous and prudent statesman must be a morally disciplined individual who must be able to distance himself from his own desires so that he can be free of their power and make some judgement about it. Such statesmanship is temperate and questioning; it approves of harmoniousness, proportion, and economy. For Aquinas, this kind of statesmanship also needs both the *espirit de geometrie* and the *espirit de finesse*—the "hard" virtues of exact workmanship along with the "disciplines" of courtesy and charity.

MAGNANIMOUS STATESMANSHIP AND THE "MIXED REGIME"

Prudent rulers can only operate when good government exists, namely, rule that is exercised for the "common good," whereby man's physical needs and the conditions for a good life produce universal (though imperfect) happiness. Those actions are prudent and magnanimous that produce happiness for the "multitude." In the *Summa* when Aquinas asks himself what is the best form of government, he states the following:

> The best form of government is in a State or Kingdom wherein one is given the power to preside over all, while under him are others having governing powers. Yet a government of this kind is shared by all, because all are eligible to govern, and because the rulers are chosen by all. This is the best form of polity, being partly kingdom, since there is one at the head of all; partly aristocracy, insofar as a number of persons are set in authority; partly democracy, that is, government by the people, insofar as the rulers can be chosen from the people and the people have the rights to choose their rulers.[21]

There exists a common interest between insufficient persons that goes beyond their legitimate private interests. No one person can determine that interest. As Aquinas states:

> Where there are many men together and each one looks after his own interest, the group would be broken up and scattered unless there were someone to take care of what appertains to the common good. . . . There must, therefore, be something which impels toward the common good of the many, over and above that which impels toward the private good of each individual. Wherefore in all things that are ordained toward a single end, there is something to be found which rules the rest.[22]

This something that rules the rest exists for the community. States-manship exists in order for the members of the community to realize their talents and to achieve their perfection. For Aquinas, it is proper for rulers to recognize themselves as their subjects' servants. However as Jacques Maritain, a great neo-Thomist, warns: "one of the most instructive chapters of a Christian philosophy would deal with what I might call the intermingling of masks and offices. Not only is the part of iniquity often played under the mask of justice [or the common good], but masks of iniquity can fill and mar the roles of justice."[23] Serious moral scrutiny must be applied to those who call themselves "servants" of justice and the common good.

There is no doubt as to Aquinas' personal preference for magnanimous monarchical rule, provided that the rule be just and prudent. Aquinas' teaching claims that there is no one form of government that is best in any absolute sense. That form of government is best that under given conditions of time, place, and culture most effectively serves the needs of the people in terms of the common good. Aquinas agrees with Augustine who expresses the view that in a civil society that is basically pervaded by a sense of responsibility and moderation the people should choose their own magistrates. Otherwise, in a situation where a society is basically corrupt and degenerate, the choice could be reserved to a few men who are both good and wise.[24] Aquinas is also appreciative of the political principle of self-rule that lies at the heart of contemporary liberal democracies. Yet he is cognizant of the dangers of excessive egalitarianism which may fail to consider the need for the "aristocratic" contribution of magnanimous statesmen in politics.

This leads us to the final theme concerning magnanimous statesmen and citizens in government—the question of human equality. Aquinas' political theory views "natural equality" as fundamental to his view of human nature. "In what pertains to the interior motion of the will," says Aquinas, "man is not bound to obey man but only God."[25] Man is bound to obey man in the external bodily actions; but even in such of these as refer to the nature of the body—for example, "whatever concerns the nourishment of the body, and the generation of offspring—man is not bound to obey man but God alone, for *all men are by nature equal.*"[26]

Aquinas teaches that every person is entitled to spiritual freedom and to the exterior conditions of human existence, whether proprietary, personal, or marital. Within this sacred, private sphere no human artifice or organization should intrude. Aquinas strictly limits even serfdom in a way quite "modern" for his time. "A serf," he says, "is his master's property in matters superadded to the natural, but in matters of nature all are equal."[27]

It follows from this that there is no such thing as natural superiority in the spiritual sense. The Aristotelian conception of the natural slave may be ultimately incompatible with Christian philosophical anthropology. Yet some of Aristotle's phraseology is retained but transformed in discussing the particular need for intellectual and moral excellence in magnanimous statesmanship. Thus the Aristotelian principle of natural inferiority and servitude was reduced by Aquinas to the following axiom of competence: "Those who are pre-eminent in intellect naturally dominate, while those who are intellectually deficient but corporally strong seem by nature to be adapted for serving, as Aristotle says in his *Politics*."[28] This idea was also applied to politics. "In human government," says Aquinas, "inordination arises from the fact that someone rules not on account of intellectual pre-eminence, but usurps power for himself by brute force, or someone is appointed to government owing to sensual affection."[29]

Thus while all men are entitled to spiritual freedom and to the exterior conditions of human existence, some hierarchical gradation is essential for human coexistence. This gradation must be based on the existing distribution of disparities and aptitudes if the magnanimous statesman is to have an opportunity to serve. Those persons who excel in active faculties ought to be directed (primarily persuaded) by those who excel in mental faculties. For Aquinas, it is impossible that the common good of the State could progress, unless there is virtue in the citizens, and those magnanimous statesmen to whom the government is entrusted. Although persons are spiritually equal, they are unequal politically. If the principle of the common good is to be made manifest and not result in a chaos of mediocrity and incompetence, the aristocratic principle in the strict and literal sense must be present.

THE MAGNANIMOUS STATESMAN AND THE VICISSITUDES OF POLITICS

For Aquinas the first intention of a ruler must be to establish and maintain the unity of peace among his people. Justice of itself is not sufficient to produce harmony and order that go to make up peace. This effect can only be produced by the virtue of charity. Aquinas says, "Peace is the work of justice indirectly, insofar as justice removes obstacles to peace: but it is the work of charity directly, since charity, according to its very nature, causes peace, for charity is a unitive force."[30] No true rulership is possible without charity.

Charity is thus "the mother" and the foundation of all the virtues, and the moral life is really the life of charity. In charity, we love our neighbors, even where we give different honors in accordance with the worth or excellence of each and where we are unable to love all with the same affection. All virtue, and action, apart from charity is necessarily incomplete. It is in charity that justice, for example, becomes full or complete justice. Aquinas claims that even just decisions involving the promotion of the welfare of the community or state can lack the sanction of the full knowledge of what is good. That is because just acts, such as the distribution and restitution of divisible goods, can be true and fair but also blind and inequitable. Even theft must be seen in the light of charity in order to determine which acts of appropriation are *morally* wrong. Inasmuch as material things are to be held in such a way as to be shared with others, the taking of the goods of another when one is in need is not really theft. Thus justice, which regulates human actions with respect to the claims of others, must truly understand these claims as the claims of neighbors and not simply of social equals or unequals.

In his insistence on charity by the ruler, Aquinas quotes the command of Moses, "Seek out from among the people wise men who fear God, in whom there is charity . . . and appoint from them leaders."[31] As we have emphasized, Aquinas' view of rulership is one of service, and sacrificial service is a manifestation of charity. There can never be charity without service; it is the fruit of charity. Indeed, it is the ultimate test of the statesman's magnanimity.

Charity on the part of the ruler begets love from the people. It inspires them to great acts of unselfishness and devotion. Aquinas relates the example of the great love that Julius Caesar manifested for his soldiers and how this was reciprocated. It is this charity that enables the magnanimous statesman to elevate and maintain without hostility the public authority. Such a ruler is always courteous and pleasant with his people. The prudent statesman is always aware that there is in the bosom of every man a secret rebellion and opposition to all authority. Experience confirms this and original sin explains it. The true statesman realizes this full well. The tyrant may utilize his coercive powers to beat a man to his knees but he will never acquire any internal submission. The magnanimous, prudent, and charitable statesman, instead of creating large numbers of enemies to his rule, diminishes such enmity by making many of them friends by his great love and sacrificial service. No better example of the pursuit of such magnanimity and charity can be found in American politics than in the presidency of Abraham Lincoln:

> With malice toward none; with charity for all; with firmness in the right, as God gives us to see the right, let us strive on to finish the work we are in; to bind up the nation's wounds; to care for him who shall have borne the battle and his widow, and his orphan—to do all which may achieve and cherish a just and lasting peace among ourselves, and with all nations.[32]

It is clear for Aquinas that few persons possess the qualities of magnanimous, prudent, and charitable statesmanship that are necessary in one who takes upon himself the perogative of making the practical judgments necessary in the governance of the political community. We have seen that for Aquinas prudence and charity are virtues that are basic to making efficacious moral judgments which are measured by the objective demands of the commonweal. It is also clear for Aquinas that political prudence should be cultivated and found in all the citizens of a civil community, since the common good is the concern of them all. But it is required in a special way in those who exercise civil authority.

For Aquinas, political prudence involves not only considering the practical political actions conducive to the common good, but it also involves an understanding of when no political rule is best. Very often some measure which of itself is most desirable must be refrained from because, given the concrete socio-cultural circumstances, it would be detrimental to the common good or to public peace. Likewise, certain hardships must be tolerated because, given the concrete circumstances, measures against them would undermine the common good. This is not considered an abandonment of principle. Rather, it is an appreciation of the view that if the common good is destroyed for the sake of a particular, legitimate, or even laudable end, the magnanimous statesman is defeating his primary task, the preservation of the public good.[33]

Aquinas' profound concern about the centrality of prudence for the charitable and magnanimous statesman is exemplified quite well in Lincoln's particular approach to the proper tactics of alcohol reform with reference to "temperance" crusades. For Lincoln, persuasion, not denunciation, is the means to be used. Without friendship even truth will fail. "If you would win a man to your cause, first convince him that you are his sincere friend. Therein is a drop of honey that catches his heart, which say what he will, is the great high road to his reason."[34] Lincoln's counsel of persuasion and friendship is not mere expediency; rather it is best to be a friend to both the opponents and supporters of "temperance."[35] Aquinas and Lincoln are one in their concern about how governments can devour themselves in the pursuit of absolute principles without concern for human weakness, present circumstances, or charity. An excessively moralistic approach on the part of the authorities can only lead to greater disorder, in bitterness and resentment in civil society, and is contrary to political prudence. As a modern Thomist, John Courtney Murray, put it:

> society must look to other institutions for the elevation and maintenance of its moral standards, that is, to the church, the home, the school, and the network of voluntary associations that concern themselves with public morality in one or other aspect.
>
> Law and morality are indeed related, even though differentiated. That is the premises of law are ultimately found in the moral law. And human legislation does look to the moralization of society. But, mindful of its own nature and mode of action, it must not moralize excessively; otherwise it tends to defeat even its own modest aims, by bringing itself into contempt.[36]

It is quite difficult to raise up a new generation of magnanimous statesmen with the "hard" virtues necessary to transcend the dogmas of their age. Deference to intellectual and moral excellence, for Thomas Aquinas, can only exist when charity and the intuition of metaphysical reason are understood to be the real sources of human dignity and magnanimous statesmanship. Leo Strauss has stated that human problems arise when political life is deprived of the sacred: "It is hardly necessary to add that the dogmatic exclusion of religious awareness proper renders questionable all long-range predictions concerning the future of societies."[37] For Thomas Aquinas, God's undiminished greatness provides for the preservation and integrity of human community. His approach to magnanimous statesmanship is grounded in the profound commitment to a fruitful relationship between revelation and reason as the basis for a healthy political life.

NOTES

1. Leo Strauss, *Spinoza's Critique of Religion* (New York: Schocken Books, 1965), 50.
2. Larry Arnhart, "Statesmanship as Magnanimity: Classical, Christian and Modern," *Polity* (Winter 1983): 263–65.
3. Aristotle, *Nicomachean Ethics*, 1124.20–1125 a. and 1123 a. 34 1124.6.
4. Cicero, *De Officiis*, trans. William Miller (Cambridge: Harvard University Press, 1951), I, xxiv, 83–84.
5. Cicero, I, xx, 66.
6. Cicero, I, xix, 64.
7. Cicero, I, xxv, 88.
8. W. Nestle, "Die Haupteinwande des antiken Denkens gegen das Christentum," *Archiv fur Religionswissenschaft* 37 (1941): 51–100.
9. St. Augustine, *De civitate Dei*, Bk. XXII, Ch. 22, trans. Marcus Dods (New York: Modern Library, 1950), 178.
10. St. Thomas Aquinas, *Summa Theologiae*, trans. Fathers of English, Dominican Province (London: Burns, Oats and Washbourne, 1935), IIa, IIae, CXXIX, art. 2.
11. Aquinas, *Summa*, I, q. 47 and 1.
12. Aquinas, *Summa*, I, q. 6. a. 4.
13. St. Thomas Aquinas, *Exposito in Job*, Ch. 13, lect. 2.
14. Aquinas, *Summa*, IIa, IIae, CXXIX, art. 3, ad 4.
15. Aquinas, *Summa*, IIa, IIae, CXXIX, art. 3, ad 4.
16. Aquinas, *Summa*, IIa, IIae, CXXXII, art 1, ad Iam.
17. St. Thomas Aquinas, *On Kingship: To the King of Cyprus*, trans. and intro. I. Th. Eschmann, O.P. (Toronto: Pontifical Institute of the University of Toronto Press, 1949), 24.
18. Aquinas, *Summa*, I-II q. 56a, ad 3.
19. Thomas Gilby, *Summa Theologiae* (London: Blackfriar's, 1949), vol. 36, appendix 4, p. 183.
20. Aquinas, *Summa*, I-II, q. 57, art. 6.
21. Aquinas, *Summa*, I-II, 105, 1 in c.
22. Quoted in Wilfred Parsons, "St. Thomas Aquinas and Popular Sovereignty," *Thought* XIV (1941): 473.
23. Jacques Maritain, *True Humanism* (New York: Scribners and Sons, 1928), 223.

24. Aquinas, *Summa*, I-II, q. 97, a.lc.

25. Aquinas, *Summa*, II-II, q. 104, art. 5.

26. Aquinas, *Summa*, II-II, q. 104, art. 5.

27. Aquinas, *Summa*, II-II, q. 104, art. 5.

28. St. Thomas Aquinas, *Summa Contra Gentiles*, trans. Vernon J. Bourke (Notre Dame: University of Notre Dame Press, 1975), 2–3.

29. St. Thomas Aquinas, *Commentary on the Politics,* trans. A. P. D'Entreves (Oxford: Basil Blackwell, 1947), iii, 17, 1288 a. 15.

30. Aquinas, *Summa*, II-II, q. 29 a. 3, ad 3.

31. St. Thomas Aquinas, "De Regime Judaeorium," in *Aquinas: Selected Political Writings*, trans. A. P. D'Entreves (Oxford: Basil Blackwell, 1948), 91.

32. Cited in Glen E. Thurow, *Abraham Lincoln and American Political Religion* (Albany: State University of New York Press, 1976), 89.

33. Aquinas, *Summa*, I-II, 96.2 ad 2.

34. Aquinas, *Summa*, I-II, 96.2 ad 2

35. Aquinas, *Summa*, I-II, 96.2 ad 2.

36. John Courtney Murray, *We Hold These Truths* (New York: Image Books, 1965), 166.

37. Leo Strauss, *Liberalism, Ancient and Modern* (New York: Basic Books, 1968), 8.

4

The Role of Prudence in Burke's Politics

Peter J. Stanlis

MISCONCEPTIONS OF
BURKE'S PRINCIPLE OF PRUDENCE

For the past century or more perhaps the most common single error of writers on Edmund Burke's politics has been the failure to understand the nature and function of "prudence" in both the theory and practice in his politics. Nineteenth-century utilitarian and positivist writers on Burke—Henry Buckle, John Morley, William Lecky, and Sir Leslie Stephen—understood Burke's principle of prudence as the basis of his political "expediency," as an empirical, rational, and pragmatic principle, wholly unrelated to religion or ethics. In Morley's words Burke's expediency overthrew "the baneful superstition that politics . . . is a province of morals."[1] Morley and his utilitarian contemporaries assumed that Burke's prudence made "expediency" or "the standard of convenience," rather than an appeal to normative ethical and legal principles, the ultimate foundation of his politics. Thus, Burke's principle of prudence was separated from ethics and law and set in opposition to traditional morality and jurisprudence. Burke's own explicit words, that "the principles of true politics are those of morality enlarged," were completely ignored.

The path chartered by Morley's interpretation of Burke's principle of prudence was followed, with some slight variations, by a whole host of Victorian and twentieth-century writers in the liberal tradition of politics. At the beginning of the twentieth century, Charles E. Vaughan, a learned authority on Burke, applied the usual Benthamite antithesis between "natural rights" based on a normative view of human nature, and "expediency" based on pragmatism and the general welfare of society, and he concluded that in Burke's politics "the last appeal is not to Rights but to expediency."[2] Vaughan noted that Burke's "expediency" differed from that of Hume and Bentham, because it was qualified by "higher principles" and "a tissue of moral and religious ideals," but like Morley he never doubted that Burke made intellectual calculation or "expediency the ultimate principle of politics." In 1913, John MacCunn, an excellent Burke scholar, also assumed that Burke was a utilitarian in politics, and concluded: "To Burke, as to Bentham, all rights . . . are not ultimate but derivative."[3] Elie Halevy supplied a variation on this theme in 1928: "From a utilitarian philosophy Burke deduced an anti-democratic political theory. . . . The utilitarian morality led Burke to social views which were profoundly different from those to which it led Bentham."[4] In 1934, Lois Whitney, a noted eighteenth-century scholar, contended: "Priestley, Burke, and Bentham are in harmony in their utilitarianism, Burke developing the doctrine in the form of a philosophy of expediency."[5] John H. Randall also stated in 1940 that Burke's political philosophy rested ultimately upon utility and pragmatic expediency, and during the 1940s other writers repeated this commonly held conviction that Burke's principle of prudence was an intellectual virtue in the utilitarian tradition.

Unfortunately, even writers who believed that politics is a branch of practical morality were led to accept the utilitarian and positivist interpretation of Burke's principle of prudence. Late in the nineteenth century, Lord Acton, whose early interpretation of Burke was filled with praise of his moral wisdom in politics, came to accept Morley's utilitarian view of Burke as valid, and condemned Burke for having separated politics from ethics. As late as 1953 this same error was repeated by Richard M. Weaver in *The Ethics of Rhetoric*. He noted that Burke frequently employed "the argument from circumstance" when he was "at grips with concrete politics," and he concluded that Burke's strict regard for circumstances was proof that he believed, with the utilitarians and positivists, that empirical observation and rational analysis were sufficient as a basis for politics, and that therefore Burke's politics was wholly separated from any normative ethical or legal principles.[6] Like the utilitarian and positivist writers to whom they were strongly opposed, Acton and Weaver identified Burke's "prudence" with the intellectual calculation of utilitarian expediency. They failed to understand that Burke's insistence upon taking all empirical circumstances into account, in dealing with politics, was not a denial of general principles of morality and law, but rather an insistence that through prudence the general principles of ethics and law could find their practical realization in all the concrete circumstances of man's social life. In brief, both the utilitarian and positivist critics of Burke, and many of their opponents, failed to understand the vital connection between Burke's principle of prudence and the normative principles of ethics, derived from Christianity and the moral natural law, and the normative principles of law, derived from English common law, in Burke's political philosophy.

PRUDENCE AND BURKE'S CONCEPTION OF HISTORY

Undoubtedly, one of the chief reasons for the common misunderstanding of Burke's principle of prudence is that in his discussions of how changes should or should not be made in civil society he frequently appealed to history. Therefore, an understanding of Burke's conception of history is essential to an understanding of his principle of prudence. The relationship among history, prudence, and politics in his total philosophy is well summarized by Burke as follows:

> My principles enable me to form my judgment upon men and actions in history, just as they do in common life, and are not formed out of events and characters, either present or past. History is a preceptor of prudence, not of principles. The principles of true politics are those of morality enlarged; and I neither now do, nor ever will, admit of any other.[7]

History is primarily a descriptive account of man's past, and as such it does not supply men with their normative moral principles; indeed, normative ethical principles are applied in judging men and events in history. Clearly, such principles derive from a source that transcends the ordinary temporal events of politics and history. For Burke, there were two sources of transcendent normative principles—the revelations of Christianity and religion, and the moral natural law perceived through "right reason." In addition, the tradition of English common law provided Burke with legal norms for judging the political actions of Englishmen. Yet if history differs from religion, ethics, and law in not providing general normative principles in morals and law, as imperatives for man's personal and social conduct, nevertheless there are lessons, even moral lessons, to be learned from history.

Burke was essentially an Aristotelian in his philosophy, and he perceived transcendent normative moral principles as immanent in the temporal affairs of men. Moral laws do not exist only in general laws, abstracted from men in civil society; the principles of morality and law are embodied in practice in systems of religion and law, and therefore they are perceived in the great patterns of historical change and continuity. Through its specific examples, history teaches the precepts of moral prudence, of temperance and restraint, as political virtues. Prudence was for Burke a moral virtue, not an intellectual virtue; it was the first of all political virtues because it was the link between politics and ethics, between the specific actions of men in history and the general laws of jurisprudence and ethics. Prudence was the virtue that made it possible for "the principles of true politics" to be "those of morality enlarged."

To Burke history itself could not be understood simply as a matter of empirical observation of human events comprehended through rational analysis and synthesis. This was how the *philosophes* of the Enlightenment and the English utilitarians and positivists viewed history. Unlike them, Burke saw history as involving the will of God as well as the will, reason, and actions of men. So far as history reflected transcendent normative principles embodied in the temporal events of mankind, it was to Burke a secondary form of revelation. History supplemented through concrete examples, empirically perceived and rationally understood, all that was revealed to man by faith through religion and by "right reason" through moral natural law. To understand what he meant by history as a "preceptor of prudence" it is necessary to understand the role of God in Burke's view of history.

At the core of Burke's view of history was his belief that a transcendent God is concerned with the temporal events of mankind. This belief occurs frequently throughout Burke's writings, and it cannot be dismissed as idle rhetoric, since it rests at the base of some of his most important political arguments. Burke regarded the great social institutions of mankind, such as church and state, as instruments given to man by a concerned and benevolent God to be used for man's spiritual and temporal self-fulfillment. In the *Reflections* (1790), he explicitly states that God is the ultimate cause of the state: "He who gave our nature to be perfected by our virtue willed also the necessary means of its perfection: He willed, therefore, the state." In *An Appeal from the New to the Old Whigs* (1791), while advancing his argument that the duties of men in civil society are not voluntaristic, Burke asserted that "the awful Author of our being is the Author of our place in the order of existence," and that He marshalls and disposes "us by a divine tactic, not according to our will, but according to His." Burke also affirmed that the general course of a nation's life is "the known march of the ordinary providence of God." In all such statements Burke was a world removed from the *philosophes*, utilitarians and positivists, whose view of man in history was based wholly upon empirical observation and rational analysis and synthesis.

Burke's view of history included the Divine will of God, acting directly, or indirectly through man's reason and will, to determine temporal events. The direct intervention of God into human affairs was very rare, according to Burke, and could be ascertained with reasonable confidence only in those enormous changes that alter the whole course of history. In his entire writings Burke mentioned only two such events: the migration of the Teutonic tribes into the Roman Empire, and the French Revolution. In *An Abridgment of English History* (1757), Burke described the invasions of the Teutonic tribes as a "resistless inundation" of "most cruel barbarians." As an historian examining this event, Burke wrote, "We are in a manner compelled to acknowledge the hand of God in these immense revolutions by which at certain periods He so signally asserts His supreme dominion, and brings about that great system of change which is perhaps as necessary to the moral as it is found to be in the natural world." Thirty-four years later, in a famous passage that Matthew Arnold praised as the finest example of magnanimity in the entire eighteenth century, Burke wrote at the close of *Thoughts on French Affairs* (1791):

> If a great change is to be made in human affairs, the minds of men will be fitted to it, the general opinion and feelings will draw that way. Every fear, every hope, will forward it; and then they who persist in opposing this mighty current in human affairs will appear rather to resist the decrees of Providence itself than the mere designs of men. They will not be resolute and firm, but perverse and obstinate.

Where God's mysterious ways were manifested in events that baffled Burke, and contradicted his most cherished convictions, he accepted a wisdom and power that transcended his own. Yet Burke continued to oppose the direction and methods of the French Revolution to his dying day, because given his convictions it was part of his role in history to oppose it to the last.

Burke believed that although many events in history could be explained by observation and rational analysis, not all historical causes or effects spring from the mind and will of man. In the *Annual Register* he remarked on "those accidents which so frequently interpose to the disgrace of human wisdom, and which demonstrate that she is far from being the sole arbitress." Beyond human reason and will and chance there were causes in history which could not be explained by science and scholarship, and these Burke attributed to God:

> It is often impossible, in these political inquiries, to find any proportion between the apparent force of any moral causes we may assign and their known operation. We are therefore obliged to deliver up that operation to mere chance, or, more piously, (perhaps more rationally), to the occasional interposition and irresistible hand of the Great Disposer.[8]

According to Burke, the ultimate cause of decisive historical events is God, acting rarely directly, most commonly acting indirectly through the agency of leaders in civil society. Burke saw no conflict between the omnipotence of God in man's temporal events and the freedom of man's will and reason in shaping historical destiny. Those events that fall within the explanations of empirical observation and rational analysis, "in their proximate efficient cause," are "the arbitrary productions of the human mind." Burke was not an historical determinist; he believed that the "arbitrary" or free will and reason of individual men and of corporate bodies of men acting through institutions determined to a great extent the events and destiny of nations.

Although the ultimate cause of man's historical destiny is in the mind and will of God, the proximate efficient causes are to be found in all the circumstances surrounding the temporal conditions of men, in geography, climate, past history, the inherited laws, customs, habits and basic institutions of a people, their nature, intelligence, temper, energy, feelings, prejudices and interests, their leadership, and their state of affairs at a particular time. These are "the internal causes which necessarily affect the fortunes of a state," and even these, Burke noted, "are infinitely uncertain," "obscure," and "difficult to trace." In studying the events and courses of history, Burke believed that the historian should follow the methods of scientific scholarship, and approach history inductively, through a close and thorough examination of the empirical evidence contained in documents and monuments of the past, and also through a rational analysis of all available records.

The following three paragraphs, from the "Preface" to the second edition of his *A Philosophical Inquiry into the Origins of Our Ideas of the Sublime and Beautiful* (1757), summarize Burke's historical method and his deep skepticism that men can arrive at ultimate truths through the study of history:

> The characters of nature are legible, it is true, but they are not plain enough to enable those who run, to read them. We must make use of a cautious, I had almost said, a timorous method of proceeding. We must not attempt to fly, when we can scarcely pretend to creep. In considering any complex matter, we ought to examine every distinct ingredient in the composition, one by one; and reduce everything to the utmost simplicity; since the condition of our nature binds us to a strict law and very narrow limits. We ought afterwards to re-examine the principles by the effect of the composition, as well as the composition by that of the principles. We ought to compare our subject with things of a similar nature, and even with things of a contrary nature; for discoveries may be, and often are made by the contrast, which would escape us on the single view. The greater number of the comparisons we make, the more general and the more certain our knowedge is likely to prove, as built upon a more extensive and perfect induction.

> If an inquiry thus carefully conducted should fail at last of discovering the truth, it may answer an end perhaps as useful, in discovering to us the weakness of our own understanding. If it does not make us knowing, it may make us modest. If it does not preserve us from error, it may at least from the spirit of error; and may make us cautious of pronouncing with positiveness or with haste, when so much labor may end in so much uncertainty.

> That great chain of causes, which, linking one to another, even to the throne of God himself, can never be unravelled by any industry of ours. When we go but one step beyond the immediate sensible qualities of things, we go out of our depth. All we do after is but a

faint struggle, that shows we are in an element which does not belong to us.

Perhaps even more than David Hume, Burke was aware of the uncertainty of man's temporal knowledge, and skeptical that empiricism
and reason were sufficient instruments for establishing the causes and
effects of truth. Clearly, Burke was so aware of the unknown and
mysterious factors that constantly operate in human affairs that it was
impossible for him to have an ideological formula or system or
method of procedure to fully explain the temporal affairs of men. In
light of these convictions, it is not surprising that Burke had no philosophy of history, and that he was skeptical of all claims that politics
was or could ever be an exact science. Burke's conception of liberty
was basic to his belief that moral prudence was the first of political
virtues.

Burke's view of history as a reflection of the will and reason of God
and man is perhaps most clearly illustrated in his conviction of how
sovereign political power is legitimately exercised by each generation
under its inherited constitution. Each generation of Englishmen was
for Burke not the master of the constitution under which it lived, but
its creature at the latest point in history. The sovereignty of constitutional law always supercedes the exercise of present political sovereignty, because present rulers are themselves under the law that they
have inherited and administer. Even when their executive or legislative acts depart from past positive laws, they do not so much break
precedents as make new precedents for the future. To make the will
of the present generation absolute and supreme over the constitution,
as Dr. Richard Price, Thomas Paine, and others advocated, was in effect to destroy the constitution and to make the present convenience
of each generation the supreme source, test, and end of government.
Burke strongly condemned such an *ad hoc* conception of sovereignty. In the *Reflections* he wrote that "the temporary possessors and
life-renters" in the nation, "unmindful of what they have received
from their ancestors," invariably become as unmindful "of what is due
to their posterity."

To Burke, history is a preceptor of moral prudence, because among
other things, it teaches men reverence for the enduring achievements
of mankind, and links the generations of men. In the *Reflections*
Burke noted that without a sense of men's achievements in the past,
"the whole chain and continuity of the commonwealth would be bro-

ken; no one generation could link with the other; men would become little better than the flies of a summer."[9] When men expunge out of their minds the achievements of their ancestors, they are guilty of an insane kind of pride and arrogance: "I cannot conceive how any man can have brought himself to that pitch of presumption, to consider his country as nothing but *carte blanche*, upon which he may scribble whatever he pleases."[10] Without reverence for history as the embodiment of what God has willed and man has achieved over many centuries, men despise prudence and become fanatical ideologues in their methods of changing society: "Rage and frenzy will pull down more in half an hour than prudence, deliberation, and foresight can build up in a hundred years."[11] By placing a check upon the arbitrary will of men, prudence conserves the best achievements of each generation and transmits them unimpaired to the future through the continuity of history.

However, Burke did not believe that the "retrospective wisdom" of history should itself ever be made the basis of speculative theory in determining the practical decisions of present politics. History does not provide statesmen with political principles on how to rule in the ever changing circumstances of the present. Burke believed that statesmen should "enter into the most ample historical detail" of a problem, in order to understand the particulars of practical wisdom. But the chief concern of the statesman is the sum total of what constitutes "the business before him," in its particular and inherent character. Historical analogies are of very dubious and limited use as guides in solving current political problems, and metaphysical speculations based upon history were as suspect to Burke as similar speculations based upon abstract philosophy or mathematical logic.

As a preceptor of prudence, history taught that politics is the practical art of governing, not a theoretical science. To Burke no pure theory was a sufficient guide in practical politics, because theory as such could never supply the practical wisdom of prudence, and by making claims for some abstract truth, theory often ignored the particular and contingent in concrete situations, and at times even prevented sound political practice. Burke insisted that not abstract truth but concrete circumstances give "to every political principle its distinguished effect." In contrast to knowledge of the general principles of government, Burke wrote in the *Reflections*: "The science of constructing a commonwealth, or renovating it, or reforming it, is, like every other experimental science, not to be taught *a priori*."[12] The distinction between false theory and sound practice in politics was probably even more important to Burke than the appeal to history, because appeals to history were themselves only useful examples of the past habits of political wisdom exercised by men or of the dire consequence of imprudent actions.

PRUDENCE AND HISTORY
VERSUS METAPHYSICAL SPECULATIONS

Burke's lifelong intense antagonism against rational speculations and "metaphysical" theories of society springs directly from his view of history as a preceptor of moral prudence. In opposing metaphysical abstractions in politics, he invariably appealed to history and moral prudence as valid alternatives to the plausible delusions of speculative theorists. Burke denied that through the study of history men could derive many general infallible laws by which to govern society: "But as human affairs and human actions are not of a metaphysical nature, but the subject is concrete, complex, and moral, they cannot be subjected (without exceptions which reduce it almost to nothing) to any certain rule."[13] From this it follows that the leaders of nations cannot possess the means to reach a single remote goal toward which the state moves the nation, because the final goal either does not exist for man, or if it does cannot be known. Since the laws that govern civil society are too complex and mysterious to be known by human reason, no metaphysical or political speculation can supply the formulas or means to shape the state to preconceived ends. In his second *Letters on a Regicide Peace* (1796), Burke illustrates this point by describing how the nations of Europe have grown up through history:

> The states of the Christian world have grown up to their present magnitude in a great length of time and by a great variety of accidents. They have been improved to what we see them with greater or less degree of felicity and skill. Not one of them has been formed upon a regular plan or with any unity of design. As their constitutions are not systematical, they have not been directed to any particular end, eminently distinguished, and superceding every other. The objects which they embrace are of the greatest possible variety, and have become in a matter infinite. In all these old countries, the state has been made to the people, and not the people conformed to the state.[14]

In short, Burke believed that nations are not formed according to any theory; rather, theories are drawn from studying the evident structure of the state. Nations change and grow by at once adhering to the design evident in old establishments, and by alterations made within the inherited structure of laws and customs. These changes are determined by past experience and present necessities, and even by happy chance which improves the design even as it seems to depart from it. Human reason and free will aid the growth of the state by preserving inherited institutions and adjusting them continuously to changing circumstances and needs.

Burke's view of the general continuity of history and of how social changes occur within history is most evident in his statements on the constitutional development of England. As he noted in the *Reflections*, the constitution of England was not the result of a theory of ideal government, but of a long series of solutions to particular problems and crises, a process that Burke called "working after the pattern of Nature":

> The institutions of polity, the goods of fortune, the gifts of Providence, are handed down to us, and from us, in the same course and order. Our political system is placed in a just correspondence and symmetry with the order of the world, and with the mode of existence decreed to a permanent body composed of transitory parts,—wherein, by the disposition of a stupendous wisdom, moulding together the great mysterious incorporation of the human race, the whole at one time, is never old or middle-aged or young, but, in a condition of unchangeable constancy, moves on through the varied tenor of perpetual decay, fall, renovation, and progression. Thus, by preserving the method of Nature in the conduct of the state, in what we improve we are never wholly new, in what we retain we are never wholly obsolete.[15]

Through constitutional changes made from generation to generation the "chain and continuity" are maintained. The evolved constitution at the furthest point in history is "a deliberate election of ages and generations," in harmony with "the peculiar circumstances, occasions, tempers, dispositions, and moral, civil, and social habitudes of the people, which disclose themselves only in a long space of time."[16] The changes in the constitution of England not only reflected the corporate character of the English people, but in their relation through history extended to all its citizens the natural and civil rights to life, liberty, and property, which were the chief object of all good government.

From Burke's view of history it should be evident that his political philosophy was not and could not be a speculative science dealing with abstract truth, but that politics was for him the practical art of governing men through moral prudence, and that the state was a moral instrument for giving orders, justice, and civil liberty to all its subjects. The politician, by Burke's definition, was "the philosopher in action," and no prudent politician-philosopher could ever assume *a priori* knowledge of principles that would enable him to attain exact mathematical certainty in the consequences of his decisions. Politics was a part of practical normative reason, not of theoretical discursive logical reasoning; it was concerned with the good, not the true. The nature and actions of men are indeed under general laws of moral necessity, Burke believed, but because the will of man is free to obey or to defy the moral law, and because his social circumstances are infinitely varied, in contingent matters and details there can be no general laws of politics. Although justice must always be maintained, the determination of what is just in each particular instance, under the different institutions and conditions of mankind, must always vary in its means, according to the infinite variations of men's temporal circumstances. The common social nature of man is infinitely modified by climate, geography, history, religion, nationality, and race, by institutions, customs, manners, and habits, by all the civil circumstances of time, place, and occasions, which cut across and qualify, but do not impair the different means by which the great moral ends of society are fulfilled. Prudence is the principle that links the Divine will, as evidenced in the changing patterns of history, with the concrete practical affairs of men: "The progressive sagacity that keeps company with times and occasions," Burke wrote, "and decides upon things in their existing position, is that alone which can give true propriety, grace, and effect to a man's conduct. It is very hard to anticipate the occasion, and to live by a rule more general." Burke's view of history and principle of prudence made his political philosophy as far removed as possible from any theory of politics based on metaphysical speculations applied deductively as an exact science. It also made his political philosophy the complete antithesis of politics as propounded by Machiavelli.

PRUDENCE AS A MORAL VIRTUE

To Burke, "no moral questions are ever abstract questions." As a moral virtue prudence was the best corrective and positive alternative to the errors of rational metaphysical abstractions in politics. Burke's best statement of this belief is in *An Appeal from the New to the Old Whigs*:

> Nothing universal can be rationally affirmed on any moral or political subject. Pure metaphysical abstraction does not belong to these matters. The lines of morality are not like ideal lines of mathematics. They are broad and deep as well as long. They admit of exceptions; they demand modifications. These exceptions and modifications are not made by the process of logic, but by the rules of prudence. Prudence is not only the first in rank of the virtues political and moral, but she is the director, the regulator, the standard of them all.[17]

Burke always maintained that the exercise of competent jurisdiction in politics is a matter of moral prudence, because "moral necessity is not like metaphysical, or even physical." Tyranny was a more common abuse in government than usurpation, Burke believed, because even under legitimate legislatures, "if the rules of benignity and prudence are not observed," oppressive actions would result. Prudence, or a strict regard for circumstances, is not merely a matter of empirical observations and intellectual calculation; it is morally imperative to regard circumstances, because otherwise political actions could mortally injure those whom the statesman wishes to serve.

Burke's conception of prudence as a moral virtue is well illustrated in his attempted economical reform of 1780. In his speech (February 11, 1780), he distinguished between his principle of prudence and mere moral weakness or equivocation:

> It is much more easy to reconcile this measure to humanity, than to bring it to any agreement with prudence. I do not mean that little, selfish, pitiful, bastard thing, which sometimes goes by the name of a family in which it is not legitimate, and to which it is a disgrace—I mean that public and enlarged prudence, which, apprehensive of being disabled from rendering acceptable service to the world, withholds itself from those that are invidious.

Burke's remark "if I cannot reform with equity, I will not reform at all" and his statement "I am not possessed of an exact measure between real service and its reward" provoked Jeremy Bentham's sarcastic reply: "Except Edmund Burke, no man is thus ignorant." Bentham's willingness to compute the ratio between public service and its reward illustrates one of the great differences between Burke's principle of prudence and the utilitarian idea of "expediency."

To Burke, prudence is the general regulator of social changes, including the reforms of abuses in society, according to the legal norms of the constitution and the moral principles of natural law. As such, prudence is the cardinal political virtue because it supplies the practical means by which natural law principles are fulfilled in the various concrete circumstances of man's social life. Burke's prudence is not the utilitarian computation of circumstances, an intellectual calculation of how far political power might be utilized before provoking opposition. Nor is Burke's prudence merely the social virtue of tact. To Burke, prudence is part of God's "divine tactic" fulfilled through man's moral temperance and political tact. Prudence is the principle that checks the impetuous will and speculative reason and will of God, as manifested in the unfolding patterns of historical events, and in accordance with revealed normative laws in religion and natural law. Understood in this profoundly Aristotelian sense, Burke's principle of prudence is nothing less than the universal, eternal, and unchangeable moral law, applied in a great variety of ways in practice through politics to each particular man, at every moment and in all circumstances, under the constitutional sovereignty of various nations. Since "the situation of man is the preceptor of his duty," prudence tells us when we should "abate our demands in favor of moderation and justice, and tenderness to indiviudals." Prudence is not intellectual calculation, but the moral discretion that enables men to live by the spirit of moral natural law and constitutional law.

The claims of utilitarian writers that Burke belongs to their political camp has obscured the absolute difference between their conception of utility and his principle of prudence. Burke had a principle of utility, but he was no utilitarian. In the "Tracts on the Popery Laws" (1765), he indicated that he derived utility from Cicero's principle of moral equity, which was based upon "original justice." It was a utility "connected with and derived from our rational nature; for any other utility may be the utility of a robber." Many years later, in his attack on Warren Hastings' "system of corruption," Burke noted the governor's "attempt to justify it on the score of utility," and he added: "God forbid that prudence, which is the supreme guide, and indeed stands first of all virtues, should ever be the guide of vices." Burke distinguished carefully between a true and false adherent of moral prudence: "Our love to the occasionalist, but not server of occasions." In any conflict between merely utilitarian convenience and law, his stand was clear: "What the law respects shall be sacred to me. If the barriers of law should be broken down upon ideas of convenience, even of public convenience, we shall have no longer any thing certain among us." When rulers follow true moral prudence they are perfectly in accord with natural law and constitutional law, from which men's true civil and natural rights are derived. Burke believed that when claims to individual "rights" conflicted with moral expediency or prudence, they were not really "rights," and not, as Morley and the utilitarian critics of Burke said, that they were personal rights but had to yield to public expediency.

Late in life Lord Acton came to interpret Burke as a utilitarian, and charged that "Burke loved to evade the arbitration of principle." Burke did indeed refuse to engage in speculations based on metaphysical theories, particularly when such theories contributed nothing but heat toward the solution of a practical political problem which did not require an appeal to ultimate moral or legal principles. But apart from Acton's failure to distinguish between principles of political policy, which are subject to arbitration, and basic moral principles, which are beyond arbitration, Burke's whole practical political career is the best answer to Acton's misinterpretation. Burke's loyalty to the Rockingham Whigs, and his moral and intellectual guidance of Whig policies for almost three decades, in the face of strong administrative opposition, is but one sustained instance of his deep personal integrity. He gave up his seat for Bristol rather than support an iniquitous economic and religious policy against Ireland. For years after most of his colleagues would have liked to have quietly dropped Hastings' trial, Burke made himself unpopular because of the moral zeal with which he pursued a just decision for India. He broke lifelong friendships and stood alone for several years, rather than give approval of the French Revolution. Goldsmith's famous line is literally true: Burke was "too fond of the right to pursue the expedient." Because of his refusal to be bought by the Crown, Burke spent most of his political life with the loyal opposition. All of these factors in Burke's political life show that neither in practice nor in theory did his

principle of prudence cause him "to evade the arbitration of principle." Acton should have read Burke more carefully than to identify his
principle of prudence with the calculated expediency of utilitarian
self-interest.

Burke once described prudence as "the god of the lower world." In
Natural Right and History Leo Strauss has wisely seen fit to note that
"Prudence and 'this lower world' cannot be seen properly without
some knowledge of 'the higher world'—without genuine *theorie*."[18]
Religion and the natural law were for Burke the basis of his moral
principles in the higher world of political philosophy, just as English
common law supplied the legal principles for his practical politics. As
a practical means of applying the principles of natural law in "this
lower world" of civil society, prudence was supreme, because only
through prudence could statesmen give full regard to men's differences, have reverence for local loyalties, and take into account all the
circumstances involved in a problem. Through the ethical norms of
natural law and the legal norms of the common law and political prudence, Burke united ethics, law, and politics within a vast framework
that included religious mysticism concerning the Divine intent in human history and the immediate desires, needs, and objectives of men
in their concrete practical affairs.

Burke's ability to combine the natural law and prudence made his
political philosophy thoroughly consistent, yet almost wholly unsys-
tematic. Religion, natural law, English common law, and prudence, all
operating together in history, enabled Burke to fuse to the limit of
their valence the most sublime moral precepts and the most concrete
empirical facts, details, and circumstances, so that political theory and
practice were one: "A statesman," wrote Burke, "never losing sight of
principles, is to be guided by circumstances; and judging contrary to
the exigencies of the moment he may ruin his country for ever." This
is the key statement behind Burke's definition of the politician as "a
philosopher in action." As a philosopher, he drew his ethical principles from religion and the natural law; as a politician, he applied his
principles in the concrete, with a full regard to historical circumstances, through his conception of prudence as a moral virtue.

For Burke, history is "the preceptor of prudence" because it reveals
"the known march of the ordinary providence of God." History was
for Burke a secondary form of Divine revelation, supplementing
Scripture and right reason in natural law. History taught practical
ethics, not directly through moral precepts, but indirectly, by incul-

cating the spirit of ethics through temperance and moderation: "Our physical well-being, our moral worth, our social happiness, our political tranquility, all depend on that control of our appetites and passions, which the ancients designated by the cardinal virtue of Temperance." Burke believed that "the restraints on men are to be reckoned among their rights." In civil society, the moral law alone was insufficient to restrain the passions of men. The most immediate restraints on men come from the established institutions and legal processes of society, regardless of its political structure. In every just social order, sound ethical norms are embodied in its established laws and institutions, so that in ordinary cases, within "the ordinary providence of God" which constitutes the historical process, society provided the practical means of solving its political problems by the legal norms of government, in harmony with the moral law. Since for Burke "the actual and the present is the rational," prudence was a sufficient guide in the ordinary political problems of men. It was not necessary to appeal to transcendental moral standards in most political conflicts; such appeals were reserved for extraordinary violations of the moral law, as in the cases of British misrule in Ireland and India and the Jacobin tyranny in France. But for "the ordinary providence of God," which constitutes human affairs in history, prudence is indeed "the god of this lower world."

NOTES

This chapter was originally published in *Religion and Society*, vol. 1, no. 5, October 1968. Reprinted with permission.

1. John Morley, *Edmund Burke: A Historical Study* (New York: Macmillan, 1867), 152.

2. Charles E. Vaughan, *Studies in the History of Political Philosophy Before and After Rousseau* (New York: Longmans, Green & Co., 1925), II, 5.

3. John MacCunn, *The Political Philosophy of Burke* (London: Edward Arnold, 1913), 193.

4. Elie Halevy, *The Growth of Philosophic Radicalism* (New York: Macmillan, 1928), 158, 161.

5. Lois Whitney, *Primitivism and the Idea of Progress* (Baltimore: Johns Hopkins University Press, 1934), 196–97.

6. Richard M. Weaver, *The Ethics of Rhetoric* (Chicago: Regnery, 1953), 58.

7. *The Correspondence of Edmund Burke* (Chicago: University of Chicago Press, 1960), II, 282.

8. *The Works of the Right Honorable Edmund Burke* (Boston: Little, Brown & Co., 1904), V, 235.

9. *Works*, III, 357.

10. *Works*, III, 440.

11. *Works*, III, 455.

12. *Works*, III, 311.

13. *Works*, XI, 69.

14. *Works*, V, 373.

15. *Works*, III, 275.

16. *Works*, VII, 95.

17. *Works*, IV, 80–81.

18. Leo Strauss, *Natural Right and History* (Chicago: University of Chicago Press, 1965), 321.

5

Bringing Prudence Back In: Leadership, Statecraft, and Political Science

Carnes Lord

In the United States today, the idea of "leadership" is very much in vogue. This is in part because of its growing prominence in the corporate world, where it has been touted as an essential supplement to traditional business "management" in an era of rapid technological change and global competition. But the phenomenon is a much wider one, reflecting impulses relating to character formation and civic engagement. Leadership has become a watchword of public discourse in contemporary America because (or so one might speculate) it provides a value-neutral and therefore generally acceptable way to foster moral and civic virtues at a time when these qualities are felt to be in decreasing supply.

All of this is no doubt to be welcomed, but it has a certain sedative effect when it comes to serious analysis of the role of leadership in politics. "Leadership" in such contexts is something almost wholly benign. It is an exquisitely democratic activity, one in which the interests of leaders and the interests of followers fully coincide, leaders are sensitive to the needs and wants of followers, and decision making is highly consensual. As such, it is a fundamentally apolitical concept, ignoring central concerns of political leadership such as power and authority. And because it assumes that leadership is a quality that can be effectively exercised in any field of human endeavor, it tends to downplay the distinctiveness of political leadership and its special requirements. In particular, it downplays the need for political leaders to have any specialized knowledge of political phenomena. Leadership so understood, to use Max Weber's well-known formulation, rests on personal "charisma" more than it does on the "rational-legal" processes of policy formation that are at the heart of modern bureaucratic governance.[1]

The theory and, indeed, much of the practice of leadership today bring to mind Aristotle's observation about the ancient "sophists" who tried yet failed to invent the discipline of political science. "For the most part," he says, "they do not even know what sort of thing it is or what things it has to do with, for otherwise they would not have laid down that it is the same as rhetoric or even inferior to it, or believed it is easy to legislate by collecting the most renowned laws—they think it possible to select the best laws, as if the very selection were not a matter of understanding, and correct judgment were not the most important thing here."[2] Some twenty years ago, in his pioneering work on leadership, James MacGregor Burns could write: "The crisis of leadership today is the mediocrity or irresponsibility of so many of the men and women in power, but leadership rarely rises to the need for it. The fundamental crisis underlying mediocrity is intellectual. If we know all too much about our leaders, we know far too little about leadership. We fail to grasp the essence of leadership that is relevant to the modern age and hence we cannot agree even on the standards by which to measure, recruit, and reject it."[3]

These words remain true enough today. There can be little question that the contemporary world—and not least, the advanced democracies—is experiencing a leadership deficit of significant dimensions, and that much of the reason for this is the lack of appropriate intellectual preparation for leadership functions in the political class. No one should underestimate the importance of the psychological and moral requirements of leadership, or the special challenges today's leaders face in this area. But democratic electorates seem sensitive to this aspect of leadership almost in inverse proportion to their insouciant disinterest in the fundamental question: what is it exactly that politicians must know in order to lead effectively? The answer plainly has little to do with the tactics and techniques of winning elections and maintaining a strong position in opinion polls—although these things are a major preoccupation for most democratic leaders today. It has to do with knowledge of what is perhaps best called by the old-fashioned term "statecraft."

Statecraft in the sense indicated is a certain kind of reasoned knowledge or expertise. This kind of knowledge is not what might be called policy knowledge. In contemporary politics, the language of policy is spoken universally. But this is a language easily learned and just as easily unlearned, one that is in constant flux as issues are thrust forward into a leader's awareness, get resolved, recede in political importance, and are eventually forgotten. It is, to pursue the metaphor, a language that a user can make very serviceable without mastering its grammar. Even politicians who speak it fluently need not master its grammar; indeed, to the extent that they are politically successful, they tend to lose the incentive to do so. Mastery of the grammar of politics is one way to think about the nature of statecraft.

Though far from absent in the language of contemporary political discourse, the concept of statecraft is rarely given sustained analytic attention or brought into relationship with the idea of leadership. Even its basic meaning is not entirely clear. The term is most commonly used to refer to diplomacy or the conduct of foreign policy in a broad and comprehensive sense. Yet it is also widely recognized that the foreign policy behavior of states cannot be adequately understood if they are treated as indistinguishable billiard balls colliding on the international stage according to a set of predictable laws. Domestic politics and the cultural and ideological imperatives that shape and motivate the decisions of leaders are as important as external factors in determining their behavior, if not indeed more so. From the perspective of statesmen themselves, the weightiest political issues are no respecters of the artificial boundaries between academic disciplines. They are connected in complex ways, their relationships governed by a particular logic that is more than the sum of their parts. The grammar that gives these issues their articulation and the logic that links them—such is statecraft in what is arguably its comprehensive and proper sense.

Carl von Clausewitz, the great theoretician of the art of war, once observed that war and politics have the same logic, but a different grammar.[4] The point is not self-evident, but whatever qualification it might need for our own age, it is a helpful point of reference in coming to grips with the concept of statecraft. Like strategy in war, statecraft is an art of coping with an adversarial environment, one in which actions generate reactions in unpredictable ways and chance and uncertainty rule. Like strategy, too, statecraft is also an art of relating means to ends. If, in Clausewitz's formulation, strategy is the art of using battles to achieve the objectives of the war, statecraft is the art of using wars and other instruments available to political leaders to achieve national goals. Statecraft must be concerned, then, both with the goals of a nation and with the resources necessary to achieve them. The exercise of leadership may amount to articulating a "vision," but statecraft properly understood is also about something more—and something arguably more difficult: the ways visions are implemented. Effective statecraft requires an understanding of the various instruments actually or potentially available to statesmen and an ability to use them in coordinated fashion in differing circumstances.[5]

If statecraft today is largely a forgotten art, much of the responsibility for this lies with contemporary social science. Over a century or more, a vast literature has grown up that claims to seek comprehensive political knowledge using methods derived more or less loosely from modern natural science. It is not to our purpose to rehearse the various inadequacies of this literature. A great deal can be learned from it that is useful for the practice of statecraft. The problem is that political science (a term I use expansively of the political or policy-relevant components of all of the social sciences), with its scientific or universalistic pretensions, in effect abandons the perspective of practicing statesmen and slights their concerns. In the eyes of most political scientists, the cognitive status of statecraft differs little from the cognitive status of witchcraft. Political science is preoccupied with the identification of law-like regularities in social and political behavior rather than the dynamics of particular political situations, the kind of knowledge that is of most practical use to politicians. It discounts the value of "mere" experience and common sense, the stuff of ordinary political judgment. It tends to focus on impersonal "systems" or "forces" as the key explanatory factors in politics, not individual leaders. And it tends to pay insufficient attention to the various instruments of statecraft and the problems statesmen face in utilizing them effectively.[6]

Woodrow Wilson was one of the founders of American political science; his own outlook on politics had been decisively shaped by the speeches and writings of the great eighteenth-century British parliamentarian Edmund Burke. Abraham Lincoln learned his politics from the Bible and the plays of Shakespeare. When Napoleon invaded Egypt in 1798, the Bible and the Koran were among a few "political" books he took along (Machiavelli's *Prince* was another). The American founding fathers sought inspiration for their "new science of politics" in political philosophers such as Locke and Montesquieu. Machiavelli turned to the Roman historian Titus Livy. In general, history was in older times the principal medium of political education. Classic works such as Tacitus's histories of early imperial Rome, Gibbon's *Decline and Fall of the Roman Empire*, Hume's *History of England*, Macaulay's *History of Greece*, and Henry Adams' *History of the United States in the Administrations of Adams and Jefferson*—most of them written with an explicit pedagogical intention—taught the secrets of despotism and the principles of republican or constitutional government to the politically active elites of the modern West over many generations.

One of the fundamental developments in political life in the West over the last century or so has been the displacement of these older sources of political knowledge by political science. In education, the general culture, and even the councils of state, expertise in politics has gradually come to be identified with political science as studied in our universities. This kind of expertise alone is now considered authoritative: it is certified in various ways by professional organizations and journals, extensively underwritten by wealthy foundations, and recognized by the government itself in the form of official commissions, funded studies, and other public roles.

What is more, as political science has become more authoritative, it has also changed its character. Though still concerned with the pursuit of pure scientific truth as it sees it, it has developed a corporate character and set of interests.[7] Moreover, it has become increasingly engaged in day-to-day struggles over public policy. Some years ago, it could be argued, political science simply neglected issues of statecraft in its concern for the timeless and the universal. Today, political scientists are eager to make their mark in the political arena and to engage current issues on their own ground. The result of this development is to reduce even more severely the scope for judgment and action by politicians. Faced with the challenge posed by political science, political leaders seem to have essentially two options. One is to defer entirely to political science expertise. The other is to ignore this expertise, in the name either of a purely tactical or pragmatic politics or of a charismatic "vision" that rejects ordinary politics altogether.

The critical question is whether or to what extent political science has succeeded in providing an objective, generally agreed, comprehensive, and coherent approach to political phenomena and the issues of contemporary politics. Even in the heyday of the discipline, few would have been hardy enough to affirm or predict this. Today, it is widely acknowledged that political science is in fundamental disarray—scarcely closer to formulating a comprehensive theory of politics than it ever was, fragmented into warring (or non-communicating) schools, and of doubtful relevance to the actual practice of politics in contemporary democracies. Partly in reaction to this situation, the discipline has moved since the 1970s to engage more directly and extensively with issues of contemporary public policy. Unfortunately, this "policy turn" has been unable to escape the technocratic and positivistic spirit that arguably continues to pervade the discipline as a whole.[8]

An unfortunate (though predictable) side effect of the greater engagement of the discipline in policy issues in recent years has been to polarize and politicize scholarly disagreements. Apart from the dangers of corruption of the academic enterprise that are inherent in this development, it further complicates the life of politicians. When political scientists behave more like lawyers arguing a brief than objective analysts, politicians cannot avoid playing the role of judges; yet they generally lack the intellectual preparation to do so effectively, or the patience to grapple with the jargon and intramural disputes of the academy. All this is curiously reminiscent of the situation confronting political leaders of late antiquity or the early modern era who refereed the theological disputes that threatened to disturb the peace in their domains.

The problematic relationship between politicians and scientific knowledge of course extends beyond political science. Given the complexity of economic life and its political importance in all contemporary states, politicians cannot afford to be wholly ignorant of modern economics. Nor can they always avoid direct engagement in highly abstruse scientific-technical matters when these involve large outlays of public funds or become politically sensitive. Even when the experts in these various fields are in agreement among themselves (and there is certainly a larger area of general consensus among economists than among political scientists), however, it is rarely easy to translate their technical knowledge into language that is comprehensible to politicians, let alone to constituencies that may require persuading or appeasing. In any event, politicians must regularly make decisions about these matters—whether only to allot funds or make key appointments—that demand an independent exercise of political judgment.

What is missing in the contemporary understanding of political knowledge is an appreciation not merely of the scope and nature of its subject matter, but also of its proper mode. The mode of knowing that is at the core of statecraft in its traditional sense is political judgment, or to use another old-fashioned term, "prudence." At its simplest, this notion implies that there is a kind of cognition that is specially suited to political decision making and action. It implies that politicians, because of their greater experience of political matters, develop an intellectual ability that enables them to make sound political decisions—sounder than the decisions that are apt to be made by those lacking such experience, whatever their intellectual capabilities or store of relevant knowledge might be.[9]

The classic articulation of the notion of prudence appears in the thought of Aristotle. In his two great works, the *Politics* and the *Nicomachean Ethics*, Aristotle in effect founded the discipline of political science in what may be called its pre-scientific form. Aristotle's term for the discipline of political science (*politike*) can equally be rendered "political expertise" or "statecraft": there is no sharp distinction for him between the theory of politics and its practice. According to Aristotle, prudence or practical wisdom (as the term *phronesis* is sometimes translated) is the mode of knowing proper to political science. Prudence differs fundamentally from scientific or theoretical knowledge. It is the faculty we use in applying general principles to particular circumstances that require decision and action. It thus requires both general knowledge of a certain kind and an understanding of circumstances that can only come from experience; an important implication of this is that prudence tends to be found mostly in mature and experienced people, not the young. Part of the general knowledge prudence requires is knowledge of the principles of morality. Prudence in this sense is then a kind of virtue. In its most common form, prudence is a virtue that comes into play in the decisions we make about our own lives. In a special sense, however, it is the virtue of political leaders.[10]

What kinds of general political knowledge do politicians need? Aristotle never fully addresses this question, but he provides several important clues. The first comes in his observation that there are five matters generally at the center of public deliberation or discussion: "revenues and expenditures, war and peace, defense of the territory, imports and exports, and legislation"—or in more contemporary terminology, finance, foreign policy, defense, trade, and constitutional law.[11] With its perhaps surprising emphasis on the economic dimension of statecraft, this list could not readily be improved upon today. It is worth noting that in the passage just referred to, Aristotle goes on to stress the importance of learning about other states as well as one's own, including lessons that might be gleaned from their domestic politics. He also mentions the value of historical knowledge, particularly as it relates to decisions to go to war—presumably because politicians are likely to have less direct experience of these relatively rare situations.

Clues may also be found in Aristotle's more theoretical remarks concerning what politics is about. In its original meaning, "politics" is simply the affairs of the "city" (*polis*, the Greek equivalent of our "state"). As Aristotle argues at the beginning of his *Politics*, the city is a kind of partnership or association. Like other partnerships or associations, it aims at some good common to its members; but what is distinctive about the city is that it is the ultimate partnership and aims at an ultimate good, one that embraces all of the lesser goods of the lesser partnerships (the family, for example). This ultimate good, Aristotle tells us at the beginning of the *Nicomachean Ethics*, is well-being or happiness.[12]

Several implications flow from this. Because the common good pursued by political leaders is comprehensive, it requires them to grasp in some way all of the lesser goods that contribute to it. Aristotle draws an analogy between the politician and the "master builder" (*architekton*)—in effect, a general contractor. General contractors do not have to have detailed knowledge of all the crafts that are needed to build a house. What they must know, rather, is how to coordinate and integrate the activities of the specialized craftsmen who work for them. And, equally important, they must be capable of judging the final products of these craftsmen, in terms both of their intrinsic excellence and of their contribution to the success of the overall enterprise. The good politician, Aristotle tells us, is someone capable of "architectonic and practical thinking." He "uses" arts or kinds of expertise such as generalship and rhetoric, but subordinates them to the overall good it is his own job to pursue. The knowledge of the "user" may well be intrinsically inferior to the knowledge of the maker or doer, but from a practical standpoint, it is superior: the ultimate test of a house is not the quality of its materials or workmanship, but how well it suits the needs of the people who are going to live there.[13]

A second and equally fundamental point has to do with Aristotle's identification of "happiness" as the ultimate good, and therefore in some sense the primary preoccupation of political science. At first sight, this seems odd and hard to justify. Americans have long been comfortable with the more restrictive formulation of the objectives of politics—"life, liberty, and the pursuit of happiness"—offered in the Declaration of Independence. This formulation implies that politicians have no business trying to achieve or even define a substantive vision of happiness, but rather should concern themselves only with providing the means necessary for the pursuit of private visions of happiness. It suggests that the primary preoccupation of politics is or should be with things that are instrumental if not simply material. Aristotle, by contrast, insists that politics is also and more fundamentally about things "just and noble." Happiness, so far from being mere subjective satisfaction or pleasure, turns out to be an "activity of the soul in accordance with virtue."[14] Politicians—or at any rate genuine politicians—must therefore give special attention to virtue, since this is what makes citizens good and law-abiding.[15] Furthermore, since happiness is a condition of the soul more than the body, politicians must have some knowledge of the workings of the human soul—of psychology.[16]

All of this sounds alien to contemporary ways of thinking; but is it in fact? It would not be difficult to make the case that Aristotle's position is closer to current American thought and practice than is the theoretical liberalism reflected in the Declaration of Independence. Consider, to cite an instructive recent example, the emerging national consensus that traditional welfare programs have not only failed to alleviate poverty but have themselves contributed to a range of social pathologies in the urban underclass. This consensus is based on a new appreciation of the importance of family stability and a culture of individual responsibility for the economic and personal success of the poor, which is to say, of the moral and psychological factors that condition social behavior. The confusion of (material) "welfare" with general social well-being that has been at the core of the problems of the

American welfare system is a mistake that would never be committed by a politician of Aristotle's stamp. To summarize an argument that has been developed at length by George Will, statecraft, even in the contemporary era, is inevitably a form of "soulcraft."[17]

A related feature of Aristotelian political science is its acknowledged imprecision. "Problems of what is noble and just, which politics examines, present so much variety and irregularity that some people believe they exist only by convention and not by nature. The problem of the good, too," he continues, "presents a similar kind of irregularity, because in many cases good things bring harmful results." Accordingly, we must not expect the same consistency in politics that we do, say, in mathematics. A properly educated or cultivated person is one who "searches for that degree of precision in each kind of study which the nature of the subject at hand admits; it is obviously just as foolish to accept arguments of probability from a mathematician as to demand strict demonstrations from an orator." This is another reason, it may be added, why political knowledge rests so squarely on experience. Young people cannot be competent politicians because of their lack of experience, though they may well be competent mathematicians or scientists. "Each man can judge competently the things he knows," Aristotle continues. "A good judge in each particular field is one who has been trained in it, and a good judge in general, a man who is generally cultivated."[18] This implies that the true education of politicians derives less from any specialized training in political science than from a general or liberal education and wide experience of the world.

Do politicians then not need any kind of specialized training in statecraft? Again, Aristotle does not openly address this crucial question; but he indicates his view clearly enough. Of the five areas of political deliberation he mentions, Aristotle has virtually nothing to say of trade, finance, defense, or foreign policy. His *Politics* is instead dedicated entirely to the last of these: "legislation"—more accurately, that aspect of legislation that concerns the fundamental political arrangements of a state, or what Aristotle calls the "regime." Why this limitation? One can surmise that Aristotle felt the economic and security dimensions of statecraft to be too variable and dependent on external circumstances to lend themselves to useful general analysis. Legislation—or perhaps better stated, the art of regime management—is more within the control of political leaders. At the same time, it appears to be at once more intellectually challenging and more problematic. It is the area of political knowledge that most attracts the attention of non-politicians, because it involves fundamental questions of justice and power and necessarily generates political controversy. It tempts intellectuals of various descriptions to propose speculative schemes of reform that are often superficially appealing, yet lack basic political sense. Politicians themselves, Aristotle lets us understand, are not entirely immune to the charm of such schemes.[19] Perhaps the most important task of political science is to provide politicians the conceptual armament to resist them. Political science so understood is the ally of prudence.

At the same time, it is critical to recognize that Aristotle's ethical treatises too are an integral part of political science as he conceives it. Knowledge of "just and noble" things is also of direct relevance for legislation, as well as for the application of law in the courtroom; and much of the theoretical account of the virtues in the *Nicomachean Ethics* can be understood as providing the necessary intellectual scaffolding for forensic (courtroom) argument and judicial decision—functions that in Aristotle's time were not sharply distinguished from political judgment. This area too, Aristotle strongly implies, cannot be mastered or mastered adequately through ordinary experience, but requires an intellectually disciplined inquiry that is capable of transcending the limitations of experience or of the cultural assumptions through which it tends to be filtered.

A detailed articulation of Aristotle's approach to political science and its implications for the practice of statecraft is beyond the scope of this discussion, but the following larger point is worth making. Under the impact of the doctrines of modern liberalism and their remote source, the thought of Machiavelli, the guiding concerns of Aristotelian political science ceased to be central to the study of statecraft. On the one hand, regime management was discovered to be superceded by the invention of the constitution, a "machine that would go of itself" or that did not require the supervision of wise statesmen or the active exercise of political leadership.[20] On the other hand, ethics or the formation of character was held to be inessential to a statecraft centered on the satisfaction of men's instrumental and material needs—not to say in important ways *inimical* to that statecraft through the opening it afforded religious institutions and elites to vie for secular power. That the moderns have the better of this argument is, to say the least, far from evident to anyone surveying the history of the century just past, or of the political health of contemporary democracies.

NOTES

1. Fundamental on this subject is Robert Eden, *Political Leadership* and *Nihilism: A Study of Weber and Nietzsche* (Tampa: University Presses of Florida, 1983).

2. Aristotle, *Nicomachean Ethics* 10.9.1181a12-18. (This and subsequent translations of Aristotle are my own.)

3. James MacGregor Burns, *Leadership* (New York: Harper & Row, 1978), 1–2.

4. Carl von Clausewitz, *On War*, ed. and trans. by Michael Howard and Peter Paret (Princeton: Princeton University Press, 1976), 605.

5. For statecraft as a strategic discipline, consider, for example, Colin S. Gray, *War, Peace, and Victory: Strategy and Statecraft for the New Century* (New York: Simon & Schuster, 1990).

6. Aspects of this critique are usefully developed by Alexander L. George, *Bridging the Gap: Theory and Practice in Foreign Policy* (Washington, D.C.: United States Institute of Peace Press, 1993), David A. Baldwin, *Economic Statecraft* (Princeton: Princeton University Press, 1985), and Daniel L. Byman and Kenneth M. Pollack, "Let Us Now Praise Great Men: Bringing the Statesman Back In," *International Security* 25 (Spring 2001): 107–46.

7. This is a principle theme of David M. Ricci, *The Tragedy of Political Science: Politics, Scholarship, and Democracy* (New Haven: Yale University Press, 1984).

8. See, for example, Douglas Torgerson, "Policy Analysis and Public Life: The Restoration of *Phronesis?*" in *Political Science in History*, ed. James Farr, John S. Dryzek, and Stephen T. Leonard (Cambridge: Cambridge University Press, 1995), 225–52.

9. See generally Ronald Beiner, *Political Judgment* (Chicago: University of Chicago Press, 1983), and Peter J. Steinberger, *The Concept of Political Judgment* (Chicago: University of Chicago Press, 1993).

10. Aristotle discusses prudence thematically in *Nicomachean Ethics* VI 7-13. For the distinction between the general and special (political) types of prudence, see 8.1141b23-42all. On the character of Aristotelian social or political science generally see Carnes Lord and David K. O'Connor, eds., *Essays on the Foundations of Aristotelian Political Science* (Berkeley: University of California Press, 1991), 1–48.

11. *Rhetoric* 1.4.1359b19-23.

12. *Politics* 1.1.1252a1-5; *Nicomachean Ethics* 1.4.1095a14 ff.

13. *Nicomachean Ethics* 1.1.1094a6-18, 2.1094a26-b11. The phrase "architectonic and practical thinking" occurs in *Eudemian Ethics* 1.6.1217a1-6.

14. *Nicomachean Ethics* 1.2.1094b14-15, 7.1097a15-98a18.

15. *Politics* 3.9.1280a31-b12.

16. *Nicomachean Ethics* 1.13.1102a5-1103a1O.

17. George W. Will, *Statecraft as Soulcraft: What Government Does* (New York: Simon & Schuster, 1983). See also Charles Murray, *In Pursuit of Happiness and Good Government* (New York: Simon & Schuster, 1988).

18. *Nicomachean Ethics* 1.3.1094b11-95a13.

19. "There are certain persons who, it being held to belong to a philosopher to say nothing randomly but rather to use reasoned argument, make arguments that are alien to the subject and empty (they do this sometimes out of ignorance and sometimes from charlatanry) and are not detected, thus taking in those who are experienced and capable of acting, though they themselves neither have nor are capable of architectonic or practical thinking" (*Eudemian Ethics* 1.6.1217a1-6). For Aristotle's critique of sophistic political science see further *Politics* 2.8.

20. Michael Kammen, *A Machine That Would Go of Itself: The Constitution in American Culture* (New York: Random House, 1986).

6

A Postscript to *Political Judgment*

Ronald Beiner

The idea of democracy presupposes an account of political judgment, for without an understanding of how human beings are capable of making reasoned judgments about a shared public world, it
would remain mysterious how one could conceive the very notion of
a democratic citizen. Judgment has become a notable theme in contemporary political theory largely owing to the efforts of Hannah
Arendt, who was inspired by her reading of Immanuel Kant's *Critique of Judgment* and tried to make his account of aesthetic judgment the basis of a political philosophy.[1] What Arendt hoped to draw
theoretically from her politically charged reading of Kant's third *Critique* is well summarized in the following passage from an early version of Arendt's Kant lectures:

> The *Critique of Judgment* is the only [one of Kant's] great writings
> where his point of departure is the World and the senses and capabili-
> ties which made men (in the plural) fit to be inhabitants of it. This is
> perhaps not yet political philosophy, but it certainly is its *sine qua non*.
> If it could be found that in the capacities and regulative traffic and in-
> tercourse between men who are bound to each other by the common
> possession of a world (the earth) there exists an *a priori* principle, then
> it would be proved that man is essentially a political being.[2]

Here Arendt more or less announces the program for a theory of political judgment drawn from Kant. Sadly, she herself never saw this
program to completion; however, her Kant Lectures help to point us

in the direction of such a theory (and my own modest efforts in my book *Political Judgment* attempt to pursue some of her thoughts, juxtaposed to some thoughts of Gadamer's).[3]

In fact, the attempt to reflect philosophically on what makes human beings capable of sizing up the "ultimate particulars" that compose moral and political life and that present themselves for judgment goes all the way back to Aristotle's analysis of phronesis, practical wisdom, in Book 6 of the *Nicomachean Ethics*[4]; and among contemporary theorists, a whole generation of neo-Aristotelian philosophers have highlighted once again the importance of concretely situated practical judgment as central to the understanding of ethical and political life.[5] The Aristotelian theme of practical wisdom is nicely encapsulated by Alasdair MacIntyre when he defines moral virtue in terms of a capacity for practical reasoning that "is not manifested so much in the knowledge of a set of generalizations or maxims which may provide our practical inferences with major premises; its presence or absence rather appears in the kind of capacity for judgment which the agent possesses in knowing how to select among the relevant stack of maxims and how to apply them in particular situations."[6] In an important sense, reflection on the theme of judgment teaches us the limits of theory, for judgment (whether in ethical or political life) attends to particulars that are beyond the purview of theory as such. As Hans Jonas makes the point: "there is no science of judgment. . . . judgment as concerned with particulars is necessarily outside science and strictly the bridge between the abstractions of the understanding and the concreteness of life." He goes on (again in reference to Aristotle): "knowledge of use . . . is acquired or learned in ways different from those of theory. This is the reason why Aristotle denied there being a science of politics and practical ethics; the *where, when, to whom* . . . cannot be reduced to general principles. Thus there is theory and use of theory, but no theory of the use of theory."[7] Or as Hans-Georg Gadamer more succinctly puts it: "There are no rules governing the reasonable use of rules."[8]

An account of political judgment that attempted to vindicate the capacities for judging and deliberating on the part of democratic citizens would be founded on the following three claims:

(1) We are constantly making political judgments. In saying "we," what is meant is not any particular group of specialists, or specially qualified persons, but ordinary people, that is, common citizens.

(2) In making these judgments, we relate to (and at the same time constitute) an intersubjectively shared public world.

(3) The active exercise of a faculty of political judgment is *good* for us as human beings.

The corollary of this is that the shrinking of opportunities for active judgment, or the increasingly passive adherence to norms and beliefs within society, indicates a dislocation, or even pathology, within contemporary political life. This places the account of political judgment within the wider context of a theory of the human good. It also characterizes reflection on political judgment as a point of departure for a more general political philosophy of citizenship. The exercise of active judgment is good for us because citizenship in general is good for us. Citizenship is an important aspect of the human good, and, it follows, so is "civic judgment," or the judging of public affairs "as a citizen."

These claims, taken together, are both descriptive and normative. They tell us (descriptively) what it is to be a political being, and they tell us (normatively) what is desirable about being a political being. The exercise of judgment characterizes both what we *are* and what we *ought to be*. This is the reason for saying that it presupposes (or serves to develop) an account of the human good, of what conduces to a proper or excellent human life.

In pursuing an argument, say between A and B, where the conflicting claims advanced clearly refer to worldly, and therefore potentially intersubjective, phenomena (as opposed to matters of mere faith), either A's judgment is more comprehensive than B's, or B's judgment is more comprehensive than A's, or both views are one-sided and need to be encompassed within some third perspective that does justice to the truth in each. Moreover, the fact that we actually take up a particular stance in the discussion *already* commits us to the presumption that there is a truth of the matter (binding on all parties), i.e., we think our own judgment is comprehensive, until we can be persuaded otherwise. Without the assumption of a practical truth that forms the object of practical reason, political judgment would be impossible *tout court*.

So it is hard to discern any grounds for denying that a resolution of the conflicting claims is *in principle* within reach. Only if our respective beliefs were matters of unshakeable faith would a resolution, in principle, be unavailable. The fact that each of the participants actually assumes that a resolution is, in principle, available is shown by the fact that each, in fact, holds fast to their respective opinions, entailing that the requisite resolution of the conflict is already at hand, viz., their own opinion. The implicit assumption is that if the other party came to a certain insight or overcame a certain blindness, they too would be converted to one's own, more comprehensive, belief. This means that each of the parties, despite their differences, already assumes that these matters are legitimately within the sphere of common judgment and amenable to common reason. Only someone who had no political opinions and offered no political judgments could coherently deny the claims of reason. (This is a variation of Jürgen Habermas's argument for communicative rationality.)[9] In matters of faith, by contrast, the resolution is, in principle, more remote since one's claims are intrinsically related to an alleged access to certain (private) experiences, and one either has these private experiences or one doesn't. No appeal to intersubjectively shareable features of our situation can validate the claims of one side or the other if one lacks the appropriate spiritual receptivity (hence Max Weber's remark that he simply wasn't religiously "musical").[10] It may be conceded that the distinction is more complex, since attaining the insights required for the more comprehensive point of view in morals and politics also depends upon having the right kinds of experience, and presupposes an analogous cognitive receptivity—analogous insofar as it too depends on a proper education of the soul, as it were. But our experiences can be enlarged (through sharing the experiences of others), and our receptivity for insights can be educated (by opening ourselves to the insights of others), though this may also be true for conflicts in the sphere of faith. *Perhaps* religious questions, as well, are amenable to rational resolution (though I doubt it), but in any case, here at least one can see clear limits in principle to shareable experience that *cannot* be identified in the political sphere.

Consider the following example of conflicting political opinions. A thinks that Israeli policies towards the Palestinians are defensible and just: Israel is a legitimate state, and its policies in relation to the Palestinians are consistent with what a state can legitimately do to secure its existence and protect the security of its people. B, on the other hand, believes that Israeli policies are a case of one nation trampling on the rights of another nation, and denying the latter its legitimate claim to determine its own destiny. It is logically impossible that *both* sets of beliefs are in this respect straightforwardly true (that Israeli policy towards the Palestinians both is and is not morally and politically defensible), though it is (logically) possible that there is some truth in both of these points of view. Either A's view is correct, or B's view is correct, or both views express partial truths in need of a more comprehensive perspective that gives each its due. The fact that all of us who make such judgments pursue the argument at all entails that we hold our own judgments to be rationally binding upon the other no less than upon ourselves (the non-cognitivist achieves coherence only by observing total silence). In principle, there are always a multiplicity of ways in which such differences can be resolved. We can appeal to facts or features of situations that are publicly available and shareable. We can await further evidence for realization of our hopes or confirmation of our suspicions. We can expand our reflections by considering the issue from every possible angle, in the hope that one of the parties will come to a new insight, or appreciate the power of an argument that was previously overlooked or not seen to be decisive. After all, the full set of considerations that led to the conclusion of one person's moral reasoning are no less available (potentially) for the consideration of the other person, and vice versa. Where in all this are there *logical* limits, or limits in principle, to the possibilities of bridging practical differences? Again, the considerations that decide the question for one person are contained in the public realm, and therefore are potentially available to influence (eventually) the deliberations of the other (or vice versa).

Or consider conflicting judgments about NATO's 1999 bombing campaign against Yugoslavia: on the one side, the view that this was a legitimate intervention on behalf of the victims of genocide rightly intended to compel the Serbs to halt their ethnic cleansing of Albanian Kosovars; on the other side, the view that it was a misguided folly that, in violation of international law, infringed upon Yugoslav sovereignty and only worsened the condition of the Kosovo Albanians. Let us consider what assumptions are shared by the two sides in this debate. Both parties assume that there is a truth of the matter here. Neither would so much as bother to articulate their position, or rather the grounds of their position, unless they thought that they had appreciated truths (or aspects of the truth) that the other side had undervalued or improperly weighted. Also both sides assume that rational argument is an appropriate way to cope with political differences. Both sides address themselves to those with similar political commitments as well as to partisans of the opposing side. The rendering of a judgment proceeds in the context of a *community* based on certain shared assumptions, or rather, the judgment brings into play a whole range of different communities of shared judgment, both universal and particular, embodying wider or narrower sets of shared assumptions. The purpose of communicating the judgment is to attempt to bridge these different communities. There are, of course, those who are not explicitly addressed in this debate (e.g., those who actually support genocidal nationalism). But the crucial point is that the immediate contenders each address their political judgments both to those who share most of their political presuppositions, and to those who do not (fully) share these presuppositions. One articulates a set of political opinions not only to consolidate the views of those who already agree, but also to appeal to those who disagree to reconsider.

These are of course mainly truisms. Nonetheless, they run counter to the prevalent view that opposing political judgments are constituted by irreconcilable "values," and that this opposition at the level of fundamental values cannot (*in principle*) be bridged by mere reason. Against this liberal ideology, it should be regarded as a matter of some considerable significance that actual participants in political discourse give the lie to this prevailing view, by the very fact of their participation in rational debate.

To help us appreciate what is most contentious in our claims on behalf of political judgment, let us consider some possible objections. First of all, it might be objected that since there are better and worse judgments, what is most important is not judging as such, but judging well, and therefore we should seek not to maximize the general exercise of judgment, but to maximize the exercise of correct judgment. It might follow that we should place a monopoly of judgment in the hands of those who are especially qualified, or those whose judgments tend to be astute. There are several ways of replying to this objection. In politics, the object of our deliberation is not external to, or separable from, the intrinsic good of deliberation itself. Encouraging people to think for themselves, assume responsibilities, and adopt a more critical and independent stance towards their life in society is part of the very good that we hope to locate in politics. Therefore the rendering of judgments is itself part of the end that we strive for po-

litically, not merely some means to an external good. If we get people to care for the common good, to take civic responsibilities seriously, and to make good judgments, that itself serves as a measure of
our political achievement.

Furthermore, we have less grounds for confidence in our judgments if we attempt to identify correct judgments in abstraction from
the process of common deliberation. In general, it is natural for us to
seek confirmation of what we take to be our best judgment by testing
it against the opinions of others. This is especially so in politics, where
the opinions of all are relevant, since what is at stake is a way of life
common to all. As Aristotle noted in book III, chapter 11 of *The Politics*, while certain people's judgments are certainly better and more
reliable than those of most people, there are compensating advantages to be found in deliberations that are conducted throughout the
whole community:

> Each of them by himself may not be of a good quality; but when all
> come together it is possible that they may surpass—collectively and as a
> body, although not individually—the quality of the few best. Feasts to
> which many contribute may excel those provided at one man's expense.
> In the same way, when there are many, each can bring his share of
> goodness and moral prudence; and when all meet together the people
> may thus become something in the nature of a single person, who—
> as he has many feet, many hands, and many senses—may also have
> many qualities of character and intelligence. This is the reason why the
> Many are also better judges of music and the writings of poets: some ap-
> preciate one part, some another, and all together appreciate all.[11]

Aristotle knew as well as anyone, probably better than anyone, that
there is a sure distinction between cognitively valid and invalid judgments, that some people's judgments are objectively more sound than
those of other people, and that good judgments are a product of the
right kind of *ethos*—that is, moral training and ethical habituation.
Proper judgments are not a matter of head-counting or historically relative contingencies. Yet it was precisely Aristotle who saw the definite
advantages of a democratization of political judgment—at least within
a political community that was habituated to civic responsibility.
Therefore we should not use the distinction between judging and
judging well to restrict the circle of those to whom we entrust the exercise of authoritative political judgment. Rather, our conclusion
should be that just as (in Kant's words) "we cannot ripen to political

freedom if we are not first of all entrusted with it,"[12] so we can only come to make good judgments through the shared active exercise of this essential human capacity.

Is judgment "natural" or is it "acquired"? Is it a universal "faculty" that we may be assumed to possess simply by virtue of our status as human beings, or is it a contingent product of particular socially instituted practices and conventions? This is a question that was posed by one critic of my *Political Judgment* book.[13] I think it rests, however, on a false dichotomy. As John Stuart Mill declares in *Utilitarianism*: if "the moral feelings are not innate, but acquired, they are not for that reason the less natural. It is natural to man to speak, to reason, to build cities, to cultivate the ground, though these are acquired faculties." As an acquired capacity, "the moral faculty, if not a part of our nature, is a natural outgrowth from it; capable . . . in a certain small degree, of springing up spontaneously; and susceptible of being brought by cultivation to a high degree of development."[14] As Mill makes clear, basic human capacities like our power of judgment are *both* natural and acquired, *both* (in principle) universal and (in actuality) dependent on socially inculcated habits and practices. To maintain that all human beings, independently of social practices and *ethos*, not merely potentially but actually possess the power of judgment is an absurd view, and cannot sustain a moment's reflection. On the other hand, to hold that human beings do not generally possess a *capacity* for rational judgment, subject to socially cultivated habituation to the *exercise* of this capacity, is an equally untenable view and a pernicious one, for it is antithetical to the idea of democratic citizenship.

The following questions may also be put to us as an objection. Of what use is a theory of political judgment if it does not actually *guide* our decisions nor help us navigate the treacherous waters of political life? What is the point of theorizing political judgment if it does not serve to alleviate our bewilderment in situations of actual practical choice? We conceded that the propositions offered as the rudiments of a theory of political judgment are mainly truisms (though maybe they do not appear as such in a society, like ours, that tends not to take politics seriously and that encourages us to put our chief energies into producing and consuming). Such reflections do not tell us what judgments to make, but merely remind us of what it is to make judgments. The claims of such a theory are extremely modest. The primary intention of the theory I have been sketching is expressed very well in the following statement by Gadamer: "practical and political reason can only be realized and transmitted dialogically. I think, then, that the chief task of philosophy is to justify this way of reason and to defend practical and political reason against the domination of technology based on science." Thus "it vindicates again the noblest task of the citizen—decision-making according to one's own responsibility—instead of conceding that task to the expert."[15] Gadamer himself understands extremely well the limits of this kind of theoretical reflection with respect to the realm of praxis. Just because a philosopher can tell us the *conditions* for *phronesis* does not mean that we should expect the philosopher also to *exercise phronesis*. Theorists who devote their lives to reflecting on what is *general* are notoriously unreliable when it comes to apprehending *particulars*, which is precisely the skill or aptitude that we associate with practical wisdom. Judgment, as opposed to the application of "principles" or "theories," is a "knack," inextricably bound to the concrete particulars that are judged. As we noted above, the study of political judgment teaches us the *limits* of theory, so attention to the role of judgment can help to moderate the ambitions of theory.

No doubt, this will draw the reproach (from those not content as theorists with remaining in the position of mere "back seat drivers") that an inquiry into political judgment conceived in this way disconnects theory and practice. Since the seventeenth century, thinkers ranging from Bacon to Marx have advanced theories that, if applied, were supposed to lead to practical salvation. The experience of modernity, if nothing else, has taught us what to expect of such promises. All of these thinkers would have accepted as a matter of course John Stuart Mill's dictum that "the test of real and vigorous thinking, the thinking which ascertains truths instead of dreaming dreams, is successful application to practice."[16] Of the great modern thinkers, Rousseau alone had a more sensible view of the relation of theory to practice. In the *Emile* he declares that he has no reason to apologize for the fact that his philosophy amounts to "dreaming dreams"; at least he gives his dreams as dreams, which others are not careful to do.[17]

Modernity has given us a sufficient experience of the consequences of the idea of an application of theory to practice. Invariably, what results is a technocratic vision of politics that stifles the natural resources of ordinary prudence. It is time that theorists adopted a far more modest conception of their vocation. Theories alone cannot tell us how to reorder the world. At best, they can alert us to some of the dangers of a bad unity of theory and practice, in the form of technocratic understandings of politics. Theory can teach us to limit the intrusions of theory itself into the practical sphere. This function is, to be sure, a negative one, but at least it has the positive effect of helping to roll back the technocratic pretensions to a successful application of theory to practice. As I have mentioned, one finds an instructive exemplification of such philosophical modesty in the return to Aristotelian practical philosophy recommended by Gadamer: "ethics is only a theoretical enterprise and . . . anything said by way of a theoretic description of the forms of right living can be at best of little help when it comes to the concrete application to the human experience of life."[18] The philosopher's quest for the ideal "is not a guide for action but a guide for reflection."[19]

We need to return to Aristotle's insight, powerfully restated by Gadamer among contemporary theorists, that it is *ethos* that is decisive in constituting sound judgments, not theoretical considerations of any kind. Whether a society possesses the *ethos* sufficient to support sound practical judgment owes very little to the influence or guidance of philosophers (as Gadamer has noted: even Aristotle could not restore *ethos* to the polis). Instead, the converse is rather the case: any influence that philosophers exercise will depend on the *ethos* that already exists. On the other hand, it is helpful to remember that we theorize in the context of a society that is to a large degree intoxicated with theory (as it has been since the Enlightenment), where the society expects much of theorists, and theorists expect much too much of themselves. In this context, to deflate the exaggerated promises of theorists may itself be a highly salutary practical effect of theory!

It should be understood that the appeal to an Aristotelian conception of ethics shared by the authors invoked at the start of this essay (Gadamer, MacIntyre, Jonas) does not entail that we can or should attempt to recover the pre-modern horizon of theory—for reasons made very clear in the essay by Jonas cited earlier. A straightforward return to the classical (contemplative) understanding of theory is not open to us today inasmuch as theory *already is* heavily enmeshed in practice, namely in those technicist or technocratic understandings of politics that are widely effectual in contemporary society. This is the thrust of Habermas's critique of Löwith, who embraces the classical conception of theory.[20] To this extent, theory must at least serve the *negative* function of restraining or repulsing the "theoretical praxis" that is *already* realized in the technicist understanding of society. It is in this sense, too, that Charles Taylor is correct in describing our society as "very theory-prone," or even "theory-drenched."[21] But rather than assuming that this demonstrates the efficacy of theory, the proper question to raise should be whether this instead exhibits the political malady of a culture that hungers for "theoretical" instruction, that is, for scientific solutions to its problems. In any case, we should cherish no illusions about the status of theory within the modern dispensation. To borrow Jonas's trenchant image: modern theory, in its commitment to modernity's unceasing dynamism, "is chained to its chariot, in harness before it or dragged in its tracks—which, it is hard to tell in the dust of the race, and sure it is only that not theory is the charioteer."[22]

Belief in the omnicompetence of theory to direct political judgment generally presupposes a deductive model whereby theory determines ultimate "principles," from which are deduced maxims for action. Much of contemporary moral theory, whether deontological or consequentialist, is premised upon such a model. If theory can be used to locate the correct principles, it is assumed, then one shall possess the key to right conduct. The problem with this picture of things is simply that it offers a wholly false account of the relation between theory and prudence (as Aristotle understood so well). In contrast to this false model, what is implied in the notion of reflective judgment, as I understand it, admits of no deduction from rules or principles. Rather, the task of judgment at its most acute is situated (sometime tragically) at the intersection of conflicting and nearly incommensurable moral and political claims: for instance, the claims of the local and particular versus those of the general and universal, the perspective of the involved participant versus the perspective of the detached "outsider" (or, in Burke's terms, the claims of "kindred" versus those of "kind").[23] No recourse to binding principles can release one from this tension-ridden seat of judgment. To attempt to reduce this (at its height) tragic responsibility of practical judgment to a deductive entailment from ultimate principles misses the genuine concreteness of the judging situation as well as the consequent pathos of the moral-political agent.

This helps explain the force of Aristotle's reference to "ultimate particulars," which again brings home to us the necessary shortfall in the relationship between theory and prudence. It is in the very nature of a particular that it cannot be adequately anticipated by theory. To put the point in a way that accords with insights by philosophers ranging from Kant to Wittgenstein: even if we had an adequate rule, we would require a further rule to *apply* this first rule, then a rule beyond that to apply this next rule, and another, and so on *ad infinitum*.[24] Eventually, we must run out of rules, and confront the particular without benefit of a rule for the subsumption of particulars. But encounter with particulars independent of rules of subsumption is precisely what defines prudence.

Hence I do not believe that a theory of political judgment can teach us how to make the right judgments in the sphere of praxis, nor am I convinced, as most theorists seem to be, that mere theory can make a notable contribution to unravelling the predicaments of our society. I am inclined to agree with Arendt that—in the words of Heidegger—"thinking does not endow us directly with the power to act."[25] However, perhaps a theory of political judgment can at least bolster our faith in the legitimacy of political reason, and renew our flagging sense of the dignity and autonomy of political discourse—within the context of a liberal society that is wallowing in subjectivism and in which the public judgments of citizens are systematically reduced to the private value-preferences of de-politicized consumers. If such a theory cannot guide our actual judgments, perhaps it can (at least to the satisfaction of our fellow theorists) defeat the presumption that such judgments are necessarily lacking in grounds, and thus stave off despair over the possibility of judging with the warrant of intersubjective validity.

Political judgment, then, is (to recapitulate our basic thesis) a capacity whose exercise is everpresent, all around us, because politics is a realm that admits of intersubjectively binding truth claims. We participate in the worldliness of political relationships, and the faculty of political judgment is an unmistakeable token of this worldliness. Judgments as such are *about* the world, and only for this reason is it possible for them to possess validity or lack validity (unless one posits a transcendental subjectivity that enables us to make universally binding claims without reference to the objective world, as Kant does in his theory of reflective judgment for aesthetic experience). In ordinary political discourse, moral-political judgments, whether of justice or of prudence, do not have status limited merely to the expression of privately held "values," or an evaluative posture towards the world; rather, they will devolve upon factual judgments concerning states of affairs in the world—past, present, and future. For instance, if Quebec were to secede from Canada, we would have a better idea whether the project of independent Quebec statehood had been a well-conceived one if, as its supporters expect, the French language remains vibrant, the new state can provide for the welfare of its citizens, it has good relations with its neighbors, and the rights of minority groups are respected; opponents of this project will tend to be vindicated if, on the other hand, there is serious ethnic conflict within the new state, if it suffers not just short-term economic crisis but longer-term economic decline, and if Québécois culture is more vulnerable within a smaller, less prosperous country. Naturally, one cannot simply "read off" normative judgments from facts in the world, since our moral and political judgments are ultimately grounded in judgments about human flourishing, that is to say, they have their ground in deeper judgments about human nature. Nonetheless, normative judgments, in politics as in private morality, obtain their force—derive their validity—from the discernment of realities.

It follows from such arguments that political judgment is the quintessential mode of relating to the world, because, as political beings, we *share* a world. If we start from this fact about our situation (namely, the fact that our subjectivity is grounded in intersubjectivity), we can perhaps go on to show the ways in which political identity is essential to our definition of ourselves and why citizenship is a crucial aspect of the human good. But this is an exceedingly ambitious argument to make, and certainly cannot be derived from formal considerations such as those presented above. If it can be shown (as I believe a full account of political judgment would seek to show) that the quality of our experience atrophies in proportion as we passively yield to the judgments of others and cede greater and greater dimensions of political responsibility (a process that is everywhere at work in modern liberal society), then we would have powerful reasons to believe that active citizenship is a major component of the human good. In actively rendering judgments upon our shared world, we at the same time resolve to comport ourselves as *citizens* (rather than as clients of the state or as privatized consumers), and thereby affirm our own nature as political beings. To judge human affairs from the standpoint of the citizen is to acknowledge this aspect of the human good. Therefore, to inquire into the nature of political judgment is not a merely formal endeavor, but involves the assertion of substantive claims about the good for human beings.

NOTES

1. Hannah Arendt, "The Crisis in Culture: Its Social and Its Political Significance," in Arendt, *Between Past and Future: Eight Exercises in Political Thought*, enl. ed. (New York: Viking Press, 1968), 197–226; and Hannah Arendt, *Lectures on Kant's Political Philosophy*, ed. Ronald Beiner (Chicago: University of Chicago Press, 1982).

2. See Arendt, *Lectures*, 141–42.

3. Ronald Beiner, *Political Judgment* (Chicago: University of Chicago Press, 1983). For a collection of commentaries on Arendt's project for a Kantian-inspired political philosophy of judgment, see *Judgment, Imagination, and Politics: Themes from Kant and Arendt*, ed. Ronald Beiner and Jennifer Nedelsky (Lanham, Md.: Rowman & Littlefield, 2001).

4. Aristotle, *Nicomachean Ethics*, trans. M. Ostwald (Indianapolis: Bobbs-Merrill, 1962), 160.

5. See, for instance, John McDowell, "Virtue and Reason," *The Monist* 62, no. 3 (1979): 331–50; Alasdair MacIntyre, *After Virtue*, 2nd ed. (Notre Dame, Ind.: University of Notre Dame Press, 1984), chapters 12 and 14–16; Hans-Georg Gadamer, *Reason in the Age of Science*, trans. F. G. Lawrence (Cambridge, Mass.: MIT Press, 1981); Hans-Georg Gadamer, *Truth and Method*, 2nd rev. ed., trans. revised by J. Weinsheimer and D. G. Marshall (New York: Continuum, 1989), First Part: I and Second Part: II.2; Ronald Beiner, "Do We Need a Philosophical Ethics? Theory, Prudence, and the Primacy of *Ethos*," in Beiner, *Philosophy in a Time of Lost Spirit: Essays on Contemporary Theory* (Toronto: University of Toronto Press, 1997), 83–94.

6. MacIntyre, *After Virtue*, 223.

7. Hans Jonas, "The Practical Uses of Theory," in Jonas, *The Phenomenon of Life: Toward a Philosophical Biology* (Chicago: University of Chicago Press, 1982), 199.

8. Gadamer, *Reason in the Age of Science*, 121.

9. For discussion of the relationship between Habermas's theoretical project and Arendt's idea of judgment, see Jürgen Habermas, "On the German-Jewish Heritage," *Telos* 44 (Summer 1980): 127–31.

10. Cf. Leo Strauss's comment in a letter to Karl Löwith: Strauss refers to "the *factum brutum* of revelation" and then adds: "I say: *factum brutum*—for

there is *no* argument *whatsoever*, theoretical, practical, existential, . . . from [agnosticism] to belief." Karl Löwith and Leo Strauss, "Correspondence Concerning Modernity," *Independent Journal of Philosophy* IV (1983), 108.

11. *The Politics of Aristotle*, ed. and trans. Ernest Barker (London: Oxford University Press, 1958).

12. Immanuel Kant, *Religion Within the Limits of Reason Alone*, trans. T. M. Greene and H. H. Hudson (New York: Harper Torchbooks, 1960), 176n.

13. Jeremy Waldron, "Appealing to the Community," *Times Literary Supplement*, 27 April 1984, 469; for my reply, see *Times Literary Supplement*, 15 June 1984, 662.

14. John Stuart Mill, *Utilitarianism, On Liberty, Considerations on Representative Government*, ed. H. B. Acton (London: Dent, 1972), 28.

15. Hans-Georg Gadamer, "Hermeneutics and Social Science," *Cultural Hermeneutics* 2, no. 4 (1975): 316.

16. Mill, *Utilitarianism*, 211–12.

17. Jean-Jacques Rousseau, *Emile*, trans. Allan Bloom (New York: Basic Books, 1979), 112n.

18. Gadamer, *Reason in the Age of Science*, 112; cf. 48, 13334. For a good summary of Gadamer's views, see Hans-Georg Gadamer, "The Political Incompetence of Philosophy," in *The Heidegger Case: On Philosophy and Politics*, ed. Tom Rockmore and Joseph Margolis (Philadelphia: Temple University Press, 1992), 364–69.

19. Gadamer, *Reason in the Age of Science*, 82. For further elaboration of Gadamer's position concerning the inherent limitations of theory, cf. "Gadamer on Strauss: An Interview," *Interpretation* 12, no. 1 (January 1984): 10, 12–13.

20. Jürgen Habermas, *Philosophical-Political Profiles*, trans. Frederick G. Lawrence (Cambridge, Mass.: MIT Press, 1983), 91, 95–96.

21. Charles Taylor, "Political Theory and Practice," in *Social Theory and Political Practice*, ed. Christopher Lloyd (Oxford: Oxford University Press, 1983), 81.

22. Jonas, *Phenomenon of Life*, 207–8.

23. Edmund Burke, "Letter to a Member of the National Assembly," in *The Works of Edmund Burke*, vol. 4 (London: Oxford University Press, 1934), 300.

24. Cf. the quotation from Gadamer cited at note 8 above.

25. Martin Heidegger, *What is Called Thinking?*, trans. Fred D. Wieck and J. Glenn Gray (New York: Harper & Row, 1968), 159; quoted as the motto to volume one of Hannah Arendt's *The Life of the Mind* (New York: Harcourt Brace Jovanovich, 1978).

II

THE SCOPE OF PRUDENCE

7

Political Judgment in Dark Times: Frederick Douglass and Slavery

Richard S. Ruderman

In trying to assess the meaning and possibilities of political judgment in liberal democracy, one can scarce do better than to meditate on the life and career of Frederick Douglass. Douglass, born into slavery and abandoned at birth by his (almost assuredly) white father, rose to become the most prominent, effective, and thoughtful abolitionist in America. Holding no political office (until after the Civil War) and breaking with William Lloyd Garrison and his allies, Douglass successfully carved out his own abolitionist position, via speeches and his own newspaper (the *North Star*), and helped to steer America toward the end of slavery. What follows is a sketch of the penetrating moral understanding and the powerful yet precise political rhetoric that enabled Douglass to achieve, without the benefit of political office, his ends.

Douglass was born into an America that denied him and his fellow blacks all rights to life, liberty, and the pursuit of happiness. The spiritual as well as physical privation that this situation entailed could and did have but one bright spot: it required Douglass to achieve for himself what white Americans could (and to some extent today still can) take for granted—namely, the understanding of human nature that might justify and render possible human liberty. For "freedom cannot, properly speaking, be granted; it must be wrested and won."[1] As we shall see, Douglass was an unusually astute judge of human nature, at both its best and its worst, and this enabled him to select an appropriate port in the stormy dispute over slavery and to chart a course capable of delivering him and his fellow Americans more or less safely at it.

Insofar as modern liberal democracy consists of a rational teaching about equal rights, we should not be surprised to find liberal statesmen offered conflicting, not to say contradictory, advice from political thinkers. From one quarter, thinkers such as Fichte encourage statesmen to ignore public opinion and to follow only the dictates of right reason. From another quarter, democratic theorists such as Benjamin Barber advise them to reject the use of "aristocratic" reason so as not to suppress or alter the communal consensus that will thereby emerge.[2] Douglass, spared the advice of either man, tended toward the classical or pre-liberal approach. He employed reason to uncover the facts of a deeply perverted human nature, and employed rhetoric to educate a confused, uncertain, and sometimes hostile public opinion, thereby enabling him to stand almost alone and to recover a Constitutional consensus that was at risk of disappearing.

ACHIEVING MODERATION

Douglass was able to help save America in part because he did not hesitate to question, criticize, and even condemn America. His was a demanding patriotism: he would only love his country when his country became lovable. Once Douglass learned, through the kindness of a white mistress, how to read, he soon was able to teach himself how to think. And given his situation, Douglass was compelled to think long and hard about the deepest questions, including the meanings of liberty and justice and the existence of a just God. Accordingly, while Douglass's ultimate political positions could be characterized as "moderate" (he rejected both slavery and Garrison's "no Union with slaveholders," both white and black arguments for cultural superiority and, at the end of the day, preferred reform to revolution), they should not be misconstrued as tepid exercises in splitting the difference.

The unusual character of Douglass's moderation can be grasped only if we recognize that he began by questioning the very principle of moderation and compromise. After discussing a plantation-owner's curious efforts to soften, but not end, the slavery of his own son (by a slave-woman on the plantation), Douglass remarks: "It was a compromise, and like most such, defeated itself."[3] Later, when analyzing the efforts of the "well-meaning" Thomas Dorr to fashion a constitution for Rhode

Island in 1841 that would expand the suffrage, but only of white citizens, Douglass notes: "In this he consulted policy rather than right, and at last shared the fate of all compromisers and trimmers, for he was disastrously defeated."[4] And during the election campaign of 1860, Douglass's greatest concern was that "the drift of northern sentiment was towards compromise."[5] Much like Lincoln, who famously argued that "a House Divided against itself cannot stand," Douglass recognized that a political community cannot long accommodate contradictory first principles. And slaves in America were treated, not only by North and South, but especially by the slaveholders themselves (a point that Douglass as well as Lincoln would exploit brilliantly and at length), as both moral agents (and thus as essentially human) and as property (and thus as essentially non-human).

The fact that Douglass refused to compromise or to support compromise on first principles should not lead us to conclude that he was a rigid moralizer who placed moral purity ahead of effective action. This was, in point of fact, his chief difference with Garrison. One of the gravest controversies within the abolitionist movement concerned the question of whether slaveholders should be paid to free their slaves. Freedom for the slaves had to be balanced against the appearance of implicit acceptance of the slaveholders' claim that slaves were property. When Douglass, residing in England following John Brown's failed efforts at Harper's Ferry (though Douglass had attempted to dissuade Brown from the act, the governor of Virginia suspected him of collusion and ordered his arrest), was offered one hundred and fifty pounds to pay for his own liberty, he did not hesitate to accept. It was to this "commercial transaction," he said, that he owed his immunity to the operation of the notorious Fugitive Slave Law.[6]

We must attempt to understand Douglass's political judgment by examining its two distinct phases. First, we will try to determine his own understanding of the moral and political injustice to be righted, and second, we must judge the means by which he sought to enlist his fellow citizens' help in righting it.

GRASPING THE BASIS OF SLAVERY

The fact that slavery is today almost universally condemned should not blind us to the fact that not a few Americans (even, as Douglass sadly noted, some slaves) in the nineteenth century viewed it as a justified and indeed divinely commanded institution. Even some of those who rejected the Biblical justification for slavery (based on Noah's curses directed against his grandson Canaan, the supposed progenitor of the black races; *Genesis* 9:22-27) and instead relied on the rational teaching of the equal rights of man faced a terrible stumbling block: they, like Jefferson, might be certain of the injustice of slavery while nevertheless remaining haunted by doubts as to the genuine possibility of black equality or accomplishment. Douglass therefore concluded that he had to demonstrate—to himself, to the slaves, to the slaveholders, and to the American people as a whole—that blacks could in deed and not just in principle be the equals of whites.

> [P]erhaps the greatest hindrance to the adoption of abolition principles by the people of the United States was the low estimate everywhere in that country placed upon the Negro as a man—that because of his assumed natural inferiority people reconciled themselves to his enslavement and oppression as being inevitable, if not desirable. The grand thing to be done, therefore, was to change this estimation by disproving his inferiority and demonstrating his capacity for a more exalted civilization than slavery and prejudice had assigned him.[7]

Unable, he felt, simply to appeal to any abstract, philosophical claim of equal treatment, Douglass accepted the need to demonstrate black equality in practice.

Understandably, Douglass began in ignorance of the relevant facts and arguments—and even the date of his own birth. Ignorance, after all, was the basis of the slave system.[8] Yet, as Douglass observed, "though civilization was, in many respects, shut out [of the slaves' world], nature could not be."[9] Few more powerful testimonials to the instructive and liberating power of nature can be imagined than Douglass's subsequent education. That education proceeded first, via a careful analysis of the differing ways of life of slaves and slaveholders, on the one hand, and free people, on the other and, second, via a profound analysis of what Spinoza famously called the "theologico-political problem."

Even before leaving slavery and discovering anything about the nature of freedom, Douglass was struck by the "rigid" way in which the "law of respect to elders" was enforced among slaves.[10] This law, we need hardly note, was more than merely a peculiarity of slave or African culture. It can be found in Biblical and other religions and, indeed, was the universal law among humanity until the discovery of nature—and the subsequent rise of philosophy—brought it into question.[11] As long as it was believed that human beings were incapable of discovering any truths vital to the conduct of human life on their own, it was inevitable (given the dependence of humans at all times on knowledge of what to do) that people would turn to elders and the tradition that they ultimately inherited from the first beings—the gods—for guidance.[12] Douglass's suspicions of tradition were strengthened when he made his first discovery about free people: they had a far weaker attachment than slaves or slaveholders did to the place of their birth.[13] "Rigid" respect for elders and a correlative strong attachment to "home" stand in opposition to the free exercise of the human mind devoted to finding its own way in the world.

However intrigued and inspired by these contrasts Douglass may have been, he was not yet in a position to reject the one and to embrace the other. Not only were there friends and family (such as it was) who would have to be abandoned in the quest for freedom; there remained the daunting prospect that perhaps God *had* fashioned one race for mastery and the other for slavery. Now, Douglass's stirring rhetoric to the contrary would seem to deny that this was ever an open question for him:

> Nature never intended that men and women should be either slaves or slaveholders, and nothing but rigid training long persisted in, can perfect the character of the one or the other.[14]

But how did Douglass—how does anyone—come to *know* what the intentions of nature are? Or that nature trumps God's will?

In a charmingly modest and self-effacing story, Douglass lets his audience gather a hint. Sent by one of his masters to be made more pliable by a notorious "slave-breaker," Douglass was one day assigned to work a field with a team of oxen. This activity was one with which Douglass was wholly unfamiliar. Moreover, he had great difficulty in absorbing his instructions. The reason for this was his utter inability to comprehend the difference between the "in" ox and the "off" ox. "Where and what is the reason," he asked, "for this distinction in names, when there is none in the things themselves?"[15] Douglass further states: "I saw in my own situation several points of similarity with that of the oxen."[16] There is, then, no more difference in nature between slave and master than between an "in" ox and an "off" ox.

Even if Douglass could conclude with confidence, however, that reason taught that all moral distinctions among groups of human beings were nominal and that nature was therefore hostile to slavery, how could he know that reason and not revelation should be our guide? Moreover, how could he determine what God's attitude toward slavery was? As he surveyed religious opinion on slavery in America, Douglass was forced to confront what we might call, with apologies to Kant, the Antinomies of Religion. Religion, that is, stood as the foundation of both pro- and anti-slavery sentiment. The Bible was routinely (and, for the most part, sincerely) cited by both slaveholders and abolitionists to justify their respective positions. Even on his own plantation, Douglass witnessed apparently sincere Christians acting with great cruelty ("religious slaveholders are the worst")[17] and heard the teachings of "Uncle Lawson" ("If you want liberty, ask the Lord for it in Faith, and he will give it to you").[18] Religion, in short, could fuel both the most extreme cruelty and the most devoted service to the cause of freedom.

Douglass foresaw that his willingness to raise such questions in print might lead him into trouble. In fact, the entire Appendix of his first autobiography (the *Narrative of the Life of Frederick Douglass*) is devoted to assuring the reader that he is an opponent solely of "slaveholding religion."[19] Now, it would of course be imprudent in the extreme to question religion (or even merely the Christian religion) as such since, by so doing, Douglass would chase away many of his friends and allies. Even if Douglass should come to have broader doubts about religion, there still remained important secular purposes to which religion could be put. After learning to read, Douglass asked leave of his mistress to teach some of his fellow slaves to read so that they could study the Bible. But, as one critic notes, while his mistress might assume, with earlier slave narratives, that Douglass was teaching them to read only in order to teach them Christianity, he seemed in fact to be teaching them Christianity only in order to teach them to read.[20] We must therefore examine Douglass's account of religion with greater care.

Douglass alerts the reader early on to the possibility that his quest for freedom might come into conflict with religion. He speaks frankly of his eagerness "to partake of the tree of knowledge."[21] Like the Biblical Adam, Douglass was assisted in his efforts by a woman: Mrs. Auld, his master's pious wife, who soon came (under her husband's influence) to rue having done so. But unlike the Biblical Adam, Douglass was not ashamed upon being discovered and, in fact, continued to strive for knowledge.

Nowhere is the meaning of that quest portrayed more tellingly than in the scene in which Douglass confronts the slave-breaker Covey.[22] Covey, who is said to come "like a thief in the night" and who crawls on his belly like a reptile (the slaves called him "Snake"), is portrayed as both a Christ-figure and a Serpent-figure. But he may represent still more: there was, notes Douglass, "no deceiving him . . . [as he made] us feel that he was always present."[23] Douglass, on the other hand, whose legs are torn by "briers and thorns" and who escapes from a "den of wild beasts," is portrayed both as Christ and as Daniel. The complex scene as a whole, carefully read, represents Douglass's struggle with all the forces opposed to his freedom.[24] It culminates in Douglass's Jacob-like wrestling with Covey. The match ends in a stand-off and Covey never again whips Douglass. Douglass stresses that he narrates his "change in condition" so that it may "help the reader to a better understanding of human nature."[25] And he concludes with a wholly secular interpretation of Covey's failure to whip him again. Covey must have been restrained, Douglass reasons, by his need to retain his "reputation" as a fearsome "negro-breaker," a reputation that would be damaged should Covey reveal the reasons for his subsequent beatings.[26] This would seem to imply that no higher power could punish a man for seeking freedom from tyranny without sacrificing its indispensable reputation for omnipotence, much less for justice.

That Douglass was capable of attaining this lofty level of independence of mind[27] is striking, not only on account of his initial situation as enslaved and forced into ignorance, but also on account of his being, by his own admission, "something of a hero-worshipper by nature."[28] Might not the latter, however, be a necessary (but, of course, not sufficient) condition for attaining genuine independence? How, especially in a democracy, can one liberate oneself from received opinion, from the tyranny of the majority, unless one admires the force and independence of those who have already done so? The alternative to admiring ("worshipping") beauty and superiority, we should remind ourselves, is envying (the typical democratic vice) or even hating it. So far from such vices was Douglass that he spoke without a trace of envy of the "treat to [his] young and gradually opening mind to behold [the] elaborate exhibition of wealth, power, and beauty" that was his new master's mansion—built, of course, on the backs of slaves.[29] Moreover, Douglass takes the Socratic position that ownership goes to the one who can use or appreciate a thing: "These [possessions] all belonged to me as well as to Col. Edward Lloyd."[30] Douglass's character was so formed for disinterested admiration that he could speak of preferring "bold and daring" slaveholders to that "fretful little soul who never used the lash but at the suggestion of a love of gain."[31] Douglass's admiration of such superiority eventually led to his wanting to partake of it—and, indeed, to transcend it insofar as he devoted his abilities to a far nobler cause.

DOUGLASS'S POLITICAL JUDGMENT

At this point, we are prepared to examine Douglass's efforts at exercising political judgment proper. As noted at the outset, Douglass tailors his speech and arguments to the audience he is addressing. Those audiences range from simple slaves, at first, through sympathetic abolitionists (both patronizing and otherwise), and finally to public opinion in the United States as a whole. To the first audience, Douglass had to preach the possibility and desirability of achieving freedom. To the second, Douglass had to offer an altogether anti-Garrisonian approach to the slave problem. And to the third, Douglass had to establish the slaves' *worthiness* for freedom and to win the respect (and not merely the pity) of white America for the black man. This in turn would require that he galvanize public opinion and bring it to bear on the gravest moral problem in America's history without, in the process, turning that opinion toward despair or thoroughgoing anti-American sentiment.

That Douglass felt the need to win the slaves themselves over to the cause of freedom will no doubt seem strange. Yet, as mentioned above, there were some among them who "were under the delusion that God required them to submit to slavery."[32] When hatching his first escape plot with some fellow slaves, Douglass found that he needed to "imbue their minds with thoughts of freedom."[33] Despite the fact, established earlier, that nature stands for freedom, a person's nature can be suppressed or perverted. The turning point occurred when Douglass discovered a copy of *The Columbian Orator*, a then-popular collection of speeches extolling freedom. This discovery enabled Douglass "to give tongue to the many interesting thoughts which had often flashed through [his] mind and died away for want of words in which to give them utterance."[34] Rhetoric, for Douglass, is far more than mere public relations at best and obfuscation at worst. It helps to form and establish ideas (especially abstract, political, and moral ones) in the minds of the audience and even the speaker himself.

The chief classical function of rhetoric is to convince one's listeners of strange, foreign, or troubling ideas by means of trustworthy images and categories and by appealing future prospects. Douglass offers a striking example in his autobiographical retelling of his first effort at escape, an example that will prove paradigmatic for the rest of his oratorical career. He succeeds in convincing his small band of fellow slaves to risk escape—with the exception of Sandy, a believer in "divination" and the most "African" among them. Sandy, expressing apprehension about the escape, reports to Douglass that he had a dream in which Douglass was attacked "by a large number of birds."[35] Douglass was unperturbed, but later, when the need to fight as well as to run began to loom, Sandy withdrew. Worse, it was almost a certainty that he betrayed his comrades to the authorities. Upon being dragged off to prison for his attempted escape, Douglass "could not help seeing the fulfillment of Sandy's dream. I was in the hands of moral vultures."[36] More than grim humor, Douglass's remark reveals his paradigmatic approach to the "divination" in which he takes no stock[37]: religion can and should be interpreted to support the moral and political quest for freedom. One can hardly imagine Jefferson, for one, employing such an approach (or passing up the opportunity to chastise religion for slavishness).

Douglass's relations with the abolitionists generally, and with Garrison in particular, are not so quickly summarized. Upon finally escaping from slavery, Douglass soon found himself in demand as a public speaker, able to portray the harrowing evil of slavery with unusual eloquence and conviction, having once been a slave himself. But several of Douglass's "handlers" wanted him merely to present the facts of slavery without entering into the policy question of how to deal with it. "Give us the facts," one of them said, "and we will take care of the philosophy."[38] Douglass, that is, was asked to proceed like a modern social scientist. More alert to the humanly impossible aspects of this approach than social scientists are, however, Douglass refused so to limit himself. "It did not entirely satisfy me to *narrate* wrongs; I felt like *denouncing* them."[39]

Several reasons might be suggested for this attitude. First, it is not possible, for Douglass, merely to depict injustice. Brute facts, even horrific ones, may elicit our unease or even our revulsion; they cannot, on their own, give a precise account of where the injustice lies and, hence, what ought to be done about it. Second, Douglass (contrary to one critic's charge[40]) is all too aware of the dark possibility that some among his audience might take a prurient interest in his tales of slaveholder brutality: "Everybody in the South," at any rate, "seemed to want the privilege of whipping somebody else."[41] A purely neutral presentation of the facts could lend itself to such lurid misuse. Third, and most important perhaps, was the risk that, in failing to give a human response to, or account of, the evils he had seen and experienced, Douglass would come to appear merely pitiable. This would, in and of itself, undermine Douglass's overarching, long-term goal of winning equality and respect for blacks:

> Human nature is so constituted, that it cannot honor a helpless man, though it can pity him, and even this it cannot do long if signs of power do not arise.[42]

Douglass, then, would find little to approve of in the efforts of today's spokesmen for the oppressed who stress the latter's "victimhood." Not only to denounce the evil of slavery, then, but to introduce into the mind of the audience the notion that he (with their help) could crush it became Douglass's goal. This latter goal, as we shall see, helped lead to his break with Garrison.

In order to understand the meaning of Douglass's break with his fellow abolitionists, we must briefly summarize the position of Garrison himself, the country's paramount abolitionist prior to the rise of Douglass. Garrison, a deeply religious man, abhorred slavery. Moreover, he can be credited with first galvanizing opposition to it, chiefly through his abolitionist newspaper, *The Liberator.* His opposition, however, was not limited to slavery. He was also, as a pacifist, opposed to war or violence. And, viewing the Constitution as a pro-slavery document, he was opposed to it as well. In addition, Garrison opposed all temporizing with evil: only immediate emancipation would satisfy him. Finally, he was opposed to any Union that included slaveholders: if they could not be convinced, through argument or ridicule alone, to abandon slavery, Garrison wished simply to let the South go.

Though he initially admired Garrison tremendously and shared his views, Douglass came to have his doubts about each of these positions. While he wavered on the question of violence, he came to welcome it (or "any political upheaval") after the scandalous *Dred Scott* decision of 1857.[43] And though he cited "immediatism" as "the only new idea brought into the anti-slavery movement by Mr. Garrison," he was compelled also to note that "fewer slaves have been emancipated under the influence of this doctrine . . . than under the old doctrine of gradual emancipation."[44] Of greater interest, however, are Douglass's efforts to teach himself both political philosophy in general and constitutionalism in particular. Upon sensing a problem with Garrison's interpretation of the Constitution, Douglass set out

> to study with some care not only the just and proper rules of legal interpretation, but the origin, design, nature, rights, powers, and duties of civil governments, and also the relations human beings sustain to it.[45]

Douglass does not identify the political thinkers that he read. Given the time and place of this self-education, however, it is hard to imagine that the architects of modern liberalism were not among those he studied. Certainly much of what Douglass came to hold could have been suggested to him by thinkers such as Locke, Montesquieu, and the American Framers. Nevertheless, there is one striking point of departure between Douglass and liberalism's basic principles. Liberalism teaches that the most fundamental human need is for self-preservation and comfortable security. It is, as Hobbes memorably argued, the "fear of violent death" that is "the passion to be reckoned upon."[46] Yet Douglass had confronted just this fear, in a way that few men ever have to, in his confrontation with the slave-breaker Covey—and he had overcome it. Despite suffering monstrous treatment at the hands of the "tyrant" Covey, Douglass feared fighting back until he had "reached the point at which [he] *was not afraid to die.*"[47] Henceforth, Douglass could purchase a distance on liberalism afforded few of its adherents. This experience enabled him, in particular, to know that the basic premise of liberalism was a fiction. He now recognized that,

while "life is not lightly regarded by men of sane minds," human beings, even and especially in the extreme situation, can prefer freedom
and human dignity to mere survival.[48] This in turn enables us to say
of Douglass, as he was later to say of Lincoln, that "he knew the American people better than they knew themselves."[49] One might go so far
as to say that, absent this crucial insight, no speaker can help but feel
he is being dishonest (and so cannot help but appear to be dishonest)
when using any rhetoric designed to transcend base self-interest.

DOUGLASS'S CONSTITUTIONALISM

In calling the Constitution pro-slavery, Garrison pointed to the troubling fact that the Framers agreed to a Union that would include or tolerate slavery. But where Garrison took the Constitution to codify existing American practices, Douglass eventually understood it to enshrine
the ideals or principles toward which American practice should aspire.
Thus he "could now speak fully the language of the law, the language
of the defense of the Constitution."[50] Douglass explains his rules for
constitutional interpretation at greatest length in two speeches: "The
Dred Scott Decision" (delivered May 11, 1857) and "The Constitution of
the United States: Is It Pro-Slavery or Anti-Slavery?" (delivered May 26,
1860). Rather than go "behind" the words in the document, in the manner of proponents of both Critical Legal Studies and Original Intention
doctrine, Douglass insists on grasping "the simple text of the paper itself." "It would," he says,

> be the wildest of absurdities, and lead to endless confusion and mis-
> chiefs, if, instead of looking to the written paper itself, for its meaning,
> it were attempted to make us search it out, in the secret motives, and
> dishonest intentions, of some of the men who took part in writing it.[51]

With this approach in mind, Douglass turns to the Constitution and
discovers that it cannot be a pro-slavery document. First, he notes that
nowhere in the Constitution "is there a single mention of the term *slave*
or *slave holder, slave master* or *slave state*, neither is there any reference to the color, or the physical peculiarities of any part of the people
of the United States."[52] Second, he notes that the phrases that do appear—"We the People," no deprivation of liberty without "due process
of law," securing the "blessings of liberty for all," and others—all "if

faithfully carried out, would put an end to slavery in every State in the American Union."[53] For, as he goes on to show, blacks were considered men and even citizens by many states at the time of the founding. He concludes, as he says in his autobiography, that the Constitution "was in its letter and spirit an antislavery instrument, demanding the abolition of slavery as a condition of its own existence as the supreme law of the land."[54]

But if the Constitution is anti-slavery, what could account for the Framers' failure to act to eradicate it? Could they, Garrison to the contrary, have temporized with evil and yet be credited with maintaining a reasonable hope of eradicating it someday? The answers to these questions bring us to Douglass's deepest point of difference with Garrison. Garrison and his followers "looked at slavery as a creature of law" while Douglass and his followers "regarded it as a creature of public opinion."[55] Thus, for the Garrisonians, eradicating slavery was simply a question of passing legislation (or drafting a new Constitution) expressly forbidding it. To Douglass, this represented irresponsible naivety. For law, especially in a democracy, can be effective only if it has the backing of public opinion. People will find ways to evade or mute the force of law whenever it conflicts with their deeply held beliefs and opinions. It is as though Garrison felt he could eschew violence because law could compel compliance on its own. Douglass, by contrast, recognized that any *effective* change in the law would have to be preceded by a change in public opinion and, hence, by a moral education of the people. As Lincoln was to say in his first debate with Stephen A. Douglas:

> In [self-governing] communities, public sentiment is everything. With public sentiment, nothing can fail; without it nothing can succeed. Consequently he who moulds public sentiment, goes deeper than he who enacts statutes or pronounces decisions. He makes statutes and decisions possible or impossible to be executed.[56]

Similarly, Douglass saw that nothing less than a moral revolution in public sentiment concerning black people would lead to their genuine emancipation.

Far from engaging in such painstaking education, Garrison dismissed Southern slaveholders as, in effect, uneducable. For his other great principle was "No Union with slaveholders." This notion, argued Douglass, amounted to the "abandonment" of the idea with which the Anti-Slavery Society had begun: "It started to free the slave. It ends by leaving the slave to free himself."[57] Garrison's principle is tantamount to washing one's hands of distasteful matters. To go out of the Union would not only leave the blacks enslaved; it would entail abandoning all constitutional and legal means by which to alter their situation. "As a mere expression of abhorrence of slavery," Douglass concludes, "the sentiment is a good one; but it expresses no intelligible principle of action, and throws no light on the pathway of duty."[58]

JUSTICE AND MORAL EDUCATION

Douglass's own views on the character of the education needed evolved over time. At first, he admits, he believed that simple enlightenment about the situation of slaves would suffice. "All that the American people needed, I thought, was light."[59] But experience soon taught him that before they could be educated about the situation of slaves, the American people had first to be induced to care about them. In many places in the North where he spoke, Douglass discovered "apathy, indifference, aversion" and sometimes worse.[60] Nor, in retrospect, should this have surprised him. The lifeblood of America, after all, was increasingly becoming commerce, "selfish and indifferent to moral considerations as it usually is."[61] It was now evident to Douglass, however, that the Montesquieuan hope (shared by Alexander Hamilton in *Federalist* #9) that commerce could soften morals and liberate individuals was, at least in this case, unfounded. Not argument, then, was needed, but rather some form of stirring rhetoric that would remind Americans of the painful gap between their transcendent ideals and their practice. "At a time like this," Douglass proclaimed at a Fourth of July Speech in 1852, "scorching irony, not convincing argument is needed. . . . For it is not light that is needed, but fire."[62]

Douglass's chief rhetorical appeals were henceforth to love of justice and love of country. For he had learned that, however weakened by liberal principles they might have become, both sentiments appeared to be ineradicable elements of human nature. Douglass had uncovered in himself the reason why patriotism (which, even in the best cases, "is not the highest form of human excellence")[63] had a less than compelling grip on him. It was for the simple reason that his country, riddled with injustice and hypocrisy, was not lovable. Slavery undermined the country's every pretense to virtue and threatened all its interests.[64] In one of Douglass's most powerful statements, he says (in an 1864 letter to Garrison):

> That men should be patriotic, is to me perfectly natural, and as a philosophical fact, I am able to give it an intellectual recognition. But further than that I cannot go. . . . In thinking of America, I sometimes find myself admiring her bright blue sky, her grand old woods, her fertile fields, her beautiful rivers, her mighty lakes, and star-crowned mountains. But my rapture is soon checked—my joy is soon turned to mourning. When I remember that all is cursed with the infernal spirit of slaveholding, robbery, and wrong . . . I am filled with unutterable loathing, and led to reproach myself that anything could fall from my lips in praise of such a land.[65]

If Douglass or any other American is ever again to enjoy the "natural" sentiment of patriotism, the country must do away with slavery.

Douglass's suspicion that the love of justice was also a permanent part of human nature found support in two instances that might at first be thought to suggest the opposite. The first involved an observation about slaveholders; the second about a curious practice in despotic China. While many interpreted the slaveholders as dead to the appeal of justice, Douglass was struck rather by its appeal even to them. Upon first living as a freeman in the North, Douglass discovered that many southern slaveholders preferred descending into poverty rather than letting go of their slaves.[66] This sacrifice of self-interest to principle suggested that slaveholders too had a sense of justice that could be educated and appealed to. Douglass's second observation occurred when he was living abroad in England. There he heard about the Chinese doctrine of "substitution" which enabled men to procure others "to suffer even the penalty of death in their stead." Justice, eviscerated but not simply rejected, "seemed not intent on the punishment of the actual criminal, if only somebody was punished when the law was violated."[67] This is surely the *ne plus ultra* of loving justice in the abstract, to the exclusion of any concern for rehabilitation or even meaningful retribution. (It is also the obverse of the American slavery system, in which it does not matter how innocent the slave may be, as long as he is punished on occasion.) Yet it reveals a deeper point: no society can function without a concept of justice, even one that has been altogether severed from the notion that justice must be good for you.

Despite the grave injustice present in his country, then, an injustice that makes his country unlovable, Douglass insists on retaining the Union and the Constitution, and on treating slaveholders as much as possible as confused beings in need of education and even pity. Nor, on the other hand, does he expect to find a pure love of justice capable of procuring some good. He pays careful attention to the conditions that might be employed to help restrict the worst in human nature. "Public opinion," he was careful to note, functioned as a "measurable restraint upon the cruelty and barbarity of masters, overseers, and slave-drivers"—whenever, that is, it could reach them.[68] On the other hand, Douglass sought to strengthen those conditions that could shore up the best in human nature. Here again, he broke with the Lockean doctrine of relying on unlimited acquisition, preferring instead the classical notion of a narrow range of distribution of wealth. In praising Rochester as the home of a "virtuous, intelligent, enterprising, liberal, and growing population," Douglass observes that its inhabitants "were not so rich as to be indifferent to the claims of humanity, and not so poor as to be unable to help any good cause which commanded the approval of their judgment."[69]

Having withstood some of the worst that slavery could offer, Douglass was able to navigate merely political battles with remarkable toughness and aplomb. His career as an abolitionist was not easy. Though it might lead to his recapture, Douglass undertook a career of public speaking in order to stand with his brethren. He sustained abuse and even at least one savage beating. After breaking with Garrison, the latter did not hesitate to print some of Douglass's articles in the "Refuge of Oppression" section of *The Liberator*—the section normally reserved for pro-slavery opinion.[70] He was rejected by much of white America as an agitator and by some of black America as an Uncle Tom who looked at white America too admiringly. It is true that he rejected arguments for race pride and for black separation (as well as colonization of the freed slaves) on the grounds that blacks, having been brutally held down and back by slavery, were in need of white culture as a model.[71] And while his steady willingness to obtain what he could did not always endear him to those who sought impatiently to have all that they deserved, the accumulated good that he did eventually won over most of his detractors. Toward the end of his life, Douglass—in the face of black opposition—accepted a small and, some said, insulting offer to stage a "Negro Day" at the Chicago Exposition of 1893. Ida B. Wells-Barnett, a fellow crusader for black civil rights, later wrote of Douglass that he

> persevered with his plans without any aid whatever from us hotheads and produced a program which was reported from one end of the country to the other. The American nation had given him his opportunity for scoring its unfairness toward Negro citizens and he did not fail to take advantage of it in the most fitting way. . . . I was so swelled with pride over his masterly presentation of our case that I went straight out to the fair and begged his pardon for presuming in my youth and inexperience to criticize him for an effort which had done more to bring our cause to the attention of the American people than anything else that had happened during the fair.[72]

Douglass's extraordinary ability to stand alone, while never abandoning his people or their cause, provides powerful testimony that political judgment works best when its possessor attends to the facts of human nature, and not uncritically to the opinions of those he would lead.

CONCLUSION

While Douglass exercised his political judgment in—and thus tailored it to—a liberal democracy, he did not, as we have seen, simply adopt the principles of liberal democracy. He rejected the liberal premises that our deepest need is for life and security and that keeping our attention on the amoral pursuit of material advantage is the surest way to achieve it. He rejected the democratic inclination, if not principle, to find one's self-worth in the esteem of others. He treated his harassment by a mob in Syracuse as doing no more harm to his esteem than would "the kick of a jack-ass, or the barking of a bull-dog."[73] When he was once made to ride in the baggage car of a train, despite having paid the same fare as the other passengers, some well-meaning white passengers apologized for his being "degraded in this manner." Thereupon:

> Mr. Douglass straightened himself up on the box upon which he was sitting, and replied: 'They cannot degrade Frederick Douglass. The soul

that is within me no man can degrade. I am not the one that is being degraded on account of this treatment, but those who are inflicting it upon me.'[74]

However much the institution of slavery could reduce a man to a "beast-like stupor,"[75] nothing could make it plainer that the actions and beliefs of others could do nothing to diminish the self-respect of a free man.

This very notion that a man must learn to make his own way in the end, must free himself in heart and mind even after he has been emancipated in body, set an ultimate limit, in Douglass's own mind, on his political rhetoric and capacities generally. However powerful, arresting, challenging, and provocative his rhetoric, it could in the end only lead a man to freedom; it could not make him free. As Douglass knew from his own experience, it is a free mind that ultimately makes a man free in the deepest sense. We should not then be surprised to find that there is a distance, not based in any way on deceit, between Douglass's rhetoric and his own deepest beliefs.

It is often said that political leadership's chief function is to inspire hope in dark and difficult times. Douglass surely did that, refusing to despair and insisting that there was reason to hope even in the darkest of days following the *Dred Scott* decision.[76] In order to bolster that hope, Douglass encourages his listeners (as well as readers of his autobiographies) to see the hand of Divine providence in events. The extent to which Douglass himself "possessed a strong sense of God's providential care," however, is uncertain.[77] The evidence of this is, as we saw above, mixed at best. What can be known with greater certainty, however, is that Douglass had overcome the chief ground of our need for Divine providence: the fear that, without it, we cannot win the release that we deserve from our torments. The distance between Douglass and his audience was nowhere greater than with regard to the need for hope. Unable to take a comprehensive view of events, and lacking a penetrating and solid understanding of human nature, Douglass's audience was indeed in need of hope, and Douglass graciously helped to supply it. But he himself had learned early on to reject hope as an obstacle, rather than a spur, to action.

During the worst time of his stay with Covey, Douglass entertained thoughts of killing both Covey and himself, but he was always "prevented by a combination of *hope* and fear" from accomplishing it.[78]

Now, it would seem good that hope (for an eventual escape from Covey) kept Douglass from taking his own life. But insofar as the same hope kept him from taking Covey's life, it left him in distress and, thereby, in need of continuing to hope. Hope, especially the hope that we will be freed from our torments because we *deserve* to be freed from them, is a kind of pleasure (or, at least, an antidote to pain) and, as such, can imperil our sense of responsibility for securing our own good. Douglass succeeded so well, in no small measure, because he never again let his hopes interfere with his calculations of what could be effected. And, in this sense, it may be the example of Douglass himself, as presented in his autobiographies, that does more than any of his political rhetoric, however moving, to advance the cause of freedom.

NOTES

1. Diana Schaub, "The Spirit of a Free Man," *The Public Interest* 140 (Summer 2001): 103.
2. Benjamin R. Barber, *An Aristocracy of Everyone* (New York: Ballantine Books, 1992), 185.
3. Frederick Douglass, *Life and Times of Frederick Douglass* (New York: Collier Books, 1962 [1892]), 63.
4. *Life and Times*, 220.
5. *Life and Times*, 330.
6. *Life and Times*, 255.
7. *Life and Times*, 257; cf. 289.
8. *Life and Times*, 78–80.
9. *Life and Times*, 39.
10. *Life and Times*, 42.
11. Respect for elders has been identified as "the crux of spirituality for [Douglass's] people." Sterling Stuckey, "'Ironic Tenacity': Frederick Douglass's Seizure of the Dialectic," in *Frederick Douglass: New Literary and Historical Essays*, ed. Eric J. Sundquist (Cambridge: Cambridge University Press, 1990), 40.
12. Consider Plato, *Laws* 662d7–e7.
13. *Life and Times*, 97.
14. *Life and Times*, 81.
15. *Life and Times*, 117.
16. *Life and Times*, 119.
17. Frederick Douglass, *Narrative of the Life of Frederick Douglass* (New York: Dover Publications, 1995), 46.

18. *Life and Times*, 91.

19. *Narrative*, 71.

20. David Van Leer, "Reading Slavery: The Anxiety of Ethnicity in Douglass's *Narrative*," in *New Literary and Historical Essays*, 122–23.

21. *Life and Times*, 86.

22. Van Leer, "Reading Slavery," 118–28. While I disagree with some of his conclusions, I am grateful to Van Leer in many particulars for his penetrating analysis of the religious overtones of this crucial scene. That Douglass was not incapable of employing esoteric teaching is suggested by his appreciation of the "double meaning" he discovered in slave songs (*Life and Times*, 159).

23. *Life and Times*, 121–22.

24. It may even bring into question Douglass's distinction between "true" and "American" Christianity. Donald B. Gibson, "Faith, Doubt, and Apostasy: Evidence of Things Unseen in Frederick Douglass's *Narrative*," in *New Literary and Historical Essays*, 87.

25. *Life and Times*, 127.

26. *Narrative*, 43–44.

27. As one critic says, with hostile intent, "Douglass's attitudes toward other men maintain the air of a leader speaking of the masses." Rafia Zafar, "Frederick Douglass: The African-American as Representative Man," in *New Literary and Historical Essays*, 112.

28. *Life and Times*, 213.

29. *Life and Times*, 40.

30. *Life and Times*, 41; cf. Xenophon, *Memorabilia*, 3.9.10.

31. *Life and Times*, 106.

32. *Life and Times*, 85.

33. *Narrative*, 49.

34. *Life and Times*, 85.

35. *Life and Times*, 163.

36. *Life and Times*, 170.

37. "I had a positive aversion to all pretenders to 'divination.'" *Life and Times*, 138.

38. *Life and Times*, 217.

39. *Life and Times*, 217, emphasis in original.

40. Van Leer, "Reading Slavery," 132–33. Van Leer there discusses a different event, Douglass's recounting of the whipping his half-naked aunt Hester received in his presence.

41. *Life and Times*, 43.

42. *Life and Times*, 143.

43. *Life and Times*, 329.

44. *Life and Writings of Frederick Douglass*, ed. Philip S. Foner (New York: International Publishers, 1950), 2: 339.

45. *Life and Times*, 261.
46. Hobbes, *Leviathan*, ch. 14.
47. *Life and Times*, 143, emphasis in original.
48. *Life and Times*, 163.
49. *Life and Times*, 492.
50. Herbert J. Storing, "Frederick Douglass," in *American Political Thought: The Philosophic Dimensions of American Statesmanship*, ed. Morton J. Frisch and Richard G. Stevens (New York: Charles Scribner's Sons, 1971), 148.
51. *Life and Writings*, 2: 469.
52. *Life and Writings*, 2: 419, emphasis in original.
53. *Life and Writings*, 2: 419.
54. *Life and Times*, 261.
55. *Life and Times*, 229.
56. *Abraham Lincoln: Speeches and Writings, 1832–1858*, ed. Don E. Fehrenbacher (New York: Library of America, 1989), 524–25.
57. *Life and Writings*, 2: 350.
58. *Life and Writings*, 2: 351.
59. *Life and Times*, 226.
60. *Life and Times*, 227.
61. *Life and Times*, 38.
62. *Life and Writings*, 2: 192.
63. *Life and Writings*, 2: 186.
64. *Life and Writings*, 2: 201.
65. *Life and Times*, 242–43.
66. *Life and Times*, 207.
67. *Life and Times*, 239.
68. *Life and Times*, 37.
69. *Life and Times*, 269–70.
70. Eric J. Sundquist, "Introduction," *New Literary and Historical Essays*, 10.
71. *Life and Writings*, 2: 173.
72. Ida B. Wells-Barnett, *Crusade for Justice: The Autobiography of Ida B. Wells*, ed. Alfreda M. Duster (Chicago: University of Chicago Press, 1970), 118–19.
73. *Life and Writings*, 3: 182.
74. Booker T. Washington, *Up From Slavery: An Autobiography* (New York: Doubleday, Page & Co., 1901), 100; see also *Life and Times*, 224–25.
75. *Life and Times*, 124.
76. *Life and Writings*, 2: 409.
77. Schaub, "The Spirit of a Free Man," 93.
78. *Life and Times*, 124–25, emphasis added.

8

Lincoln and the Emancipation Proclamation: A Model of Prudent Leadership

Joseph R. Fornieri

The moral integrity of a democratic republic requires a virtuous citizenry who will aspire to enduring standards of excellence and who will hold their leaders accountable to such standards. As Plutarch understood nearly two millennia ago when he wrote the *Lives of the Noble Greeks and Romans*, virtue is more readily identifiable when it is manifested concretely through the actions of a particular individual who embodies its qualities and characteristics. Traditionally, Abraham Lincoln has been lauded for performing one of the greatest acts in American history: the Emancipation Proclamation. Yet, increasingly, in the contemporary climate of public opinion which denigrates magnanimity and debunks heroism, he has been derided on both the left and right wing of the political spectrum for this same act. Critics on the right contend that Lincoln was our most unconstitutional president; that the Emancipation Proclamation was illegal; and that his broad use of executive power during the war established a precedent for the Imperial Presidency. Critics on the left deride him as an unrepentant racist who was spurred on by the more principled radical abolitionists, who, in their view, are the true heroes of the Civil War era.[1]

While it may be an exaggeration to claim that Lincoln was solely responsible for freeing the slaves, it is altogether false to deny that his role was less than instrumental in securing the joint goals of preserving the Union and extending equality to all human beings. The traditional view of Lincoln as "The Great Emancipator" who freed the slaves is much closer to the truth than the deconstructionist view of him as an unprincipled, Machiavellian leader, indifferent to the plight of African-Americans. It is the purpose of this essay to show how Lincoln's decision-making on emancipation serves as a model of prudent leadership in its application of universal moral principle to a myriad of constitutional, social, and political circumstances. His prudence in this regard may be understood further as a mean between the political vices of pragmatism and moral idealism.[2]

In response to contemporary critics, it should be noted that Lincoln was assailed from both extremes of the political spectrum in his own time as well. His ability to navigate the ship of state between the moral idealism of the radical abolitionists, who demanded "Liberty first, Union afterwards," and the pragmatism of the War Democrats, who demanded, in effect, "a Union without Liberty," prudently achieved the correlative aims of preserving the Union and ending slavery. According to Lincoln, the preservation of a Union dedicated to the rule of law in the Constitution and the moral principles of the Declaration of Independence was the *sine qua non* of attaining the loftier goal of extending the principle of equality to African-Americans. Consequently, those legal concessions that he made to slavery during emancipation were prudent means adapted to the Union's preservation, an objective that implied the eventual end of slavery. By failing to appreciate the extent to which the application of moral principle is constrained by the limits of politics, Lincoln's critics inevitably fail to appreciate his prudent leadership. This failure to recognize Abraham Lincoln as a prudential statesman *par excellence* deprives students and citizens alike of a moral compass and a valuable resource to evaluate the actions of contemporary leaders.

Prudence may be defined as the ability to judge well in practical matters; it is tantamount to right reason applied to the realm of moral and political action.[3] Prudent judgment involves the just application of means to achieve noble political ends. The ultimate political end sought by the prudent leader is the common good of the regime, as opposed to an apparent good that is illusory or the selfish interest of a particular faction. In making decisions to benefit the common good, the prudent leader must consider both universal ethical principles and the application or determination of these principles to legal, social, and political contingencies.[4] Prudence thus involves the harmonization of universal moral precepts under the circumstances. St.

Thomas Aquinas states: "It is necessary for the prudent man to know both the universal principles of reason and the singulars with which ethical action is concerned."[5] In Lincoln's case, the end or common good of the American regime represented the perpetuation of a Union dedicated to the safety and happiness of the people. More specifically, this meant a Union dedicated to the moral precepts of the Declaration and the legal framework of the Constitution.

Comparatively speaking, the virtue of prudence may be understood further as a mean between the two extremes or vices of political idealism and pragmatism. Each of these vices involves a crucial defect or omission in right reasoning through precipitous or thoughtless practical judgment. Political idealism precipitously omits the consideration of particular circumstances in decision-making.[6] It involves "a negligence and blindness to the concrete realities" that surround political action.[7] The idealists' tenacious adherence to moral principle in its abstract purity blinds him to the contingencies under which these principles are to be applied and to the inherent limits of politics. The policy of prohibition provides an instructive example of political idealism. Through its precipitous disregard of the extent to which alcohol consumption was an ingrained custom in American culture, the prohibition movement had the unintended consequence of stimulating the activities of organized crime in purveying bootleg liquor. The moral crusade to abolish the evils of alcohol actually backfired by undermining respect for the law and by enhancing the public status of organized crime.

Political pragmatism, on the other hand, fails to consider adequately universal moral principles in practical judgment. The pragmatist decides policies in the ethically relative terms of utility, expediency and/or self-interest. Political pragmatism thus involves a defect or omission in the application of principle to practice; it suffers from an ethical myopia that is blind to the preeminence of moral claims in guiding public policy. In this sense pragmatism resembles "cunning (*astutia*) . . . the most characteristic form of false prudence."[8] Those politicians who rely almost exclusively upon public opinion polls to decide policies without any consideration of higher moral obligation provide a vivid contemporary example of political pragmatism.

Because prudence involves the harmonization of moral principle to political practice, a presentation of Lincoln's decision-making on emancipation must consider the moral precepts that governed his leadership. The "universal principles of reason" that guided Lincoln's prudent judgment were promulgated in the Declaration of Independence. He once noted that "All the political sentiments I entertain have been drawn . . . from the Declaration of Independence."[9] Lincoln viewed the Declaration as the moral covenant of American Republicanism. He regarded it as the foundation of the American experiment; the principles of Jefferson were the "definitions and axioms of free society."[10] Indeed, Lincoln interpreted the Declaration as a declaration of natural law and right.[11] Its universal moral precepts and self-evident truths are rational expressions of man's participation in God's eternal law. As an expression of the natural law, the Declaration provides a transcendent rule and measure—a normative standard to judge the moral and political progress of the nation. Its moral precepts of equality and consent include positive injunctions to extend freedom and negative prohibitions that prevent its deprivation.[12] Among the principles of the Declaration, Lincoln assigned priority to the self-evident truth of equality which he understood to be "the father of all moral principle" and the "central idea" of the American regime.[13]

The moral precepts of the Declaration are validated by "The Three Rs" or traditions that inform Lincoln's political thought and action: republicanism, reason, and revelation.[14] The teachings of these traditions coincide, complement, and confirm one another in providing guidance for public life. For example, Lincoln maintained that the Declaration's assertion of equality coincides with the biblical precept of *Genesis 1: 27* which teaches that all human beings possess an equal rational and spiritual dignity because they are created in the image of God (*imago Dei*): "nothing stamped with the Divine image and likeness was sent into the world to be trodden on, and degraded, and imbruted by its fellows."[15]

In addition, the Bible's teaching of "The Golden Rule" in *Matthew 7: 12* likewise confirms the moral principle of equal consent in the Declaration: "As I would not be a slave so I would not be a master. This expresses my idea of democracy. Whatever differs from this, to the extent of the difference is no democracy."[16] Because no one would wish to be treated as a slave himself, no one is entitled to enslave others: "I never knew a man who wished to be himself a slave. Consider if you know any good thing, that no man desires for himself."[17] However, the moral precepts of the Bible are publicly authoritative for Lincoln because they are complemented by natural theology and confirmed by unassisted human reason: "I think that if anything can be proved by natural theology, it is that slavery is morally wrong. God gave man a mouth to receive bread, hands to feed it, and his hand has a right to carry bread to his mouth without controversy."[18]

Although the Bible may serve as a guide to public life, Lincoln did not believe that its general precepts could be applied directly and literally to politics without prudential mediation. The Bible does not provide, nor intends to provide, specific legal determinations for public policies. Though revelation promulgates general principles of moral conduct, God did not endow human beings with the capacity of practical judgment and free will only to render it null and void by promulgating an answer in the Bible to each particular moral circumstance. Lincoln conveyed the limitations of a literal interpretation of the Bible to a group of abolitionist ministers who urged immediate emancipation during the war:

> The subject presented in the memorial is one upon which I have thought much for weeks past, and I may even say for months. I am approached with the most opposite opinions and advice, and that by religious men, who are equally certain that they represent the Divine will. I am sure either the one or the other class is mistaken in that belief, and perhaps in some respect both. I hope it will not be irreverent for me to say that if it is probable that God would reveal his will to others, on a point so connected with my duty, it might be supposed he would reveal it directly to me; for, unless I am more deceived in myself than I often am, it is my earnest desire to know the will of Providence in this matter. *And if I can learn what it is I will do it!* These are not, however, the days of miracles, and I suppose it will be granted that I am not to expect a direct revelation. I must study the plain physical facts of the case, ascertain what is possible and learn what appears to be wise and right. The subject is difficult, and good men do not agree.[19]

Lincoln's acknowledgement that "good men do not agree" on difficult moral questions reflects a humility that is directly opposed to the dogmatism and dualism indicative of contemporary ideological thinking that seeks to demonize political opponents. His rare combination of a humility that acknowledges the distance between the Divine and human will and his striving for greatness in the service of God and others manifests a biblical magnanimity that combines elements of the Christian and pagan traditions.[20]

Lincoln's view of the harmony between reason and revelation es-
chews the contemporary extremes of a purely secular political rationalism that rejects the authority of revelation and a fideism that rejects
the authority of reason. Contrary to either extreme, he stresses the
participation of human reason in accordance with Divine reason; human reason is illuminated through man's openness to God's grace.[21]
Both reason and revelation cooperate in the determination of prudent
judgments.

Given the variability of time and circumstance, it is quite conceivable that "Divine law" may be ambiguous—that is, not immediately
manifest, on particular questions. As St. Thomas Aquinas explains,
"the general principles of the natural law cannot be applied to all men
in the same way on account of the great variety of human affairs: and
hence arises the diversity of positive laws among various people."[22]
Lincoln recognized that the Constitution of 1787 made concessions to
slavery that as a statesman his oath of office bound him to uphold. Interpreting the Founders' affirmation of equality at the time of the Revolution, he noted that the authors of the Declaration

> did not mean to assert the obvious untruth, that all were enjoying
> equality, nor yet, that they were about to confer it immediately upon
> them. In fact they had no power to confer such a boon. They meant
> simply to declare the right so that the enforcement of it might follow as
> fast as circumstances should permit. They met to set up a standard
> maxim for free society, which should be familiar to all, and revered by
> all; constantly looked to, constantly labored for.[23]

Even though the principle of equality was applied imperfectly due to
the inherent limits of politics, it nonetheless serves as an aspiration
and normative guide to public life. The standard is to be approxi-
mated under the circumstances even if it cannot be fully reached.

Once prudent statesmen have acknowledged the initial preeminence of moral claims in guiding public life, they must subsequently
address a set of derivative, but equally important questions—that is to
say, they must address the specific legal and constitutional determinations of policy-making. The application of moral principle to practice is circumscribed by different jurisdictions of authority. Moral rectitude in the abstract does not account for the various circumstances
that attend statecraft. Despite slavery's inherent moral evil, before the
war Lincoln rejected the coercive use of national authority to bring
about its extirpation in the states where it already existed. The use of

such force was *ultra vires*. While Lincoln believed that slavery was inherently evil, he distinguished legally between slavery as a national, state, and territorial institution. Although the national right to slavery was never expressly and distinctly affirmed in the Constitution by the Founders (as Judge Taney mistakenly contended in *Dred Scott*), the federal division of powers prohibited the national government from interfering with the institution where it already existed in the states at the time of the Constitution. However, since the territories fell under national jurisdiction, the federal government had both a compelling legal authorization and moral obligation to restrict it in this area. In dealing with the slavery issue, Lincoln endorsed the prudential council of his Whig predecessor: "Mr. Clay says it is true as an abstract principle that all men are created equal, but that we cannot practically apply it in all cases."[24] Prior to the exigencies of the Civil War and the passage of the Thirteenth, Fourteenth, and Fifteenth Amendments, the forcible abolition of slavery where it existed in the states was unconstitutional; it would have constituted a gross usurpation of state and local authority by the national government.

Before the war, Lincoln's prudential reconciliation of moral obligation to the Declaration and legal obligation to the Constitution may be understood as a mean between the disunionist extremes of the northern radical abolitionists and southern fire-eaters. Both northern radical abolitionists and southern fire-eaters alike saw the Constitution as a pro-slavery document. Consequently, before the Civil War, both welcomed disunion as a means of establishing a more suitable form of government consonant with their own political ends. Lincoln's adherence to the rule of law may be contrasted to the political idealism of radical abolitionists such as William Lloyd Garrison who burnt a copy of the Constitution, repudiating it a "covenant with death" and an "agreement with hell." Garrison triumphantly proclaimed that "if slaves have a right to their freedom, it ought to be given them, regardless of the consequences."[25]

Likewise, Charles Sumner declared that: "The Antislavery Enterprise is right; and the right is always practicable."[26] Contrary to these extremists, Lincoln prudently acknowledged the limits of politics: "The true rule, in determining to embrace, or reject any thing, is not whether it have any evil in it; but whether it have more of evil, than of good. There are few things wholly evil, or wholly good. Almost everything, especially of government policy, is an inseparable compound of the two; so that our best judgment of the preponderance between them is continually demanded."[27] Because few things in human life are absolutely good or absolutely evil, the prudent statesman must work to minimize evil and maximize good.

The radical abolitionists of Lincoln's own time failed to appreciate his prudence. Wendell Phillips derisively referred to the President-Elect as the "slave hound from Illinois" for his concessions to slavery in order to preserve the Union and arrogantly described him as an unwitting pawn of radical abolitionists:

> Not an Abolitionist, hardly an antislavery man, Mr. Lincoln consents to represent an antislavery idea. A pawn on the political chessboard, his value is in his position; with fair effort, we may soon change him for knight, bishop, or queen, and sweep the board. . . . The Republican party have undertaken a problem, the solution of which will force them to our position. . . . Not Mr. Seward's 'Union and Liberty,' which he stole and poisoned from Webster's 'Liberty and Union.' No: their motto will soon be 'Liberty first,' 'Union afterwards.'[28]

Phillips' substitution of "Liberty First,""Union Afterwards" for "Liberty and Union, One and Inseparable" expresses rather concisely the moral idealism of the radical abolitionists. Unlike Lincoln, he was quite willing to risk the dissolution of the Union and the abandonment of the Constitution to achieve the abstract promise of equality. As political idealists who completely disregard the rule of law, expediency, and the limitations of sociopolitical circumstances, Phillips and the other radical abolitionists were unaware that their abstract commitment to principle actually undermined their own moral aspirations. Phillips' political immoderation, so reminiscent of French Jacobinism, alienated southern moderates, further impaired rational dialogue, and thereby hastened the Civil War. In fact, a member of the South Carolina state legislature quoted Phillips' speech "as one justification for his state's secession from the Union."[29]

From the start of the war and after secession, the radical wing of the Republican Party constituted by former abolitionists like Garrison and Phillips pressured Lincoln to decree immediate and unconditional emancipation throughout the entire Union, including the Border States—those states that remained loyal to the Union despite having slaves.[30] Secession provided radicals with an opportune moment to implement their utopian agenda since the southern states no longer stood in the way of their moral aspirations. Though Lincoln opposed slavery in principle, his fidelity to the Constitution and his oath of office prevented him from issuing an emancipation without proper legal authorization and without broad public support. Lincoln defended his prudent position in a reply to Albert Hodges, editor of a Frankfurt, Kentucky, newspaper, who visited the White House to inform the President of "much dissatisfaction" in his state over the "enlistment of black soldiers":

> I am naturally anti-slavery. If slavery is not wrong, nothing is wrong. I can not remember when I did not so think, and feel. And yet I have never understood that the Presidency conferred upon me an unrestricted right to act officially upon this judgment and feeling. It was in the oath I took that I would, to the best of my ability, preserve, protect, and defend the Constitution of the United States. I could not take the office without taking the oath. Nor was it my view that I might take an oath to get power, and break the oath in using the power.[31]

Critics point out that the Emancipation Proclamation did not apply to the border states, that it was justified as a necessary war measure, and that it was not issued until after two years of war as incontrovertible proof that Lincoln's commitment to ending slavery was a sham. Lincoln's revocation of two prior emancipation edicts and statement that his "paramount objective" in the war was to preserve the Union, not the immediate abolition of slavery, is cited further as evidence of his indifference to black freedom. The deconstructionist view of emancipation teaches that Lincoln was a cunning Machiavellian leader who treated blacks as nothing more than pawns on a political chessboard. If this was indeed the case, Lincoln should no longer be praised as the "Great Emancipator," but condemned as the "Great Manipulator."

Yet, Lincoln's critics fail to take into account the concrete alternatives at the time. His position on emancipation should be viewed in its proper historical context as a prudential mean between the Radical Republicans who demanded immediate, uncompensated emancipation and the War Democrats who not only opposed extending the principle of equality to African-Americans, but who were also most willing to reverse any strides made in the direction of black freedom. This is not to mention northern "Copperheads" who sympathized with the South, assailed the administration, and vehemently opposed the Union's war effort. An immediate emancipation may have assuaged the North's feelings of self-righteousness in the short term; but, in the long term, it would have jeopardized the support of War Democrats and the border states necessary to win the war. The loss of the war by the North and the dissolution of the Union would have rendered the discussion of black freedom moot; it would have resulted in the abandonment of African-Americans to a Confederacy dedicated to the principle of human inequality. On the other side of the political spectrum, a coalition of War Democrats, border states, and Conservative Republicans retarded steps toward black freedom by proposing a return to the *status quo antebellum* in regard to slavery. The pragmatic outlook of this coalition would have resulted in "a Union without Liberty"—that is to say, a Union dedicated exclusively to white freedom and the retraction of all strides toward ending slavery. Lincoln's prudent leadership served the greater public good of both Liberty and Union by avoiding the extreme alternatives proposed by the Radical Republicans and War Democrats from the border states.

Lincoln's response to Horace Greeley is often cited as proof that emancipation was merely an expedient devoid of any higher moral aspiration. In August of 1862, Horace Greeley, editor of the *New York Tribune*, wrote an editorial to the president entitled "The Prayer of Twenty Millions" criticizing Lincoln for his reluctance to emancipate: "We think you are unduly influenced by the councils, the representations, the menaces, of certain fossil politicians hailing from the Border States." Mindful that his response would be scrutinized in papers throughout the nation, Lincoln cautiously stated the North's objective during the war:

My paramount object in this struggle is to save the Union, and not either to save or to destroy slavery. If I could save the Union without freeing any of the slaves I would do it; and if I could save it by freeing some and leaving others alone I would also do that. What I do about slavery, and the colored race, I do because it helps to save the Union; and what I forebear, I forebear because I do not believe it would hope to save the Union. . . . I have here stated my purpose according to my *official* duty; and I intend no modification of my oft expressed *personal* wish that all men everywhere could be free.[32] (Italics are Lincoln's)

Though Lincoln admits that his "paramount object" is to save the Union, it does not follow that this objective excludes the ultimate goal of extending the principle of equality to African-Americans. Critics who cite the letter to Greeley in defense of the claim that the president was unprincipled in his efforts to preserve the Union neglect Lincoln's many efforts towards compensated emancipation in the border states, disregard his commitment to the Constitution and rule of law, and ignore his vision of an inclusive and moral Union dedicated to the principle of equality in the Declaration.[33] Consequently, they neglect the concluding sentence of the letter where Lincoln conveys his "personal wish that all men everywhere could be free." In a word, they posit a false dichotomy between the joint goals of preserving the Union and ending slavery by presuming that the two objectives are mutually exclusive. On the contrary, Lincoln envisioned the goals of preserving the Union and freeing the slaves as compatible. David Herbert Donald explains the relationship between these two:

> In Lincoln's mind there was no necessary disjunction between a war for the Union and a war to end slavery. Like most Republicans, he had long held the belief that if slavery could be contained it would inevitably die; a war that kept the slave states within the Union would, therefore, bring about the ultimate extinction of slavery. For this reason, saving the Union was his 'paramount object.' But readers aware that Lincoln always chose his words carefully should have recognized that "paramount" meant "foremost" or "principal"—not "sole."[34]

As Donald explains, a careful reading of Lincoln's reply to Greeley would recognize that the word "paramount" does not mean "sole" or "only," but rather "foremost" or "principal." Lincoln's language makes clear that although the preservation of the Union is the priority, it is not the only political objective. The preservation of the Union was a necessity if slavery was to be ended. In order to maintain the support of a broad coalition of Border States and War Democrats, Lincoln equivocated when he spoke of his paramount objective in the war. This equivocation is also apparent in a subsequent letter to James Conkling on August 26, 1863, which (like the letter to Greeley) was also published throughout the nation. The letter to Conkling not only helps one to appreciate the various factions the president had to balance in maintaining a winning war coalition, but it also subtly reveals his view of the inseparable relationship between preserving the Union and the promise of equality: "You say you will not fight to free Negroes. Some of them seem willing to fight for you; but, no matter.

Fight you, then exclusively to save the Union. I issued the proclamation on purpose to save the Union." Lincoln then justifies his decision to use black soldiers in the emancipation: "I thought that whatever Negroes can be got to do as soldiers, leaves just so much less for white soldiers to do, in saving the Union . . . but negroes, like other people, act upon motives. Why should they do any thing for us, if we will do nothing for them? If they stake their lives for us, they must be promoted by the strongest motive—even the promise of freedom. And the promise being made, must be kept."

As Lawanda Cox has noted in her important work *Lincoln and Black Freedom*, Lincoln saw the use of black soldiers as a prudent measure to achieving equality for blacks.[35] At the end of the letter, Lincoln affirms the Union's dedication to higher moral principles by offering thanks to all, "For the great republic—for the principle it lives by, and keeps alive—for man's vast future." To be sure, the principle the Union lives by is the principle of equality. Thus, preservation of the Union and the republic means preserving the principle of equality and its promise of freedom for all. Finally, Lincoln chastises the political pragmatism and cynicism of those whites who would deprive black people of their deserved freedom:

> Peace does not appear so distant as it did. I hope it will come soon, and come to stay; and so come as to be worth keeping in all future time. It will then have been proved that, among free men, there can be no successful appeal from the ballot to the bullet; and that they who take such appeal are sure to lose their case, and pay the cost. And then, there will be some black men who can remember that, with silent tongue, and well poised bayonet, they have helped mankind on to this great consummation; while, I fear there will be some white ones, unable to forget that, with malignant heart, and deceitful speech, they have strove to hinder it.[36]

Lincoln's reference to a peace "worth keeping in all future time" is a subtle reminder that a meaningful peace must honor the promise of freedom to African-Americans. A peace that returns blacks to slavery, as the War Democrats and General McClellan (Lincoln's opponent in the election of 1864) desired, was not worth keeping in Lincoln's view. The caustic tone of Lincoln's reference to "some white ones . . . with malignant heart, and deceitful speech" is uncharacteristic of the president's usual sobriety. This strong language conveys his righteous indignation for those who sought to hinder America's mission as an exemplar of democracy and as a standard bearer of the principles of equality in the Declaration. It is important to note that Lincoln refers to whites generically; he does not distinguish between Confederates and Northern Democrats, but implicates both in denying freedom to African-Americans.

The joint objectives of emancipation involved a short-term and long-term goal. The primary objective was the immediate and most crucial—that is, defeating the enemy and restoring the territorial integrity of the Union; the long-term objective of applying the moral principles of the Declaration was dependent upon the success of the first. The final version of the Emancipation Proclamation conveys this dual intent: It is "sincerely believed to be an act of justice, warranted by the Constitution, upon military necessity."[37] Lincoln's scrupulous attention to legal detail should not obscure the moral intention of emancipation as an "act of justice." Indeed, the South recognized that Lincoln was a principled and implacable foe of slavery—that is why they seceded in the first place. They correctly understood that slavery was eventually doomed to extinction in a regime committed to the principles of the Declaration and to a leader who would contain the spread of the institution.

Textual evidence further confirms that Lincoln envisioned the inseparability of Liberty and Union to imply the complementary goals of preserving the Union and ending slavery. At Peoria in 1854, he emphasized that the Union must be "worthy of . . . saving."[38] The Union was only worthy of saving in view of the moral principles it represented; those foundational principles conveyed by the Declaration. Preserving the Union thus meant preserving the principles and aspirations the Union stood for. Similarly, Lincoln noted in a speech at Bloomington the same year that "the Union must be preserved in the purity of its principles."[39] And, as seen above, his praise for "The Great Republic" was based upon "the principle it lives by." Lincoln maintained that the consistent application of the Declaration's principle of equality to blacks was linked to the success of the American mission in guaranteeing equality to all human beings: "In giving freedom to the slave, we assure freedom to the free—honorable alike in what we give, and what we preserve. We shall nobly save, or meanly lose, the last, best hope on earth."[40]

While en route to his inauguration, Lincoln delivered a speech at Trenton, New Jersey, an important historical site of the Revolutionary War, in which he vowed to uphold the Founding Fathers' revolutionary legacy of freedom: "I am exceedingly anxious that this Union, the Constitution, and the liberties of the people shall be perpetuated in accordance with the original idea for which that struggle was made."[41] Of course, the original idea of the revolutionary struggle was encapsulated by the Declaration. After the border state of Maryland had pledged to abolish slavery, Lincoln revealed the intimate connection between black freedom and the Union's preservation: "Maryland is secure to Liberty and Union for all the future."[42] Because the Union was dedicated to legitimate moral ends, Lincoln warned the border states that slavery would eventually become a casualty of the war: "If the war continue long, as it must, if the object be not sooner attained, the institution in your states will be extinguished by mere friction and abrasion—by the mere incident of the war." In a letter to August Belmont, Lincoln explained that "broken eggs cannot be mended," implying that the fragile shell of slavery would inevitably be smashed by the war.[43] Finally, the intention of the Gettysburg Address demonstrates Lincoln's commitment to equality. That address is perhaps the quintessential statement of America's creed and a poignant reminder of its moral aspiration to extend equality.

In *A New Birth of Freedom*, Harry V. Jaffa explains that Lincoln's immediate political intention in the Gettysburg Address was to ask the American people to ratify the Emancipation Proclamation issued the same year.[44] Lincoln's affirmation of equality as the central proposition of the nation and his subsequent reference to "a new birth of freedom" offers the American people the possibility of a Union freed from the moral blight of slavery which had soiled the regime's "republican robe" and its founding legacy. These myriad utterances testify to the inseparable connection between preserving the Union and extending liberty in Lincoln's mind.

Even if the preservation of the Union implied the eventual promise of equal rights for all, the abstract resolution of a moral claim does not prescribe a detailed set of guidelines for the determination of public policy. The concrete application of a moral principle like equality must be weighed and balanced against competing legal, political, social, and economic claims. Lincoln confesses that "the difficulty is not in stating the principle, but in practically applying it."[45] An appreciation of Lincoln's prudent decision-making on emancipation thus requires an understanding of the circumstances he confronted at the time. What contingencies and variables did Lincoln have to consider?

First, Lincoln was unsure about his constitutional authority to emancipate the slaves. He had consistently and repeatedly pledged that he could not touch slavery where it existed in the states from his earliest statements on slavery until his presidency. As much as he hated slavery, he had sworn an oath to uphold the Constitution and that meant upholding its concessions to slavery as well. As noted, prior to the Thirteen Amendment, the federal division of power prohibited interference with slavery where it already existed at the time of the Constitution. Indeed, a House Resolution in 1790 explicitly denied Congress the power to abolish slavery in the southern states.[46] A proclamation of black freedom in defiance of the Constitution would lack legitimacy and would confirm the suspicion of southerners and northern moderates alike that the Republican Party was composed of fanatics who had no respect for established legal procedure and the rule of law. Given his constitutional reservations, Lincoln believed that emancipation could only be legally justified as a "War Measure" under a broad reading of the president's power in Article 2 as "Commander in Chief" of the armed forces. Lincoln maintained that the emancipation was a necessary and reasonable means (a war measure) taken by the nation's Chief Executive to impair the South's ability to make war: the act would encourage slaves laboring for the Confederacy to flee and support the advancing Union armies. In fact, this did happen and the Union's war effort benefited greatly from it. The legal status of the Emancipation Proclamation as a war measure also explains why it did not apply to the border states that remained loyal to the Union despite having slaves.

To some, the fact that the Emancipation Proclamation reads like a lawyer's brief detracts from its significance. Richard Hofstadter noted that the act had "all the moral grandeur of a bill of lading."[47] However, the act's language manifests Lincoln's attention to legal detail, his respect for the rule of law, and his careful effort to balance both legal and moral obligation. In his profound textual analysis of the Emancipation Proclamation, George Anastaplo praises Lincoln's legal language as "the lawyer's art in its perfection."[48] For example, Lincoln was careful not to use the word "abolition" in the document to distinguish his lawful action from the unlawful measures of the radical abolitionists. The language of the act also prudently discourages wanton violence as a measure of its legal and moral propriety: "And I hereby enjoin upon the people so declared to be free to abstain from all violence, unless in necessary self-defense."

Even if it was constitutional (legally authorized), was emancipation politically expedient? How could the act be enforced in rebel territory? Lincoln's primary political consideration was to maintain a fragile war coalition composed of radical and moderate Republicans who favored emancipation on the one hand and War Democrats, Conservative Republicans, and the border states, on the other hand, who opposed emancipation. The support of border states like Kentucky, Maryland, and Missouri was crucial to the strategic success of the Union. Alienating them would upset the balance of power in favor of the South. Lincoln once said, "to lose Kentucky is to lose the whole game." He correctly discerned that it was both illegal and inexpedient to abolish slavery in the border states without their consent! The needed support of War Democrats and the border states to win the war constrained Lincoln's political possibilities. As seen, to maintain a winning coalition he prudently equivocated on what preserving the Union meant in his reply to Greeley and elsewhere to placate those who feared that the war would degenerate into an abolitionist crusade.

As a prudent commander in chief, Lincoln was forced to consider the effect of the emancipation on the Union Army's already low morale by late 1862. In order to defeat the South it was necessary to maintain unity in the northern army. Some Union officers were so hostile towards blacks that they returned fugitive slaves to the Confederacy during cease-fires. And some soldiers in the field had already threatened to desert if the cause of the Union was identified with abolitionism. After General Fremont unilaterally proclaimed emancipation in Missouri, a Union regiment threw down its arms and deserted. In fact, Lincoln had revoked two prior emancipations because he considered them to be illegal. Lincoln's commander for the Army of the Potomac, General George B. McClellan, a War Democrat, so vehemently opposed emancipation that he wrote a letter to his troops apologizing for Lincoln's actions in this regard.[49]

Lincoln also had to consider whether or not domestic opinion would support an emancipation. Leaders must consult public opinion and be responsible to it if democratic government is meaningful. According to Lincoln, public opinion and public policy are reciprocal. Public opinion disposes the enactment or rejection of public policy. Prudent leaders must guide public opinion without moving too far ahead of it and be constrained by public opinion when it is recalcitrant. As he said: "a universal opinion, whether good or bad, cannot safely be disregarded."

Lincoln had reservations about the credibility of an Emancipation Proclamation without a Union victory. Perceptions do count in politics. After winning many of the initial battles of the Civil War, the South hoped for foreign intervention to recognize or assist their cause. Lincoln presented a first draft of the Emancipation Proclamation to his cabinet as early as July 22, 1862. Secretary of State William Seward voiced reservations that without a Union military victory, emancipation would lack credibility in the nation and in the eyes of the world. Instead of a sublime triumph of freedom, it would be viewed as an act of desperation, "the last shriek on our retreat."[50] Lincoln and Seward both feared a British intervention that would force peace and guarantee the independence of the Confederacy. Thus he prudently delayed emancipation until it could be crowned with a Union victory to bolster its credibility at home and abroad. The battle of Antietam on September 17th gave the Union the victory it needed. Although it was more or less a stalemate in terms of casualties (about 20,000 total dead and wounded), Antietam was a symbolic victory because Lee was driven out of Maryland.

The preliminary Emancipation Proclamation was signed on September 22, 1862, but did not go into effect until January 1, 1863, a hundred days afterward. This interval was yet another prudent means to prepare public opinion for the subsequent transformation of freeing three million people. There were some notable differences between the preliminary and final drafts of the Emancipation.[51] The first draft mentioned compensation to slaveholders for their freed slaves if they rejoined the Union. The final draft, however, makes no mention of compensation to the rebel states. Furthermore, the final draft authorizes the use of black soldiers for the Union, not mentioned in the first draft. Lincoln saw this as both an expedient means to support the Union cause and an important step toward black freedom. By proving their manhood on the battlefield, the sacrifice of black soldiers for the Union cause would further dispose public opinion toward the goal of equality. The withdrawal of an offer to compensate slaveholders who

returned to the Union and the authorization of black soldiers in the final version of the Emancipation are consistent with Lincoln's belief
that the institution of slavery would become a casualty of the war. To
placate the fears of moderates who feared a universal, servile insur-
rection, the final version of the Emancipation prudently includes an
admonition to the freed slaves to "abstain from all violence, unless in
necessary self-defense."

As a prudent leader, Lincoln had to consider the social impact of
emancipation. This involved considerations of racial adjustment between whites and blacks. While many northerners were opposed to
slavery in the abstract, they nevertheless opposed the full social and
political equality of blacks and still viewed them as an inferior race.
What would be done with the blacks once they were emancipated?
How could they be assimilated into society given their servile condition and the prevailing opinion amongst both southerners and northerners that they were an inferior race? An example of public hostility
to black freedom in the North can be seen in the New York City Draft
riots that erupted shortly after the emancipation. A black orphanage
was burnt and blacks were lynched as a demonstration that many
were unwilling to support a war for equal rights.

Ultimately, Lincoln decided that the advantages of emancipation
outweighed its disadvantages. After judging the various contingencies,
he decided that the act was salutary in both its principle and in its effects or consequences. The transforming circumstances of the Civil
War made emancipation "an indispensable necessity" at the time,
thereby furthering the joint ends of the Union's preservation and slavery's demise. The prudent leader takes into consideration not only intentions, but the consequences of actions and ideas as well. Prudent
leadership involves foresight; it anticipates unintended consequences.
Aquinas notes that the word "prudence" is derived from providence—
that is, foresight. What were some of the positive consequences of
emancipation? It crippled the South's capacity to make war by encouraging slaves to escape from their southern masters and to support the approaching Union army. It authorized the use of black soldiers to aid the Union cause. It achieved an important moral
aspiration of the Union by extending the Declaration's principle of
equality to African-Americans in the South. It prevented diplomatic
recognition of the Confederacy and intervention. The Emancipation
Proclamation helped to discourage the foreign intervention of Great

Britain and other nations that would be forced to recognize the moral high ground of the Union's cause. It provided a strong moral incentive to preserve the Union. In addition to preserving the territorial and legal integrity of the Union, it would give the North a concrete moral cause to fight for.

The sober language of the Emancipation Proclamation, its legal authorization as a war measure, its delay until a Union victory, and its exemption of the border states and other Union-held areas demonstrate that it was a prudent act that considered a variety of contingencies. Lincoln was a principled opponent of slavery in both speech and deed. The contention that he was a hypocrite because emancipation did not apply to the border states is refuted by his many efforts to abolish slavery legally in those states through his policy of compensated emancipation. In March of 1862, Lincoln steered a joint resolution through Congress that offered financial aid to any border state that would take measures toward gradual, compensated emancipation. He argued that 1 million dollars, or less than half of the cost of the war for one day, would buy all the slaves in Delaware at 400 dollars a head. Because the border s142tates remained loyal to the Union, they had to consent to the abolition of slavery; compensated emancipation was thus a legal means to achieving an important moral principle. If Lincoln was less committed to black freedom, he would not have invited border state men to the White House and appealed to them on several different occasions to adopt his plan for compensated emancipation.[52]

The border states' refusal each time to accept the offer is an indication of the recalcitrance of public opinion in this part of the war coalition against extending equality to African-Americans. Lincoln's commitment to the principle of equality is demonstrated further by his demand that abolition of slavery be a necessary condition for the readmission to the Union of any southern state during Reconstruction, by his vigorous support of the Thirteenth Amendment that abolished slavery throughout the country, by his abolition of slavery in the District of Columbia which was under federal jurisdiction, and by his approval of African-Americans in the Union Army.

Finally, Lincoln's commitment to black freedom is demonstrated through his efforts toward black suffrage in Louisiana, the first state readmitted to the Union which would serve as a model for reconstruction. Towards the end of the war, he recommended to Governor

Hahn of Louisiana in a personal letter that some blacks be given the franchise. Prior to the Fifteenth Amendment, suffrage was left to the discretion of the states and beyond the authority of the national government to regulate. Lincoln's letter thus conveys a personal moral aspiration to the governor: "I barely suggest for your private consideration, whether some of the colored people may not be let in—as for instance, the very intelligent, and especially those who have fought gallantly in our ranks. They would probably help, in some trying time to come, to keep the jewel of liberty within the family of freedom."[53]

Lincoln's metaphor of freedom as a precious gem, the "jewel of liberty," is consistent with his earlier reference in the *Peoria Address of 1854* where he described the principles of the Declaration as "the chief jewel of the nation—the very figure head of the ship of State." In both cases, the jewel represents the legacy of freedom to which all members of the human family are heirs by their very humanity. By analogy, the founders' legacy of liberty should be bequeathed unto the entire family of mankind. The metaphor affirms Lincoln's understanding of the American regime as being crowned by the defining moral end of equality. His consistent use of the gem metaphor in describing equality as "the jewel of the nation" at Peoria and black suffrage as the "jewel of liberty" in the letter to Governor Hahn demonstrates the connection in Lincoln's mind between the preservation of a moral Union and the eventual promise of black freedom.[54]

Lincoln's unwillingness to retract the Emancipation Proclamation in order to gain public support during the early summer of the election of 1864 further testifies to his principled leadership.[55] In 1864, the Democratic Party ran George B. McClellan, who sought to retract the Emancipation. McClellan's letter of apology to the army after Lincoln issued the Act has already been mentioned. In his acceptance speech to the Democratic Party, McClellan voiced his opposition to the Emancipation Proclamation and his desire to retract it: "The preservation of our Union was the sole avowed object for which the war was commenced. It should have been conducted for that object only."[56] Unlike Lincoln, McClellan was a pragmatist; he saw the preservation of the Union as devoid of any moral principle and promise of equality to African-Americans. It is therefore tragic that in our contemporary climate of public opinion Abraham Lincoln is now mistakenly identified with the unscrupulous position that he courageously and prudently opposed during his presidency.

In the early stages of the campaign it looked as though Lincoln was sure to lose. There was a great deal of pressure to renounce the Emancipation Proclamation during the summer months of 1864. The Union was exhausted by war: some 360,000 of its soldiers had died. The existence and growth of a substantial peace movement led by northern Copperheads increasingly voiced opposition to Lincoln's war policies.[57] A miscegenation hoax perpetrated by the *New York World* newspaper attempted to stir up racism and to humiliate the Republican Party by claiming that emancipation was done to promote interbreeding among the races.[58] In his reply to Charles D. Robinson, a War Democrat who expressed concerns about his emancipation policy, Lincoln stated: "I am sure you would not desire me to say, or to leave an inference, that I am ready, whenever convenient to join in re-enslaving those who shall have served us in consideration of our promise. As matter of morals, could such treachery by any possibility, escape the curses of Heaven, or of any good man."[59] And after the election in December 1864, Lincoln stated:

> I repeat the declaration made a year ago, that while I remain in my present position I shall not attempt to retract or modify the emancipation proclamation, nor shall I return to slavery any person who is free by the terms of that proclamation, or by any of the Acts of Congress. If the people should, by whatever mode or means, make it an Executive duty to re-enslave such persons, another, and not I, must be their instrument to perform it.[60]

Lincoln's campaign for re-election sunk to a low point in the early summer of 1864; on August 23rd he circulated a blind memorandum to his Cabinet asking them to sign the unseen document that conceded defeat in the election. Inside the sealed envelope, the memorandum stated:

> This morning, as for some days past, it seems exceedingly probable that this Administration will not be re-elected. Then it will be my duty to so co-operate with the President elect, as to save the Union between the election and the inauguration; as he will have secured his election on such ground that he cannot possibly save it afterwards.[61]

If Lincoln was the astute Machiavellian described by critics, he surely would have retracted the Emancipation Proclamation in the name of expediency rather than suffer defeat in the name of principle. Thus, despite great pressure and contrary to his own momentary popularity and standing in the polls, Lincoln prudently adhered to his principles. Fortunately, Sherman's victory at the Battle of Atlanta and McClellan's endorsement of peace with the Confederacy all but ensured Lincoln's victory in 1864. If McClellan had won the election of 1864, the many strides toward black freedom would have been reversed.

The words of Frederick Douglass at the Dedication to the Freedman's Monument on April 14, 1876, in commemoration of Lincoln's Emancipation Proclamation provide a valuable insight on the sixteenth president's prudent leadership. It should be remembered that as an abolitionist and former slave, Douglass was impatient with Lincoln for delaying emancipation. Though earlier in his speech Douglass refers to Lincoln as the "white man's President" and blacks as his "stepchildren," his recognition of Lincoln's prudence places these earlier remarks in a wider context that appreciates the many contingencies the president had to balance in applying moral principle under the circumstances:

His great mission was to accomplish two things: first, to save his country from dismemberment and ruin; and, second, to free his country from the great crime of slavery. To do one or the other, or both, he must have had the earnest sympathy and the powerful cooperation of his loyal fellow-countrymen. Without this primary and essential condition to success his efforts must have been vain and utterly fruitless. Had he put the abolition of slavery before the salvation of the Union, he would inevitably driven from him a powerful class of the American people and rendered resistance to the rebellion impossible. Viewed from the genuine abolition ground, Mr. Lincoln seemed tardy, cold, dull, and indifferent; but measuring him by the sentiment of his country, a sentiment he was bound as a statesman to consult, he was swift, zealous, radical and determined.[62]

NOTES

1. See Lerone Bennett Jr., *Forced into Glory: Abraham Lincoln's White Dream* (Chicago: Johnson Publishing Co., 2000).

2. Ethan Fishman, "Under the Circumstances: Abraham Lincoln and Classical Prudence," in *Abraham Lincoln: Sources and Style of Leadership*, ed. Frank J. Williams, William D. Pederson, and Vincent J. Marsala (Westport, Conn.: Greenwood Press, 1994), 4–7.

3. St. Thomas Aquinas, *Summa Theologica: Volume Three: II-II* (Westminster, Md.: Christian Classics, 1981), II-II, Q. 47–51, 1383–1406. (Hereafter cited as *S.T.*)

4. Yves Simon, *A General Theory of Authority* (Notre Dame: University of Notre Dame Press, 1980), 144.

5. *S.T.*, II, II, Q. 47, A. 2-3, 1384–85.

6. *S.T.*, II, II, Q. 53-55, 1410–20.

7. Joseph Pieper, *The Four Cardinal Virtues* (Notre Dame: University of Notre Dame Press, 1966), 19.

8. Pieper, *The Four Cardinal Virtues*, 19.

9. Abraham Lincoln, *The Collected Works of Abraham Lincoln*, ed. Roy P. Basler, 9 vols. (New Brunswick, N.J.: Rutgers University Press, 1955), 4: 240. (Hereafter cited as *CWAL*.)

10. *CWAL*, III: 375.

11. Harry V. Jaffa, *A New Birth of Freedom: Abraham Lincoln and the Coming of the Civil War* (Lanham, Md.: Rowman & Littlefield, 2000), 122–25, 509.

12. Joseph R. Fornieri, "Abraham Lincoln and the Declaration of Independence: The Meaning of Equality," in *Abraham Lincoln: Sources and Style of Leadership*, ed. Frank J. Williams, William D. Pederson, and Vincent J. Marsala (Westport, Conn.: Greenwood Press, 1994), 45–69.

13. Harry V. Jaffa, *Equality and Liberty* (New York: Oxford University Press, 1965). See also Harry V. Jaffa, *How to Think About the American Revolution* (Durham, N.C.: Carolina Academic Press, 1978).

14. Joseph R. Fornieri, "Biblical Republicanism: Abraham Lincoln's Civil Theology," Ph.D. dissertation, Catholic University of America, 1966. For a more in-depth exploration of this theme see the forthcoming *Lincoln's Biblical Republicanism* by the same author.

15. *CWAL*, II: 544–47.

16. *CWAL*, II: 532.

17. *CWAL*, VII: 260.

18. *CWAL*, IV: 3; X: 44–45.

19. *CWAL*, V: 419–20.

20. See in this volume Kenneth L. Deutsch, "Thomas Aquinas on Magnanimous and Prudent Statesmanship."

21. *CWAL*, V: 478; VII: 535–36.

22. *S.T.*, I-II, Q. 95, A. 3.

23. *CWAL*, II: 406.

24. *CWAL*, III: 303–4.

25. William Lloyd Garrison, *Selections From the Writings and Speeches of William Lloyd Garrison* (New York: Wallcut, 1852), 118.

26. David Herbert Donald, *Charles Sumner and the Coming of the Civil War* (Chicago: University of Chicago Press, 1981), 228.

27. *CWAL*, I: 484.

28. Quoted from James M. McPherson, *The Struggle for Equality: Abolitionists and the Negro in the Civil War and Reconstruction* (Princeton: Princeton University Press, 1995), 27–28.

29. McPherson, *The Struggle for Equality*, 28.

30. See Harry T. Williams, *Lincoln and the Radicals* (Madison: University of Wisconsin Press, 1972).

31. *CWAL*, VIII: 281–83.

32. *CWAL*, V: 388–89.

33. Rogan Kersh, *Dreams of a More Perfect Union* (Ithaca: Cornell University Press, 2001), 153–97.

34. David Herbert Donald, *Lincoln* (New York: Simon & Schuster, 1995), 368.

35. See Lawanda Cox, *Lincoln and Black Freedom: A Study in Presidential Leadership* (Columbia, S.C.: University of South Carolina Press, 1994).

36. *CWAL*, VI: 406–10.

37. *CWAL*, VI: 30.

38. *CWAL*, II: 276.

39. *CWAL*, II: 340–41.

40. *CWAL*, V: 537.

41. *CWAL*, V: 537.

42. *CWAL*, VIII: 148.

43. *CWAL*, V: 350.

44. Jaffa, *New Birth of Freedom*, 73–152.

45. *CWAL*, VII: 302.

46. Joseph Ellis, *Founding Brothers* (New York: Knopf, 2000), 81–119.

47. Richard Hofstadter, *The American Political Tradition* (New York: Vintage Books, 1961), 93.

48. George Anastaplo, *Abraham Lincoln: A Constitutional Biography* (Lanham, Md.: Rowman & Littlefield, 1999), 204.

49. Benjamin P. Thomas, *Abraham Lincoln* (New York: Knopf, 1968), 345.

50. Thomas, *Abraham Lincoln*, 334.

51. Anastaplo, *Abraham Lincoln*, 197–227.

52. *CWAL*, V: 144–46; 160–61; 317–19; 324; 527.

53. *CWAL*, VII: 243.

54. See David E. Long, *The Jewel of Liberty: Abraham Lincoln's Reelection and the End of Slavery* (Mechanicsburg, Pa.: Stackpole, 1994).

55. David E. Long, "I Shall Never Recall a Word," in *Abraham Lincoln: Sources and Style of Leadership*, ed. Frank J. Williams, William D. Pederson, and Vincent Marsala (Westport, Conn.: Greenwood Press, 1994), 89–108.

56. Long, *Jewel of Liberty*, 276.

57. Long, "I Shall Never," 89–108.

58. Long, "I Shall Never," 89–108.

59. *CWAL*, VII: 500.

60. *CWAL*, VIII: 152. Also see Anastaplo, 201.

61. *CWAL*, VII: 514.

62. Frederick Douglass, *Selected Speeches and Writings*, ed. Philip S. Foner (Chicago: Lawrence Hill, 1999), 618–21.

9

Prudence, Imprudence, and the Puzzle of Bill Clinton

Wynne Walker Moskop

Recent scholarly debates about Aristotelian prudence construct a dichotomy that is problematic for contemporary political leaders. One side of the dichotomy casts philosophy as the source for moral principles that guide political action, and the other casts public rhetoric as the source, thereby pointing leaders toward a choice between two untenable models, the philosopher and the demagogue. There is little room for the practical truth that develops in the soul of Aristotle's *phronimos*.

The purpose of this chapter[1] is to show that the terms of this scholarly discussion are too narrow to encompass the multifaceted deliberative process that Aristotle's prudent statesman uses. My approach is to elaborate Aristotle's descriptions of the different kinds of information that prudent leaders consider and, based on these descriptions, to outline a model of prudence. To illustrate the complexities of prudence, I apply it to the leadership practice of Bill Clinton, which is multifaceted enough to puzzle analysts and, it is likely, multifaceted enough to illustrate all of the categories in the model.

Some detail on the dichotomy in the scholarship on prudence will be useful for understanding what the model is intended to refute. According to Richard Ruderman, proponents of prudence in the 1980s and 1990s tend to separate it from philosophy and link it to public rhetoric to avoid fallout from postmodernism's attack on amoral, hegemonic, Hobbesian rationalism.[2] They see Aristotle's rejection of Plato's philosopher-king as a denial to science of "the

right to impose . . . undebatable political 'solutions,'" and a corre-
sponding encouragement for "citizens to participate in, and
thereby to strengthen, political life." They intend to follow in his
footsteps when they turn to prudence as the basis for "political
judgment, a kind of reasoning that will be more compatible with
politics than is theoretical reason," because it emerges from democratic practice. The reason why advocates of political judgment resist a role for philosophy, Ruderman believes, is because their
"core project"—"the 'full affirmation of deliberation and rhetoric'—
requires one to 'portray politics as *fully* discursive.'"[3] To Ruderman, this means that the content of ends is drawn from public deliberation and speech rather than from any source, like philosophy,
that is external to culture.

Ruderman counters the rejection of philosophy with the claim that
it is essential to prudence. Philosophy helps "prudence to gain critical distance on popular but misguided views and to resist the often
rigid moralism of the community or regime." Philosophy juxtaposes
against public opinion knowledge of the absolute best regime,
shedding light on "the incomplete nature of justice of every regime."
Without the objective knowledge supplied by philosophy, it is not
possible to transcend the values of one's own regime and judge
wisely. To illustrate prudence's need for philosophy, Ruderman reminds us of what Pericles, Aristotle's prudent statesman, learned
from his studies with Anaxagoras, his philosophic mentor: The study
of philosophy "rendered Pericles superior to 'all arts of popularity.'"
Without philosophy, "*phronesis* . . . always tends toward partisanship."[4] Ruderman goes on to reject any democratically constituted source of moral principles, claiming that, "if there is a case to
be made for a prudent participating citizenry, Aristotle does not
make it."[5]

Aristotle's descriptions of prudence question the terms of this
scholarly debate by agreeing, and disagreeing, with both sides. Prudence has a theoretical component, he teaches, but it is not philosophy. Rather prudence carries its own theoretical knowledge, knowledge that is better suited than philosophy to the changeable realm of
action.[6] As the model outlined below shows, the practical truth that
prudence embodies is compatible with democratically constituted
morality but does not cater to it. Without disagreeing with Ruderman's
point that prudence benefits from philosophy, that Pericles benefits

from Anaxagoras,[7] I want to emphasize the obvious: Pericles is not Anaxagoras. They know different things, as Aristotle testifies so clearly. He defines the *phronimos*, or prudent man,[8] as one who "can aim at and hit the best thing attainable to man by action." To illustrate, he contrasts prudent statesmen like Pericles, who "have the capacity to see what is good for themselves and for mankind," with philosophers like Anaxagoras, who "do not know what is advantageous to them." "We admit that they know extraordinary, wonderful, difficult, and superhuman things," he writes, "but call their knowledge useless because the good they are seeking is not human."[9] They are wise but not practical.

Given that philosophy does not supply Pericles' knowledge, what does? I hope to demonstrate what the prudent leader should know by outlining a model and using it to diagnose Bill Clinton's problems as a leader.

On the one hand, Clinton seems to know a lot and, in fact, is known for his mastery of policy detail. His political brilliance is widely acknowledged. At times, he seems capable of governing moderately and effectively.[10] On the other hand, observers are understandably puzzled that someone with such highly touted capabilities can act so often without regard for what he should know and often seems to know. How can he intend to avoid widely recognized errors of Jimmy Carter's—"an inexperienced White House staff and proposing a grandiose legislative program"—and still repeat them?[11] How can he understand the similar mistakes of his first term as governor of Arkansas, as the "corrections" of his second term testify, yet repeat these same mistakes in his first term as president?[12] Why does he take inconsistent policy positions? Why does he betray friends and break promises? How can he risk his presidency and damage the institution[13] by having sex with a White House intern? Given these persistent questions about Bill Clinton, it is easy to understand Fred Greenstein's comment that, while some political leaders are "of a piece" in their governing styles—Jimmy Carter, for instance, exhibited a consistent "concern for detail and insistence on the correctness of his own positions"—Bill Clinton is not.[14] To most of the scholars and journalists who write about him, Bill Clinton remains a bundle of contradictions. The challenge to the model of prudence is to explain Clinton's multiple facets in such a way that Clinton's leadership style is "of a piece."

ARISTOTLE'S PSYCHOLOGY AND THE
ORGANIZATION OF PRACTICAL TRUTH

To see how prudence combines diverse kinds of information, we have to start with Aristotle's "psychology," as scholars have labeled his description of the soul. Aristotle's assumption that human nature is to live according to reason dictates his division of the soul into two logical components, a rational part—home of intellectual virtues—and an irrational, appetitive part—home of moral virtues. Because human nature is to live according to reason, the rational side rules.[15] Prudence is the intellectual virtue that engineers this rule of reason over appetite.[16]

To Aristotle, prudence has an architectonic function.[17] This means that it is a "superlative" virtue, without which the less comprehensive virtues—either moral or intellectual—cannot operate.[18] Prudence, in effect, rules other virtues in the sphere of action by informing them about what human good requires of them in existing circumstances. Prudence offers technical knowledge about what existing circumstances are and ethical knowledge about what is good for humans generally.

The technical component of prudence "informs" the other virtues through its "knowledge of reality," as Josef Pieper explains. Before the political leader can do good, she must know what the situation is. As proponents of democratic deliberation explain, cultural ideals and the way people interpret them are crucial to the leader's understanding of problems and ability to shape solutions. Insofar as prudence begins with cognition, and focuses upon what is already real, it must incorporate public rhetoric. When prudence moves to volition and focuses on what has not been realized, it requires foresight, "the capacity to estimate, with a sure instinct for the future, whether a particular action will lead to the realization of the goal." Failure to grasp the necessariness in the present precludes foresight and leads to inaccurate prediction of the consequences of action.[19]

The ethical component that skill must serve comes from the agent's knowledge of human good. Neither absolute nor abstract, this knowledge comes when the person who lives well gradually acquires from experience, inductively and over time, a general concept of good that serves as a constant end for action. The prudent person's motive for any action begins with the general concept of human good developed through pursuing pleasures of the right kind.[20] This motive, the ultimate end of action, is drawn toward a specific end by the apprehension of the actual circumstances that set conditions to which one who would do good must conform. The agent's goodness depends on accurate perception of and willingness to conform to the best in the circumstances, on the ability to internalize as a specific end what the situation demands.[21]

An example of how prudence combines technical and ethical information is Aristotle's prudent household manager and how he goes about obtaining wealth. The manager considers the extent to which the acquisition of wealth serves the good of the household (a human good) in a given situation and then limits the amount of wealth accordingly.[22] The example teaches us that the agent is supposed to tailor the technique of acquiring wealth to the service of human good.

However, even the right ordering of technical and ethical knowledge is not sufficient for prudence. Since prudence operates in the sphere of action, the cooperation of appetite, or will, is crucial. The prudent household manager not only must know how much wealth is conducive to the good of the household; the manager also must desire only that amount of wealth. This means that prudence has a moral component. The role of moral virtue in prudence is to make sure that the irrational part of the soul, the will, "partakes" of reason by submitting to the authority of the intellect.[23]

Moral virtues—courage, self-control, justice, generosity—operate when we do something, when we act, not when we make something (as in art) and not when we merely think (as in science and philosophy). According to Aristotle, these virtues of character develop as persons learn through habit to feel an appetite for, to find pleasure in, the right things in the right circumstances. Then, when prudence informs appetite about the right course of action, moral virtue will generate in the appetitive part of the soul pleasure at doing whatever contributes to prudence's judgment and pain at doing whatever hinders it.[24] For example, in situations that call for courage, prudence identifies for appetite specifically what constitutes courage, as opposed to cowardice or foolhardiness. And appetite, having been prepared by long habit, is pleased to pursue what courage requires.[25]

If we follow Aristotle's account, prudence develops as intellect and character interact appropriately over time. When the individual applies a general concept of good to specific situations, the concept

itself is gradually refined and strengthened. As experience reinforces it intellectually, habit reinforces it morally.[26] The result is a
particular psychological state, to Aristotle a state of the soul that bal-
ances intellectual and moral components to achieve human good.
The prudent person is the living expression, the form,[27] of human
good; she fulfills human nature as she fulfills her own. As J. A. Stewart puts it, prudence "is the good man himself—a second nature,
which, having once put on, he cannot put off. . . . It directs him un-
erringly in the interest of the noble life, as instinct directs an animal
in the interest of the physical life."[28]

PRUDENCE AS A MEAN

When has this optimum psychological balance been achieved? How
do prudent persons bring all the necessary considerations to bear on
a decision to act? Aristotle's famous answer is that they deliberate to
find a midpoint, or mean,[29] between an ideal good and an existing reality. While the process of locating this mean is inexact, Aristotle does
offer some guidance. He advises us to identify the extremes relative
to a particular situation—the extremes of excess and deficiency that
hinder success, avoid them, and seek a moderate path.[30] An example
from politics is Aristotle's notion of the best constitution that is workable in most circumstances. Working from knowledge of what constitution is absolutely best and knowledge of circumstances, he concludes that the best possible constitution is a middle path between
democracy and oligarchy, either of which is an extreme in its pure
form. Democracy governs too little, and oligarchy too much. The mixture of the two, to which Aristotle gives his own label, polity, "should
look as if it contained both democratic and oligarchic elements—and
as if it contained neither."[31]

Using Aristotle's prescription as a foundation, I conceptualize prudence as a mean in relation to both character (appetite) and intellect.
While the content of prudence, human good, cannot be established
beyond argument by this approach or any other, certain parameters
of prudent action can be identified.

From the information that prudence is an intellectual virtue that
cannot be exercised without moral virtue, we can identify two primary sources of error, or imprudence—one a defect in the rational

side of the soul, seat of intellectual virtue, the other a defect in the irrational side, seat of moral virtue. Imprudence results if the rational
side does not have an accurate knowledge of what is good or if the
irrational side is not conditioned by habit to follow the rational side's
dictates. Following Aristotle's advice for locating the mean, we can
identify two extremes of intellectual error and two extremes of moral
error, any one of which can lead to imprudence. This approach iso-
lates prudence as a mean in the context of four categories of error, or
imprudence, to be avoided.

One extreme of moral error is readily apparent from Aristotle's observation that one who would always do what one knows to be right
needs "a firm and unchangeable character."[32] This strength of character allows the prudent agent to retain allegiance to a constant vision
of good—over time and in the face of changing circumstances. One
type of moral error, then, is being overly changeable. The character
who is "fickle and changeable" lacks the moral strength needed to
obey the commands of reason. Such a person will be easily distressed
or corrupted in the face of misfortune.[33]

The other extreme of moral error, paradoxically, is being too unchangeable. Since the best possible good will vary with circumstances, and sometimes may not be very good at all, the prudent person must be sufficiently flexible to choose obtaining good results over
maintaining absolute moral integrity. Being too good, or too principled, to adapt to circumstances, in the mode of Socrates or Jesus, is
one reason for being less flexible than changing circumstances require. Another reason is simple stubbornness, in which unreasoned
attachment to a particular course of action prevents the individual
from seeing the need to adapt to the environment and keeps her from
correcting mistakes.[34] While principled individuals choose not to be
limited by the situational constraints they see, stubborn individuals
appear to ignore situational constraints altogether. Prudent individuals are more flexible morally than are either completely principled or
stubborn individuals; but they are not so flexible that they lack
strength of character.

The extremes of intellectual error are implicit in the way Aristotle
himself describes prudence. He distinguishes it from two other intellectual virtues, science and art. While prudence entails elements of
both, it is an error to treat action either too much like science or too
much like art. We can see this best perhaps by understanding that the

respective ends, or "starting points," of science, art, and prudence involve varying degrees of certainty.

The starting point of science is the most certain, because it lies outside the agent, in nature or necessity. Things occurring in the realm of
science, laws of nature, for instance, have their source of motion in
themselves and are not subject to change by other forces.[35] The necessariness, or certainty, that is inherent in the scientist's end is apparent from the fact that science, as an intellectual virtue, occurs entirely
in the realm of thought. Pure science (not applied science) aims at
discovery or understanding of natural phenomena without any intent
to change them, precisely because such phenomena are eternal and
unchangeable.[36]

The starting point of art, in contrast, is not necessarily tied to laws
of nature or to any particular thing that is external to the agent. According to Aristotle, the starting point of art, its source of motion, lies
"in the producer."[37] This makes it internal and subjective. Though the
artist, as artist, stays within certain boundaries—i.e., rational pursuit
of artistic purpose—nonetheless, she is free to create, to select the
particular form her art will take, or to change her medium and her
technique. No given situation requires her attention. Art is not natural
but contrived, or made up, because it does not have to confront a particular reality.

In comparison to science and art, prudence has an ambiguous relationship to reality. The starting point of prudence is the end "at
which our actions are aimed."[38] Insofar as it exists through the agent's
motive, through the agent's perception and character, the end is inside the agent and involves some of the creativity associated with art.
After all, the agent must deliberate about what human good requires
in a given situation, make a decision, and carry it out. And the best
course of action is by no means certain, even in retrospect. Prudence,
like art, functions in a changeable realm where things can be other
than they are, where the appearance of good changes with circumstances, and where humans can have an impact.[39]

However, the starting point of prudence may also be considered
external and necessary. Recall that the prudent person's end is
grounded in two requirements that are external to the individual: existing circumstances and a concept of human good that, while developing through the agent's experiences, must be generalizable to a variety of persons and circumstances in order to be considered
minimally human. Good action transforms existing circumstances in a

particular concrete recreation of the agent's general concept of human good. In sum, while science studies reality and art invents reality, prudence intervenes in reality. In matters of human good, the person who is overly scientific attempts too little, and the person who is overly artistic attempts too much.

Prudence's close interaction with reality is reflected in Aristotle's insistence that the means of action participate in the goodness of the end, that is, that the means be principled instances of the end.[40] His reasoning is that, as the means of action progress toward the desired end, they automatically make an impact of their own on the existing circumstances of life because they themselves are part of life.[41] If the means are not consistent with the version of human good they are intended to serve, they work against it.

To elaborate: The prudent person's deliberation about means is essentially ethical; it concerns not just whether X will produce good but whether X is good. The artist's deliberation about means, on the other hand, is essentially technical; it concerns only whether X is the most efficient instrument for producing the desired end.[42] In Aristotle's discussion of household management, it is clear that the "natural" form of acquisition is ethical because it limits wealth to an amount necessary for the good of the household, thereby participating in a principle of human good. Against this, Aristotle contrasts the "retail" form, which is technical because it pursues unlimited wealth without regard for human good.[43] However, if the retail form of acquisition enters the life of the household, its impact is not strictly technical; its implicit end of unlimited wealth undermines the human ends of the household. The example shows that, although the uncertain realm of action gives the prudent person some room to judge and to maneuver, it does not give the prudent person the artist's freedom to invent.

A MODEL OF PRUDENCE

To summarize the major components of the argument: An agent who is overly scientific can have either a changeable or an unchangeable character. The same is true of the agent who is overly artistic. Four combinations of intellect and character, then, are possible. Prudence is a mean on both scales—in intellect, a mean between science and art, and in character, a mean between changeability and unchangeability.

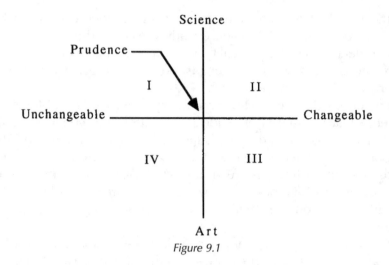

Figure 9.1

The framework that combines these ideas is diagrammed in Figure 9.1. The extremes of intellect—from science to art—are indicated by the vertical axis, which is overlaid by a horizontal axis indicating extremes of character—unchangeable to changeable. At the center, of course, is the mean: prudence. The four quadrants resulting from this intersection represent four kinds of error, four sources of imprudence. Category I would be an overly scientific agent with an unchangeable character. Category II is an overly scientific agent with a changeable character, and so on. These four combinations provide a method for classifying actions that deviate from the mean and hinder the individual from achieving good.

Actions which fall into Categories I and II are closer to science than they are to art, but in different ways. Individuals whose actions combine the most unchangeable character with science (Category I), try to live according to what is best and, in particular situations, prefer upholding the principle of the absolute best to achieving the best possible. These are philosophical politicians who share with the scientist the search for a universal truth, and who want to make that truth concrete by acting consistently with it, even in the face of ridicule or certain failure, or at the risk of life and limb. Socrates would be the prime example—had he entered politics. But he knew, according to Plato's *Apology*, that he was too honest to survive in politics.[44]

Politicians whose actions fit into Category II are equally concerned with science but from an entirely different perspective. Since their characters are too changeable to adhere steadfastly to any principle, they seek truth through empiricism, by adapting closely to existing circumstances and using them as a guide for change. They are opportunists who lack a consistent guiding end. They deliberate about means as instruments for achieving a variety of short-term ends, so that their actions are reasoned without being principled. Over the long run, the absence of a guiding purpose means that opportunists can pursue short-range goals that conflict, a pattern that is ultimately self-defeating. The patterns of action in Categories I and II usually are successful on their own terms, because the character types they represent are internally consistent. That is to say, one who follows principle recognizes no failure except compromise and the loss of integrity, and one who is guided by empirical circumstance recognizes no failure except imperfect perception.

What politicians in Categories I and II have in common that distinguishes them from politicians in Categories III and IV is that they recognize an external necessity—the demands of either an overriding principle of good or an immediate situation—to which they must respond to achieve their goals. Persons falling into Categories III and IV, on the other hand, do not recognize any necessity arising outside themselves. They resemble the artist who is not compelled to address particular situations. The problem is that the artist's freedom to invent does not exist in the realm of action. That means that the starting points, or ends, of politicians in Categories III and IV are out of touch with reality. As a result, agents in these categories fail to achieve their goals more frequently than do those who fit in the first two categories.[45]

Individuals who have changeable characters and yet do not use actual circumstances as a guide to how they should change (Category III) operate erratically, according to whim. Even if a person such as this has a good end, it doesn't contribute consistently to goodness or practical success; either appetite interferes with the ability to pursue it unwaveringly, or it is narrowly conceptualized and relates only to certain kinds of situations, leaving the agent without guidance in others.

Like persons in Category III, persons in Category IV fail to recognize external constraints. The difference is that Category IV agents have unchangeable characters. These individuals pursue a constant end and are not plagued with lack of strength to resist appetites; the trouble is that the end is emotionally rather than rationally derived—a product of the irrational part of the soul. The same passion that gives constancy and willpower blocks perception of circumstances by the intellect. The agent has difficulty correcting mistakes through observation and experience and devising means that will work, because the agent lacks the respect for empirical conditions that we find in Category II. Such persons cannot be persuaded by reason to change their minds. Aristotle labels them "obstinate."[46]

This model of prudence shows how it is possible to identify patterns of imprudence, patterns of error that should be avoided, without adopting a narrow or rigid view of human good. In each of the patterns designated by Categories I–IV, the explanation for imprudence has to do with a specific, empirically identifiable problem with the way persons prone to that type of error select ends and means. Such patterns can be observed in a person's speech and action over time.

By locating sources of imprudence, the model narrows the possibilities for what might be considered prudent action. The prudent political leader needs the philosopher's knowledge of what is good without the philosopher's ties to personal purity, and the opportunist's ability to adapt to circumstances without the opportunist's eagerness to do so. From the standpoint of prudence, the philosopher's literal translation of an absolute standard of good into action saves the philosopher but sacrifices the state, and the opportunist's literal compliance with environmental demands is also an abdication of the public leader's responsibility. In addition to striking a balance between rigidity and flexibility of character, the ideal politician should rely less than the politicians of Categories I and II on environmental sources of certainty—on either absolute principle or empirical factors—and adopt some of the artist's creativity. Within the confines of a specific political environment and a guiding concept of human good, the prudent politician has some room to reshape things and must figure out the best possible way to do that.

My concern with contemporary scholarly debates about prudence is that, in positing the need to choose between philosophy and democratically constituted morality, they misrepresent ingredients—the various kinds of information—that go into the phronimos' deliberative process and cover up the path to practical truth. Fortunately, leadership scholars who include normative elements in their analyses have tried to follow this path or similar ones anyway. Presidency scholars Erwin Hargrove and Ethan Fishman, who turn to Aristotelian prudence to include moral issues in their ideas about leadership, lean on prudence's capacity to integrate principle and circumstance.[47] Leadership scholar Ronald Heifetz envisions a similar process. He interprets leadership as "adaptive work" that tries to clarify "a community's guiding values"; these values, he says, "are interpreted in the context of problems demanding definition and action."[48] From the perspective of prudence's truth content, these three scholars make strong contributions to the study of leadership by their efforts to demonstrate how leaders balance ideals and circumstance. However, they rely, implicitly or explicitly, on sets of cultural values that it is beyond their frameworks to critique. If the content of prudence were spelled out more, specifically, if it could provide a transcendent basis for looking at cultural values, leaders and those who study them could develop frameworks that could better order and choose between cultural values.

A final word for applying the model of prudence: it is important to remember that most leaders, and most persons, are hampered by more than one kind of imprudence. To be relatively prudent is not to be infallible. The usefulness of the model lies in its potential for identifying the kinds of errors that particular leaders are likely to make and the situations that are likely to elicit those errors. Translating the standards of prudence in these fairly concrete and personal terms offers some warning to leaders and their followers about how to guard against the kinds of imprudence to which they are prone.[49]

THE PUZZLE OF BILL CLINTON

What I look for in the remainder of this essay is the difference between the form of prudence and the form (or soul, or character psychology[50]) of Bill Clinton. The discussion takes the position, stated well by Clinton biographer David Maraniss, that, with Bill Clinton (and, from an Aristotelian perspective, with anyone), it is a mistake "to separate the good from the bad, to say that the part of him that is indecisive, too eager to please and prone to deception, is more revealing of the inner man than the part of him that is indefatigable, intelligent, empathetic, and self-deprecating. They co-exist."[51]

CLINTON AS CHAMELEON: CATEGORY II

At first glance, Clinton appears to be the overly empirical agent of Category II, a "chameleon" who fit himself so completely to changing circumstances that he lost sight of ideals.

> Within hours in one day, he could eat pork ribs and listen to the Delta Blues music at Sim's Bar-B-Que in the lowlands of Little Rock's predominantly black south side; then drive up to the Heights for a round of golf at the Country Club of Little Rock, an elite hideaway with manicured fairways and no black members; then, on the way home, he might pop in his favorite tape of white Pentecostal gospel music from the Alexandria Sanctuary Chorale. Clinton could go from a meeting with deer hunters in Scott County, furious because the state Game and Fish Commission would not let them run their dogs in December, to an education summit in Charlottesville, staying up all night crafting an agenda of education goals for the fifty governors and the Bush administration, to a West Coast fund-raising dinner at Norman Lear's house where he mixed with the Hollywood glitterati. If Clinton had the ability to move easily through so many different worlds, he could also appear a chameleon, forced to balance one world off against another.[52]

So completely did Clinton mold himself to circumstances that he appeared to aides to identify with whatever person or policy was brought before him. Consequently, even his allies were uncertain of where he stood and doubted his loyalty.[53] In the White House, he exhibited so many facets that George Stephanopoulos compared him to a "kaleidoscope."[54] Leadership analysts note his eagerness to please people, his excessive dependence (even among politicians) on interpersonal relations, his verbal facility and persuasiveness, and his high degree of empathy,[55] all factors that testify to skill at adapting to the different worlds he sees. As Stanley Renshon points out, though, his empathy, like the other mechanisms through which he conformed to the environment, was often more "strategic" than altruistic, since it was combined with "a tendency to exploit others for his own purposes."[56] Renshon's award-winning *High Hopes* ties Clinton's problems as a leader to the fact that he moved through these different worlds and adapted to them in pursuit more of ambition than ideals.[57] Most accounts reinforce this point, casting Clinton as a politically brilliant opportunist, adept at manipulating people and circumstances for his own advantage. Clinton's Category II faults are recorded from the time of his college years (for instance, when he managed to avoid the draft and then to avoid the consequences of his maneuvers to avoid the draft[58]) through his presidency (which he began by abandoning the New Democratic stance that got him elected).[59] Clinton's change-ability, mostly in response to the changing worlds or pieces of reality he encountered, fed the popular image of "Slick Willie," who seemed way too flexible to retain any allegiance to principle.

Despite Clinton's well-known talent for adapting to different environments, in office, he did not adapt equally well to all situations. A political leader who completely fit the characteristics in Category II would be technically accurate and successful in his own terms, most of the time. One of the things that puzzles analysts about Clinton is that, as president, he alternated between periods of moderate and effective governance and periods of chaos and controversy.[60] Clinton was especially effective in situations or areas where his extraordinary interpersonal skills and mastery of policy detail were particularly relevant. The question is what happened in other areas? Why did he not "see"? What accounts, for instance, for the fact that Clinton was able to apply the lessons learned from his first term as governor to his second term as governor but not to his first term as president? Did he forget? In Aristotle's terms, there are three possibilities: That he deliberated but failed to abide by the result of deliberation, that he deliberated poorly, or that he did not deliberate at all. When scholars observe that Clinton is disorganized, self-indulgent, impatient, and overconfident, they offer grounds for all three possibilities.

First, if one deliberates about each of several worlds independently, without a coordinating picture (or organizing mechanism), the results will be different and conflicting purposes, a reputation for shiftiness and disloyalty, and failed commitments. This suggests that Clinton neglected the lessons of his first gubernatorial term because he segregated that experience, as being part of another world that was not so relevant to the White House.[61] In this scenario, the reality he deliberated about was not broad enough.

The second explanation for Clinton's intermittent blindness is that, because he went beyond superficial manipulation of the different worlds he confronted, because he often genuinely empathized with people and really tried to enter their worlds, he could be indecisive.[62] He was so involved and so well informed that he sometimes got "lost in the facts,"[63] especially facts pertaining to the latest reality he confronted.[64] It is fair to say that he got lost in personal details too, whether it was inviting numerous Arkansas businessmen to visit him in Little Rock and not being available when they came[65] or being unable to resist sexual opportunities. This answer suggests that Clinton was too distracted by current realities to recall the lessons of a previous reality and the results of previous deliberation.

In addition to pursuing conflicting purposes and getting lost, a third explanation for what derails Clinton is self-indulgence. According to Aristotle, self-indulgent persons miss the mean of the best possible, not because they are overcome by pleasure as morally weak persons are, but because they pursue pleasure as the result of deliberation and choice.[66] Naturally, the self-indulgent do not regret their actions and tend to repeat them.[67] Their error falls within Category II because they are still absorbed with immediate circumstances, but the scope of those circumstances is much narrower than the scope of circumstances relevant to political action. Aristotle links self-indulgence to moderate appetite[68] that doesn't interfere with duty (or wouldn't if it weren't discovered). Of course, Clinton's repeated sexual exploits did interfere with his duty—not because he abandoned the duties of office for sex, but because the sexual misconduct was discovered. In an era when the president's life is public, when previous scandals have plagued Clinton, when public trust in government is an overriding issue,[69] Clinton's form of self-indulgence did interfere with his understanding of circumstances that are relevant to presidential duty. For instance, when Clinton's opponents looked for "an explanation beyond ideology for policy changes," the character issue that Clinton's sexual misconduct had provided was "presented as evidence of the contention that the man has no standards at all, and that he is wholly lacking in principles."[70] The choice to pursue an immediate pleasure directed his deliberation away not only from any ideal but from the relative accuracy that frequently characterizes deliberation in Category II. In self-indulgence, the agent may perceive circumstances accurately; the problem is that the scope of relevant circumstances shrinks severely. Like the first two answers to the question of why Clinton sometimes seems blind, this one suggests that he neglected the lessons of Arkansas because he seems to deliberate within the particular worlds that he enters, but not across them. There is no coordination of the larger picture.

CLINTON'S EMOTIONALISM: CATEGORY III

While the image of "Slick Willie" rests securely in Category II, the home of excessive empiricism, all of Clinton's imprudent actions do not fit here. Actions that are marked by impatience, a volatile temper, lack of discipline, usually illustrate changeability that is not tied to empirical referents. They link Clinton's errors to Category III, where action is erratic and unguided.

Like Category II leaders, the leaders in the third category have a changeable character; but they differ from the opportunists of Category I in taking a more subjective or artistic approach to action. Without empirical circumstances as a guide, their flexibility is not rational. While Category II leaders act from choice, as their careful adaptation to the situation testifies, the leaders who commit Category III errors usually do not. Category II leaders are not diverted by appetite from following the result of their deliberation; if they pursue appetite, they do so deliberately. That is why self-indulgence falls into this category. In contrast, Category III leaders tend to be morally weak, as appetite interferes with the operation of their intellect; it keeps them from deliberating or from acting on the results of deliberation. Given this tendency, one characteristic associated with Category III is the regret that accompanies knowledge of one's failing, but the most prominent trait is a lack of foresight. Having neither the philosopher's goodness nor the opportunist's accuracy, Category III leaders do not recognize either of the perspectives that truth in matters of life and action requires—either the ideal or the real. As a result, the leaders cannot do good or achieve concrete success consistently. They fail in intellect or character or both, and they fail more often from their own perspective than do leaders in Category II.

The clearest evidence of Category III imprudence is Clinton's tendency toward two kinds of emotionalism. The first precludes deliberation. For example, when Clinton became governor of Arkansas, some staffers called him "Baby." Baby was known for his impatience, volatility, and tendency to excuse himself and blame others for whatever went wrong.[71] This suggests that a kind of immature emotionalism interfered with Clinton's capacity to deliberate about the actions he should take.[72]

Also, Clinton was sometimes just too impatient to deliberate. Some of his deadlines, such as picking his whole cabinet before Christmas

or passing a "a sweeping package of legislation during the first hundred days" were "self imposed and unnecessary," totally unrelated to
any requirements imposed by circumstances.[73] This illustrates Clinton's "lack of self-discipline and imperfect impulse control . . . a major source of his troubles, whether in the form of a tendency to over-
load the policy agenda, or to give excessively long speeches, or to be
scandal-prone in his private life."[74]

A second type of emotionalism, described by Garry Wills, involves
some deliberation—but from the wrong starting point and about the
wrong things.

> Clinton is so temperamentally adjustable that his mind, dragged along on
> the emotional roller-coaster ride, can veer into purest dither. What kind
> of world had he tacked and triangulated himself into when he said, 'I un-
> derstand more about agriculture than any former President?' Whom is
> Clinton kidding? He is kidding Clinton, of course, But why? When he said
> he understood farming, he really meant that he understood farmers. . . .
> He feels for farmers, so he understands agriculture. . . . He is a virtuoso
> empathizer. . . . His wildest or most improbable claims are based on what
> he grasps as an emotional truth.[75]

Being led by emotional information involves deliberation that is
based on "knowledge" that does not grasp real circumstances and cannot accurately forecast the result of different courses of action. Clinton
did not know farmers and farming in the way that he could know a particular farmer. The latter falls within the range of his empirically
oriented interpersonal skills and the latter obviously does not. The role
of emotion in Clinton's psychology (his soul, in the Aristotelian sense)
fits Aristotle's description of moral weakness: "When in the grip of emotion, a morally weak man either does not have this premise [of good],
or he has it not in the sense of knowing it, but in the sense of uttering
it as a drunken man may utter verses of Empedocles." Because the
morally weak person is temporarily ignorant of the link between
the general end that motivates action and particular circumstances, he
or she is incapable of deciding rationally.[76] That is why Clinton's action
was often unguided.

According to descriptions of his emotionalism, Clinton exhibited a
lack of intellectual awareness, a lack of self-consciousness, about the
content that determined his action. This neglect of the need to gather
accurate information and organize it toward an end extended, in the

White House, beyond personal behavior to lack of interest in, or awareness of, how the organization of the White House might facilitate or impede progress toward Clinton's policy goals. Fred Greenstein complains that "Clinton's talents cry out for management, but he is insensitive to the need to back himself up with a well-ordered support system."[77] Thus, when Clinton entered the White House, he had no "system to deal with demands," except "postponement." Rather than a central policy mechanism, there was only a "rogue process."[78] In short there was no institutional deliberative process.

These shortcomings were visible in the demise of Clinton's health care plan. The health care initiative was led by Hillary Rodham Clinton and Ira Magaziner, an old friend of the Clintons known for his tendency to complicate process and policy. As Elizabeth Drew points out, in Magaziner, the Clintons "had turned to a pal when they needed a shrewd, experienced pol." There were few experienced political operatives or Washington insiders around. In addition, the task force, which met in closed sessions of experts, was out of touch with reality, and had no check for recognizing that. One senior aide described task force meetings: "If you have that many people [fifty-some] in the room, senior people aren't going to conduct a real debate in front of the junior people. The are too many possibilities of press leaks, especially if you know you're talking about something the President disagrees with, and the President is volatile, and the First Lady is emphatic." Under these circumstances, there was no deliberation that recognized the limitations of what the Clintons favored, no serious consideration of alternatives, and no way to gage disagreement. "If the internal debate [over health care] was stifled, the Clintons allowed it to be stifled."[79] There was no reality check.

The well-known result of this process was an incredibly long and complex health care bill that engaged many conflicting interest groups, alienated New Democratic followers, and handed Republican opponents a field day. On top of that, there was little effort by the White House either to muster a supporting coalition or to educate the public about the bill.[80] When explanations were offered, rhetoric tended to veer away from Clinton's centrist campaign appeal to middle-class health security and toward "universal coverage" and "rights," helping to raise more doubts in the minds of potential, but already skeptical, supporters.[81] The situation invited Republican opposition, and the vacuum in the White House allowed Republicans to portray the Health Security bill as a big government plan, when as Garry Wills points out, much of its complexity resulted "from the fact that it was not a 'big government' solution."[82] Rather it was largely market driven and decentralized. The problem was that Clinton, through inattention and lack of organization, lost, really abdicated, the power to define his own bill.[83] That Clinton eventually did face up to the failings of his initial White House set up indicates the regret that Aristotle associates with a person who gives in to some impulse or emotion without sufficient deliberation.[84]

CLINTON'S UNCHANGEABLE UNDERCURRENTS: CATEGORY IV

Changeability does not exhaust the reasons for Clinton's imprudence. For all his apparent vacillations, Clinton's biggest weakness may have been in a particular stubborn streak that remained constant, a Category IV error. This pull on Clinton from an unchangeable, nonrational source helps to explain why someone who seemed so politically skilled and could recognize and correct mistakes was so often unguided. In Aristotle's eyes, those who fail to recognize and respond to mistakes, despite evidence that is visible to everyone else, are stubborn.[85]

Stanley Renshon identifies Clinton's driving instinct as an overwhelming need—not to be liked, as some have argued—but to be validated. Clinton made "efforts to be acknowledged [by important others] for the specific ambitions, skills, and accomplishments by which he defined himself."[86] A frequently told story about Clinton's overinvolvement in policy detail, to the exclusion of more pressing realities, relates directly to his need for validation. He held an economic conference right after being elected. At a time when he needed to pay more attention to organizing the White House and thinking about his legislative agenda (both undeveloped at the time), he was more eager to impress people with his knowledge.[87]

Clinton's reach for validation operated not only in his relations with other people but in his relationship with himself, leading him "to either avoid or discount evidence from his own behavior that all is not as he believes it to be." Renshon notices:

> how few doubts [Clinton] entertains about his own motives, values, and candor. . . . He presented himself as fair, open, honest, and genuinely

interested in and responsible to others' points of view and concerns. Critical to his self-image (as well as to his campaign strategy) was a view of himself as a victim. . . . These characteristics . . . reflect a strong component of *self-idealization.*[88]

Clinton's idealized view of himself and his efforts to defend that view were visible in poor judgment, "difficulty acknowledging his mistakes in a straightforward way," failure to see "discrepancies between what he says and what he does,"[89] and a tendency to take large risks on the grounds that he is smarter than everyone else.[90] Clinton's need for validation from himself and others also resulted in overconfidence, and even "grandiosity." It was naiveté born of this excessive self-confidence that made Clinton think he could implement a large policy agenda without an organized White House staff or a plan of action.[91]

Clinton's Category IV need for validation was the unchanging instinct that influenced his Category II and Category III changes. It explains Clinton's aptitude for focusing more clearly on, and deliberating about, particular pieces of reality and neglecting others. Specifically, the need for validation pushed Clinton toward chameleon-like Category II errors in familiar situations that reinforced his idealized self-image, and toward apparently unguided Category III errors in unfamiliar situations where he was swayed by emotion or misplaced self-confidence.[92] Clinton paid attention to interpersonal relations and policy details, because those are the areas where his personal experience has provided continuing validation. He has sought friends and offices all of his life. The same is true of academic accolades. He was used to winning in these areas. When his instinctive immersion in one of these was not adequate for handling a situation, he was undisciplined and should have been unsure. Much of the time, however, he was not. He extended his justifiable confidence in relational skills to other areas, where it was misplaced. Overconfidence hid the need to deliberate across worlds, or to deliberate at all, and derailed Clinton from pursuit of his goals. Seeing Clinton through the constancy of Category IV explains "why someone as intelligent and politically adept as Clinton should be so dependent on external correction."[93]

The complimentarity of the three types of imprudence identified so far helps us see Clinton as less of a puzzle, as if he is "of a piece." His need for validation goes hand-in-hand with the two other kinds of error. That Clinton might suffer from the remaining kind of imprudence,

that he might be overly philosophic, is too much at odds with the evidence to be considered. However, that he is not philosophic does not
mean that he has no general concept of good that could guide action
if his deliberation were derailed less often.

CONCLUSION: POSSIBILITIES FOR PRUDENCE?

Does Clinton have a general concept of good that allows him to take
a critical view of the culture around him and work toward some good?
Some former staffers, journalists, and biographers say "yes." They cite
his activism, his genuine empathy, his long-term efforts to carve out a
third way, his efforts to preserve some positive role for government,
and especially his life-long interest in civil rights, as indications that
he does have an idea of what is good for humans and he does try to
pursue it.[94] When Clinton was teaching at the University of Arkansas
Law School, his black students called him "Wonder Boy," because he
supported them when others did not and when there was no advantage to himself.[95] Dick Morris claims that Clinton had "a very true
compass," that did not vary much with public opinion. From this perspective Clinton's maneuverings were directed by an end. "Within the
general proposition he wants to go north, he will take an endless variety of routes. He's constantly maneuvering, constantly picking the
routes he wants to get there, maneuvering his opponents into positions where they can't get a clear shot at him."[96] In the context of the
middle class's reasons for supporting health care reform and divisions
in the political environment, Clinton's search for a "third way" might
actually have functioned as a kind of principled accommodation to
the environment.[97] Policy-oriented analyses by Baer, Berman, and
Skocpol also suggest that Clinton had both genuine interest in health
care and long-term understanding of why the Democratic Party had
to become "New" in order to build a supporting coalition for it.[98] They
also point out that he understood how he was caught between New
Democratic supporters and liberal Democrats in Congress. From their
perspective, it would have been very difficult to get health care
through, and Clinton's deficiency was not in his vacillations but in his
failure, in Hargrove's terms, to teach and persuade.[99] He knew what
the context was; he just lacked the organization and discipline, personally and institutionally, to deal with it.

However, this sketchy evidence that Clinton might hold to a principle of good is not strong enough to counter Renshon's conclusion about Clinton's principles. After noting Clinton's own defense against the charge that he had no core values—that the charge may stem from the "the fact that his philosophy has 'some liberal and some conservative elements'"—Renshon remarks:

> A flexible political identity gives Clinton a great deal of political latitude. By choosing this strategy, however, he raises several critical issues. Is Clinton unwilling or unable to articulate the real basic principles that guide him across instances or integrate his philosophy? If so, why? Is he unwilling to do so because it will cost him politically? Then he is masking his views for political advantage. That may be a clever short-term tactic, but for a president about whom issues of honesty and integrity have been raised so often, it is a dangerous one. By failing to articulate his fundamental views and the basis on which he reconciles the liberal and conservative elements in his political identity, he has abdicated the very important presidential responsibility of educating the public about his solutions to their problems.

Renshon concludes that "Clinton seems not to have developed a real synthesis and integration of the ideals, values, and principles that would make it possible to proceed on other than a case-by-case basis."[100]

Is there a way to encourage such a synthesis by guarding against Clinton's partial view of reality, self-indulgence, and rigid adherence to an exalted opinion of himself? Once we see that the need for validation led Clinton to prefer sets of circumstances in which he could be certain of validation, it is clear that he needed help incorporating and coordinating information from other sets of circumstances, from other realities. He needed people who are able and willing to point out when he ignores too much of the rest of reality. He needed politically experienced people who were "screamers" like former Arkansas Chief-of-Staff Betsy Wright or older, parental-type advisors and people who were willing to buck his deceptions of himself and others.[101] Most of all, he needed a supplemental search for the real world beyond the stimuli to which he knows how to react. Ideally this would also help him understand the problems with his self-indulgent appetites. But the only real remedy there is maturity, self-restraint, more alternative modes of validation and, above all, an external mechanism for keeping Clinton on track. And there is that possibility. Clinton's ability to correct suggests that his illusions only go so far. Greenstein says he was "measured and effective" when outside constraints dictate—but they do have to be forced on him.[102]

When Clinton replaced his initial White House staff (in the face of new Republican opposition in Congress) with such "seasoned aides as David Gergen, Leon Panetta, and Michael McCurry," he exhibited an "uncommon ability to rebound in the face of misfortune and . . . readiness . . . to admit his own failings, qualities that account for the claim that he is incapable of sustained error."[103] His grasp of the environment and his deliberative capacities returned. His "mid-course correction"[104] both as governor and as president illustrates his "learning curve"[105] and supports the opinion of Betsy Wright, who claimed that he would eventually figure things out. "He always does."[106] With the right kind of help, the consequences of Clinton's imprudent tendencies could at least be mitigated.

There may also be grounds for optimism in the fact that, at times, Clinton seemed willing to take direction, as if he were aware that he needed it. Clinton sometimes exhibited a passive side that welcomed outside direction, according to Dick Morris.[107] He could take guidance from father figure Mack McLarty (who was slow to figure this out),[108] as well as from pollster Morris. Hiring Morris and initiating the "permanent campaign" were ways of institutionalizing Clinton's personal propensity to adapt liberally to circumstances. The permanent campaign tailored his policy direction and appeals to respond to polls that identified voters' preferences, and relied on paid public relations consultants rather than the news media to get his message out to voters.[109] The tendency of the permanent campaign to emphasize style over substance, to market and sell, continued, albeit inconsistently, into his presidency[110] (for instance in the rhetoric about an undefined crisis in health care).[111] This institutionalized form of deliberation was a way to extend the reach and accuracy of Clinton's chameleon orientation and reliance on interpersonal relations. It had the same major deficiency as the embodied first-hand version—it lacked an architectonic point of view for ordering and following up on the information it took in. Though the permanent campaign did not meet criteria for institutionalizing prudence, it was an effort toward institutionalized deliberation.

These possibilities for moving toward prudence, it should be clear, are not possibilities for moving either toward philosophic good or toward a good that is completely defined by cultural values and public deliberation. By the standards of philosophy, Clinton is worthless, as are all real politicians, because they operate in a different realm and according to different standards. Neither a move toward prudence nor a move toward cultural values is totally defined through public deliberation. Clinton's allegiance to civil rights in Fayetteville arguably opposed any good tied too closely to cultural values. To move toward prudence requires using the perspective of human good; that is the perspective that teaches us that Clinton in fact saw multiple cultural worlds and, on different occasions, molded himself to them individually. From the perspective of prudence, public rhetoric in different worlds provides no coordination. That must come from a core concept of good that operates in cultures, but keeps a reflective distance.[112] Examining Clinton's psychology for a core concept yields some possibilities, but they cannot be fulfilled without supplemental help that keeps Clinton's imprudent tendencies within limits. Aristotle's explanation of the multiple facets of prudence helps us figure out what in Clinton's psychology is useful for achieving human good and what has to be restrained.

NOTES

I thank Kathryn Kuhn for commenting on drafts of this essay.

1. A portion of this chapter was previously published in "Prudence As a Paradigm for Political Leaders," in *Political Psychology* 17, no. 4, December 1996. Copyright © 1996 by Blackwell Publishers. Reprinted by permission.

2. Richard S. Ruderman, "Aristotle and the Recovery of Political Judgment," *American Political Science Review* 91, no. 2 (June 1997): 409–20.

3. Ruderman, "Recovery," 409–10, 417. Here, Ruderman speaks particularly of Ronald Beiner. See Ronald Beiner, *Political Judgment* (Chicago: University of Chicago Press, 1983). While Ruderman's point is not overstated, his critique of Beiner may be. See n. 111 below.

4. Ruderman, "Recovery," 416.

5. Ruderman, "Recovery," 411–13, 18.

6. For an additional perspective on the theory in prudence, see Georgios Anagnostopoulos, *Aristotle on the Goals and Exactness of Ethics* (Los Angeles: University of California Press, 1994), 88–101.

7. Ruderman, "Recovery," 418.

8. Aristotle, of course, refers to the prudent man and argues that, while women have a "deliberative faculty," "it is without authority." *Politics* 1260a13, trans. Ernest Barker (New York: Oxford University Press, 1958). The gendered nature of Aristotle's concept is not part of its logic or the logic of my argument.

9. Aristotle, *NE* 1141b4–13, 1140b7–10. All references to *Aristotle's Nicomachean Ethics* (NE) are from Martin Ostwald, trans. (New York: The Liberal Arts Press, 1962).

10. Fred I. Greenstein, "There he goes again: the alternating political style of Bill Clinton," *PS: Political Science & Politics* 31, no. 2 (June 1998), <www.web4infotrac.galegroup.com/itw/infomark> (9 July 2001).

11. Erwin Hargrove, *The President as Leader: Appealing to the Better Angels of Our Nature* (Lawrence, Kans.: University Press of Kansas, 1998), 42.

12. Garry Wills, "The Clinton Principle," *New York Times Magazine*, 19 January 1997, 28, <we.lexisnexis.com/universe/document> (18 June 2001).

13. Ethan Fishman, *The Prudential Presidency: An Aristotelian Approach to Presidential Leadership* (Westport, Conn.: Praeger, 2001), 85.

14. Fred I. Greenstein, "Style of Bill Clinton," 1.

15. Aristotle, *NE* 1097b25-1098a4,1102a26–31, 1102b25–28. Exactly how the moral and intellectual components of prudence work together is controversial. In scholarship on Aristotle, there is a longstanding controversy about whether intellect or moral virtue determines the end of prudent action. For the history of this controversy, see J. D. Monan, *Moral Knowledge and Its Methodology in Aristotle* (London: Oxford University Press, 1968), 49–50; Norman Dahl, *Practical Reason, Aristotle, and Weakness of the Will* (Minneapolis: University of Minnesota Press, 1984).

16. The hierarchical rule of reason over appetite, inherent in Aristotle's teleological definition of human good, is not necessarily elitist and need not disturb democratic leadership analysts. As Stephen Salkever argues, the human good that Aristotle sees as a guide for action is not, as a practical matter, necessarily different from the general conceptions of good through which most of us evaluate action. The alternative to formulating and following a more or less consistent notion of good is incoherent, inconsistent, and self-defeating action. Salkever's argument, which cannot be elaborated here, shows that prudence provides a practical way to think about human good in a contemporary context. See Stephen Salkever, *Finding the Mean: Theory and Practice in Aristotelian Political Philosophy* (Princeton, N.J.: Princeton University Press, 1990). See also Martha Nussbaum, "Human Functioning and Social Justice: In Defense of Aristotelian Essentialism," *Political Theory* 17, no. 4 (December 1996): 202–45.

17. *NE* 1.2, 6.8.

18. W. R. Newell, "Superlative Virtue: The Problem of Monarchy in Aristotle's *Politics*," *Western Political Quarterly* 40, no. 1 (March 1978): 159–78.

19. Josef Pieper, *The Four Cardinal Virtues: Prudence, Justice, Fortitude, Temperance* (New York: Harcourt, Brace and World, 1965), 7, 9–11, 17. Though Pieper is describing prudence via Thomas Aquinas rather than interpreting Aristotle, his explanation of the proximity of the prudent persons' ends to reality coincides with Aristotle's, especially with *NE* 1143b4–5, where Aristotle says that the ends of principles of good action arise out of the "perception of particular facts."

20. Richard Sorabji, "Aristotle on the Role of Intellect in Virtue," *Proceedings of the Aristotelian Society* 74 (1974): 114; Aristotle, *NE* 1151a16–17, 1141b16–21, 1144b32–1145a3, 6.1.

21. David Wiggins, "Deliberation and Practical Reason," *Proceedings of the Aristotelian Society* 76 (1975–76): 40.

22. Aristotle, *Politics* 1256b27–29.

23. Aristotle, *NE* 1102b12–1103al.

24. Aristotle, *NE* 1102b12–1103al. Persons "are corrupted" through the opposite course, "through pursuing and avoiding pleasures and pains either of the wrong kind or at the wrong time or in the wrong manner" (*NE* 1104b22–23).

25. Aristotle, *NE* 2.6–9.

26. Aristotle, *NE* 1103a17, 1100b17–18, 1103a26–b2, 1140b29–30.

27. Takatura Ando, *Aristotle's Theory of Practical Cognition*, 3rd ed. (The Hague: Martinus Nijoff, 1971), 149–51; Pieper, *Cardinal Virtues*; Wynne Moskop, "Political Science and Aristotle's Extra-Political Writings," *American Political Science Association Proceedings*, 1989, 4–8.

28. J. A. Stewart, *Notes on the Nicomachean Ethics of Aristotle*, 2 vols. (New York: Oxford University Press, 1892): 2:34.

29. Aristotle, *NE* 1106b8–12.

30. Aristotle, *NE* 1108b11–12, 1109a19–23.

31. Aristotle, *Politics* 1294b15–18.

32. Aristotle, *NE* 1105a33.

33. Aristotle, *NE* 1101a9–11, 1100b15–1101a13, 1154b20–32.

34. Aristotle, *NE* 1151b4–17.

35. Aristotle, *NE* 1140a33–b1.

36. Aristotle, *NE* 6.3. When a scientist applies scientific knowledge in some practical way, it is no longer science in the strict sense; its new purpose transforms it into either art or action, depending on whether one considers it from the perspective of some technical good or the perspective of human good.

37. Aristotle, *NE* 1140a13–14.

38. Aristotle, *NE* 1140b 16–17.

39. Aristotle, *NE* 1140a1.

40. Aristotle, *NE* 1140b19–20, 1144a32–36.

41. Aristotle, *Politics* 1.4.5.

42. Anthony Kenny, *Aristotle's Theory of the Will* (New Haven, Conn.: Yale University Press, 1979), 148–53.

43. Aristotle, *Politics* 1.8.13–14; 1.9.12–13.

44. Plato, *The Apology,* in *Great Dialogues of Plato,* trans. W. H. D. Rouse (New York: New American Library, 1956), 437.

45. The opportunistic politician of Category II also bears some resemblance to the artist in that the means of opportunistic action are not principled. Because they serve the end without embodying it, the opportunist's means are technical rather than ethical. The difference between the Category II and Category III politicians is that only the former change rationally, with circumstances. The opportunist's action is rational production—art successfully imposed on life, at least from the agent's point of view—while action in Categories III and IV is irrational production because the agent lacks empirical accuracy.

46. Aristotle, *NE* 1151b4–17.

47. Hargrove, *President As Leader*; Fishman, *Prudential Presidency.*

48. Ronald Heifetz, *Leadership Without Easy Answers* (Cambridge: Belknap Press of Harvard University Press, 1994), 22–23.

49. Aristotle, *NE* 1109b2–6.

50. Stanley Renshon's character psychology is similar to the idea of a form, as the term is used here. It emphasizes "the psychology that underlies a person's behavior, the circumstances that will affect it, and the relationship between." It is useful for prediction because it relies on "consistency of behavior." Renshon, *High Hopes,* 13.

51. David Maraniss, *First in His Class: A Biography of Bill Clinton* (New York: Simon & Schuster, 1995), 355.

52. Maraniss, *Biography,* 451.

53. Renshon, *High Hopes,* xii; John Brummett, *Highwire: From the Backroads to the Beltway—The Education of Bill Clinton* (New York: Hyperion, 1994), 12.

54. Renshon, *High Hopes,* 82.

55. Renshon, *High Hopes,* 92.

56. Renshon, *High Hopes,* 117; Renshon, "After the Fall," 17.

57. Renshon, *High Hopes,* x–xiii.

58. Maraniss, *Biography,* 198–99.

59. Renshon, *High Hopes,* xiii; Kenneth S. Baer, *Reinventing Democrats: The Politics of Liberalism from Reagan to Clinton* (Lawrence: University Press of Kansas, 2000), 211–12.

60. Wills, "Clinton Principle."

61. Wills suggests that he may have felt "exhilarated by an apparent liberation from the shackles of the Arkansas Constitution and could take on new challenges—even take on the Pentagon." Wills, "Clinton Principle," 5.

62. Brumett, *Highwire*, 17; Maraniss, *Biography*, 402, 409.

63. Maraniss, *Biography*, pp. 362–63; Brummett, *Highwire*, 6.

64. Renshon, *High Hopes*, 260.

65. Brummett, *Highwire*, 6.

66. Aristotle, *NE* 1148a15–17, 1150a11–24.

67. Aristotle, *NE* 1150a21.

68. Aristotle, *NE* 1148a18–20.

69. Renshon, *High Hopes*, 31.

70. Stephen Skowronek, *The Politics Presidents Make: Leadership from John Adams to Bill Clinton* (Cambridge: Belknap Press of Harvard University Press, 1997), 459–60.

71. Maraniss, *Biography*, 334–35, 364.

72. Elizabeth Drew, *On the Edge: The Clinton Presidency* (New York: Simon & Schuster, 1994), 96; Renshon, *High Hopes*, 110.

73. Renshon, "After the Fall," 8.

74. Greenstein, "Style," 3–4.

75. Wills, "Clinton Principle," 2.

76. Aristotle, *NE* 1147a24–b19, 1148a16–17, 1151a6.

77. Greenstein, "Style," 4.

78. Drew, *On the Edge*, 232, 305.

79. Drew, *On the Edge*, 304–5, 309, 194, 195.

80. Theda Skocpol, *Boomerang: Clinton's Health Security Effort and the Turn against Government in U.S. Politics* (New York: W. W. Norton and Company, 1996), 131–33, 171; Drew, *On the Edge*, 419.

81. Rachel L. Holloway, "The Clintons and the Health Care Crisis: Opportunity Lost, Promise Unfulfilled," in *The Clinton Presidency: Images, Issues and Communication Strategies*, ed. Robert E. Denton Jr. and Rachel L. Holloway (Westport, Conn.: Praeger, 1997), 180, 177–78.

82. Wills, "Clinton Principle," 6.

83. Skocpol, *Boomerang*, 98; Baer, *Reinventing Democrats*, 212.

84. Greenstein, "Style," 4.

85. Aristotle, *NE* 1151b4–17.

86. Renshon, *High Hopes*, 99–100.

87. Renshon, "After the Fall," 8.

88. Renshon, *High Hopes*, 85.

89. Renshon, *High Hopes*, 130, 138, 9.

90. Drew, *On the Edge*, 305.

91. Renshon, *High Hopes*, 90, 92.

92. Adding the perspective of Category IV casts Clinton's Category III errors as misguided (by his need for validation and self-idealization) rather than unguided.

93. The question is Fred Greenstein's. Greenstein, "Style," 4.

94. Drew, *On the Edge*, 420; Wills, "Clinton Principle," 8; Renshon, *High Hopes*, 81; Maraniss, *Biography*, 416–17, 113, 293–94.

95. Maraniss, *Biography*, 293–94.

96. Renshon, *High Hopes*, 81.

97. Skocpol, *Boomerang*, 45–46, 459; Baer, *Reinventing Democrats*, 208–11.

98. Baer, *Reinventing Democrats*; William C. Berman, *From the Center to the Edge: The Politics and Policies of the Clinton Administration* (Lanham, Md.: Roman & Littlefield, 2001); Skocpol, *Boomerang*.

99. Hargrove, *President as Leader*, ch. 2.

100. Renshon, *High Hopes*, 83.

101. Brummett, *Highwire*, 41–43.

102. Greenstein, "Style," 4.

103. Greenstein, "Style," 4.

104. Wills, "Clinton Principle," 1.

105. Greenstein, "Style," 4.

106. Brummett, *Highwire*, 30.

107. Renshon, "After the Fall."

108. Brummett, *Highwire*, 43.

109. Maraniss, *Biography*, 407–8.

110. Renshon, *High Hopes*, 276–78.

111. Holloway, "Health Care Crisis," 177.

112. Beiner, *Political Judgment*, 102. Beiner's incorporation of a Kantian judicious-spectator perspective in political judgment suggests that Ruderman's critique of his rhetorically constituted ends is overstated.

10

Prudence and the Constitution: On the Year 2000 Presidential Election Controversy

George Anastaplo

And in those days Peter stood up in the midst of the disciples, and said (the number of names together were about a hundred and twenty), "Men and brethren, this scripture must needs have been fulfilled, which the Holy Ghost by the mouth of David spoke before concerning Judas [Iscariot], who was guide to them that took Jesus. . . . And it is written in the book of Psalms, 'Let his habitation be desolate; and let no man dwell therein': 'and his bishopric let another take.' Wherefore of these men which have companied with us all the time that the Lord Jesus went in and out among us, beginning from the baptism of John, unto the same day that he was taken up from us, must one be ordained to be witness with us of his resurrection."

And [the disciples] appointed two, Joseph called Barsabas, who was surnamed Justus, and Matthias. And they prayed, and said, "Thou, Lord, which knowest the hearts of all men, show which of these two thou hast chosen, that he may take part of the ministry and apostleship, from which Judas by transgression fell, that he might go to his own place."

And [the disciples] gave forth their lots; and the lot fell upon Matthias; and he was numbered with the eleven apostles.

—Luke[1]

INTRODUCTION

The year 2000 presidential election provides us an opportunity to consider, once again, the workings of prudence in applications of Constitutional provisions. One way of doing this is to follow the development of and responses to an unusual electoral controversy which proved to be quite instructive.

I provide here the responses I happened to make at three stages of the Year 2000 contest and its aftermath. The first (in Part A of this chapter) was while the outcome of the presidential election was still in doubt. The second (in Part B) was shortly after the inauguration of the president settled upon. The third (in Part C) was a few months later. (Parts A and C incorporate responses originally prepared for law school audiences. All of the notes were written when this chapter was prepared in the fall of 2001.)

The observations found here and the judgments made should be applicable to other aspects of the study by us both of prudence and of the Constitution.[2]

A. PRESIDENTIAL POLITICS, PRUDENCE, AND THE CONSTITUTION[3]

I.

My point of departure is the so-called Electoral College arrangement in the Constitution for selection of the president of the United States, as that arrangement has been applied by statutes (congressional and state), by election officials, and by judicial interpretation.[4] My decision to speak about this subject, upon being asked last week to prepare something for this faculty workshop, was prompted by the developments of the past fortnight in the wake of the election held on November 7.[5]

The Electoral College issue is dramatized, of course, by what has been happening in Florida and elsewhere this month. Thus, the *Times* of London has been quoted, on National Public Radio, as having referred to the Electoral College as the "swollen appendix" in the American constitutional body.

Concerns about the Electoral College are expressed from time to time, especially when a presidential election promises to be close.

Thus, the issue had been discussed the week before the election this year by two Illinoisians, Senator Dick Durbin and Representative Ray LaHood, to whom I will return.[6] Particularly disturbing for critics is the prospect of an election in which one candidate has an advantage in the Electoral College vote while the other candidate has surpassed him in the popular vote. This is the horror story that is conjured up again and again—and it is this that some believe we now have, a development that is seen to undermine the political (not the legal) validity of a president chosen in this way.

It is not appreciated by such critics, however, that rather than creating a crisis in legitimacy this time, the Electoral College arrangement has reduced significantly the problems and uncertainty that would otherwise have had to be contended with. Uncertainties have been localized (this time, primarily in Florida), permitting them to be dealt with fairly easily, at least compared to what would have happened if we had been obliged to have all votes, nationwide, recounted in a more exacting manner than that which can be provided by machines.

There are bound to be anomalies everywhere in so comprehensive an election as we have for the presidency. But is it not obvious that the Electoral College system "takes off the board," very early in the count, more than four-fifths of the country's precincts? It also means, among other things, that it makes no sense in most states to run the risk of fraudulent conduct in a presidential contest. Although Electoral College critics have been revived by what is happening now, it does seem to be evident to an increasing number of informed observers that the Electoral College arrangement has spared us from considerable grief this time around. It may be some time, for instance, before we can be sure about who is first in the popular vote—and it would probably take even longer if the popular vote were determinative.

Even so, considering the nature of our regime and the way it is discussed in the mass media, it can be difficult to make the point publicly that the popular vote is not significant when that vote had not been understood to be decisive when that voting began. It is as if the league standings, at the end of a football or basketball season, were determined not by the record of wins and losses in discrete games but rather by the total number of points scored by each team during the season.

II.

It can be instructive to notice how the mass media have responded to the events of the past fortnight. Anyone who is believed to know anything about such matters has been besieged, as I have been, by callers from newspaper and other media men and women around the country—in my case, from Florida, Washington, D.C., California, and of course Illinois. There was also an interesting chap from Wyoming. Such are the marvels of an electronic age.

I can say more in detail about the kinds of inquiries one gets—or, rather, the waves of inquiries, for each development (especially in Florida) would stimulate the working of the phones by mass media people to find someone with a new angle. One is not likely to be of much sustained interest for such callers, however, if one tends to be moderate in one's responses. I was surprised, therefore, to see a November 12, 2000, Gannett News Service report featuring, in a Sioux Falls, South Dakota, newspaper (and perhaps elsewhere), one such moderate response by me.

There is, of course, no lack of confidence and even self-righteousness on all sides in the current controversy. An illustration of the passions that can be mustered here may be found in the debate between Paul Gigot and Mark Shields on the *News Hour with Jim Lehrer* on November 16. Be that as it may, I have insisted to several callers that this is a close presidential contest, not a major constitutional crisis.

The constant shifting in telephone inquiries is illustrated by a call I received last Friday afternoon when it appeared that a manual counting of ballots would not have to be accepted by the Florida secretary of state. (This was after a trial judge had ruled, but before the Florida Supreme Court indicated that things were still up in the air.) That Friday afternoon call, with a deadline pressing upon my caller, was as to what "the president-elect" should say. I asked her to tell me first, if she would, who that was.

III.

Speculations about these matters (some of them rather wild) should be discouraged, except perhaps as parlor-games. Even more to be discouraged are the complaints that too many lawyers have become involved in the Florida proceedings. Litigation can be useful in such matters, especially when state public officials (in Florida, the secretary of state and the attorney general) are at odds about what the law of the state calls for with respect to manual counting and other important issues. It is hard to see where the authoritative guidance is going to come from, if the courts (and especially the Florida Supreme Court) are not relied upon when matters have gotten into the condition they now are. Critical to such guidance seems to be the need to determine, in a fair and efficient way, what the intention of the voter is in any circumstance when the law and established practices are ambiguous.

I find it particularly puzzling that conservatives allow themselves to appear as hostile to law and lawyering as they seem to be these days. They do not seem to appreciate how much the propertied classes usually rely upon the law, upon judicial proceedings, and upon legal technicalities.[7]

Of course, after awhile (if not from the beginning), it is difficult to rely much on what either side in such a controversy says. Each side finds plausible reasons for handling the Florida evidence in a way that favors it—and both sides are switching, when circumstances change, to arguments they had previously disparaged.[8] (Peculiarly absent, in this wholesale switching, is evidence of a sense of humor among the combatants.)

Particularly instructive here are the arguments about the efficacy of a manual count. Of course, properly designed machines can be 99.9 percent accurate, or so we are assured. And usually, that is far more than close enough accuracy. But a troubling problem arises when it becomes obvious that differences between candidates come down to one-tenth of one percent, or even less, of the total vote in a large state. The machines cannot then suffice, something that their manufacturers evidently recognize.[9] Also troubling, no doubt, is the question of how that one-tenth of one percent can be properly counted in circumstances where the temptation for manipulation and fudging is great.[10]

It is obvious, when things get this tight, that the partisans of the loser, whoever he may turn out to be, are likely to say, and may even believe, "We wuz robbed!"

IV.

An editorial of November 11 in the *Times* of London invokes "natural justice" in recommending that the most scrupulous means be used in determining the Florida tally. It is also indicated in that editorial that a "political solution" and "common sense" are called for in this situation.[11]

Considerations of both natural justice and a political solution led me to suggest, on November 10 (I want to emphasize the date, as important for indicating the circumstances)—these considerations led me to suggest, in a letter to editors, a recourse to lots in these extraordinary circumstances, preferably well before either a "winner" or a "loser" was evident. This seemed to me a prudent way of avoiding what could be unseemly, and otherwise harmful, developments—and would give all of the principals an opportunity to set aside personal self-interest in an obviously patriotic manner.[12]

I have suggested to students, in thinking about my proposal, that they particularly notice the elements in such a situation that bear upon how sensible negotiations and settlements should be approached. It is the "natural" reaching for an additional advantage that can ruin an evenhanded deal that might have been good for everyone involved.

The current situation is useful for reminding us of what is and is not done in and by a routine election. One of the original purposes of the Electoral College arrangement, it should also be noticed, was to permit sound political judgment to be exercised by presidential electors. That is no longer expected (and, indeed, is not wanted) from such electors—but that does not mean that citizens at large, and especially those who aspire to leadership, cannot resort to prudent innovations in extraordinary circumstances.[13]

It is not irrelevant here that lots are resorted to "all the time" in American election law and elsewhere in public life.[14] And, of course, lots were used to determine which young men were sent to fight and perhaps die in Vietnam. The more complicated the situation has become in Florida, the more attractive my original proposal can seem; but the longer the standoff continues, the more remote such a highly unlikely resolution will be.

Even more instructive may be the recognition that the way matters have developed in Florida means that the election there will be in effect decided by lot, but in a far less satisfactory way than I suggested two weeks ago. Considerable embitterment is likely to result, in the weeks ahead, in part because it will be virtually impossible to "prove" that a fair count has been reached, no matter what methods are used or which side wins. That is, chance will be much more critical in the final result in Florida than is usually the case in an American election—and that will not be as healthy a state of affairs as it would have been if that disturbing chance element had been faced up to and hence refined (if not even sanctified) by a deliberate recourse to lots by public servants speaking in the most elevated terms and tone.[15]

In any event, silly talk should be discouraged. Thus, one Chicago daily newspaper proclaimed in its front page headline, "Recount Chaos,"[16] when that was hardly the case. Thus, also, I have heard the mournful statement, "We don't have a president a week after the election." Nonsense, we should say, we have a president more than eager to serve until January 20—and it is almost certain that a successor will be more or less ready to take over on that day.

V.

I refer in my November 10th letter to "a big 'if.'" One important consideration today, which should be taken advantage of in minimizing the political "fallout," however this matter is finally resolved, is that the public at large simply did not clearly prefer one candidate to the other. Nor were most of their positions dramatically different. It *is* a toss-up, and that should guide us in assessing how it does happen to be decided.

Certainly, if either Mr. Bush or Mr. Gore had emerged as the obvious winner on the evening of November 7, most of the country would soon have been reconciled to the outcome of the election. That should be pointed out, again and again, once someone is settled upon, somehow or other. Neither will "deserve" to win; neither will "deserve" to lose. But the country deserves, or at least would probably benefit from, a recognized successor to the current president on January 20.

Such reflections can help us appreciate that, except in the most serious situations, it is usually more important that *someone* be settled upon for key offices among us in a plausible and otherwise acceptable manner than that any particular person be chosen. It is salutary here that everyone—candidates and public alike—be submitted to the discipline of the electoral process, whatever reservations the more perceptive may have as to whether the best candidate really wins on any particular occasion.

Indeed, is it not almost always the case that the simply best man or
woman for an important office in this country is not even running for
it—and indeed may not want it, except as a duty to be undertaken if
the community somehow or other insists upon it?[17] In considering all
of these matters, it is prudent to be reminded that we may make far
too much of the presidency.

I am raising in various ways the question of what it is we are entitled to expect from an election. Proper answers to that question can
moderate our responses when we do not get the "winner" we may
happen to prefer.

VI.

An instructive feature of the maneuvers of the past fortnight is what
is revealed about the "style" of the two candidates and their principal
supporters. The votes cast by November 7, we now know, indicate
that neither candidate had a significant edge over the other.

But would this be true if a selection should now be made on the basis of how each side has handled matters since November 7? Who has
been more of a leader as this contest has developed? Or is it that each
side has exhibited traits and talents appropriate for different circumstances? Which set of traits is more appropriate for the circumstances
of the country today?

Are these and like questions likely to be involved, one way or another, in the contest (perhaps already under way) that will culminate
in the 2004 election? I had occasion some years ago to argue that an
American election has something for everybody, that one could always find something to cheer about somewhere, even as one nursed
one's wounds in other places. This election, more than any other that
I recall, seemed to offer little that was solid for anyone, perhaps because of its general sense of inconclusiveness.

Still, perhaps something substantial can be salvaged from all this
when we reflect upon what does usually happen in our elections and
why—and how the differentness of this election points up the relia-
bility of the way we do things for the most part.

Perhaps "for the most part" is all that can be reasonably expected,
which means that we should be able to keep ourselves from making
too much of the occasional anomalies that are inevitable in any complex system.

VII.

I return, in closing, to the Electoral College issue, particularly as it has been developed by Senator Durbin (a Democrat) and by a Republican colleague from Illinois in the House of Representatives.

It should be noticed that important changes can be made here without recourse to a constitutional amendment. Thus, the "faithless" elector can probably be eliminated by state statutes, if not the actual electors themselves. Also, votes can be allocated as they are done in Maine and Nebraska, for the most part by congressional districts. But a caution is in order here: this particular change could be, in effect, a significant step toward a parliamentary form of government, something that should be seriously debated before it is ventured.

As for the Durbin-LaHood proposal, the prudence of several of its features should be questioned. Do we want a system in which run-offs might become routine (that is, if 40 percent of the popular vote is not received by the candidate initially ahead in the popular vote)? *Would* run-offs become routine? It is hard to predict what would happen. It is predictable, however, that unanticipated consequences will follow, ranging from changes in modes of campaigning to changes in the development of issues and in party alignments.

Legitimacy—or the appearance of public support—may then become much more of a problem than it has been up to now. Senator Durbin reports, "Since 1824, when the popular vote first began to be recorded along with the [Electoral College] vote, winners of presidential elections have averaged 51 percent of the popular vote as compared to an average of 71 percent of the electoral vote. In comparison, the losing main opponents have averaged 42 percent of the popular vote, but just 27 percent of the electoral vote. Year to year statistics vary greatly."[18] If we are to have presidents, is it not generally better to have it widely believed that they have been clearly and decisively elected, not merely by 51 percent of the relevant vote?

One likely consequence of a switch to reliance upon a popular vote for the president would be a nationalization of our election laws. This would be in order to discourage local aberrations that might seem to permit either fraud or incompetence that would have nationwide consequences. One consequence, in turn, of the nationalization of our election laws might be, it seems to me, to increase the power of incumbency.[19] It is a striking feature of our present arrangement that the president of the United States has remarkably little control over how votes for president are cast and counted in the multitude of election districts all over the country—and that seems to me a healthy state of affairs.

I should not close this faculty workshop without noticing that it is highly unlikely that a constitutional amendment simply abolishing the Electoral College would get the assent needed from three-fourths of the states. Are there not too many small states that would have to sacrifice some of their influence by such a change? In fact, such a proposal would have difficulties even in the Senate, where the influence of the small states remains considerable.

Although it is highly unlikely that this constitutional amendment will be recommended by Congress (by the required two-thirds vote) and ratified by the states, it is altogether possible that irresponsible talk about the anachronism and unfairness of the Electoral College arrangement can undermine the political morale of the country and hence the perceived legitimacy of our national institutions. One corrective here is to investigate and explain what does and does not happen in our elections. It can also help to have would-be leaders truly lead when the occasional impasse seems to threaten an orderly transition. This is not to deny that, in the present situation, the American people still seem to be more intrigued than threatened by what is happening in their continuing presidential contest.

B. THE ELECTORAL COLLEGE REVISITED[20]

I.

Among the responses to the long-contested Year 2000 presidential election has been widespread examination, if not even a condemnation, of the Electoral College system of choosing presidents in this country. My own immediate response to the November 7, 2000, balloting may be seen in a letter to the editor of November 10 which was published in several newspapers, beginning on November 13:

It is possible that our Presidential contest will remain "undecided" for weeks to come, partly because of uncertainties in Florida. If (a big "if")—if prolongation of this standoff threatens to damage the country and to subvert the authority of the next Administration, would it not be prudent for the two major candidates to announce an immediate recourse by them to the drawing of lots in order to settle this matter? The Electoral College votes could thereafter be easily adjusted by their supporters accordingly.

Would not this be a statesmanlike resolution of this "crisis" by both candidates, dramatizing their character and fitness and making more likely an era of national good will thereafter? This approach would best be taken before the official recount, including the absentee ballots, is announced in Florida, thereby making less likely the risk of having it appear that the "loser" won the draw. It is fortunate that the major candidates have roughly the same amount of popular support nationwide, making it much easier for the country to accept this kind of self-denying compromise.

These candidates have long been extolled as pious patriots. Would not a voluntary recourse by them to the drawing of lots in these extraordinary circumstances, for which there are American legal as well as Biblical precedents, testify both to their faith in Providence and to their dedication to the common good? Certainly, this kind of resolution would be salutary as a reminder that what always unites us as a people is much greater than what may chance to divide us from time to time.[21]

It was my opinion then that the contest, as it was developing in Florida and elsewhere, was not susceptible of a satisfactory resolution. There were bound to be hard feelings, no matter how the contest was "decided," if the contenders continued with their counting and litigation. The contest was simply too close to be resolved routinely or amicably—and deepseated resentments could be expected to follow, no matter how it was resolved. That is, this was not an occasion for routine techniques to be used and for routine judgments to be relied upon.

The prudent thing to do here, it seemed to me, was to avoid a decision by ordinary means, relying instead upon something extraordinary, the drawing of lots, a measure for which there are sound precedents, both ancient and modern, both secular and spiritual. Such reliance would have displayed the contenders as self-effacing and patriotic. And this, I believed, reflected the "realities" of the situation, a situation that would remain "unsettled," no matter what was done by "fighting it out" to the end.

A *Wall Street Journal* reporter who called me on the eve of the parties' critical oral argument before the United States Supreme Court seemed intrigued by my suggestion that the Chief Justice should open proceedings by asking counsel to consult with their clients as to whether they would be willing to proceed immediately to the draw-ing of lots (perhaps even in the Court itself) in order to lay the much-vexed matter to rest. I continue to believe that the country would have been well served by *this* kind of intervention by the Court and by the candidates' acceptance of it. In short, it can be prudent, and "political" in the best sense of the term, for the parties engaged in a quite messy situation to exhibit an obvious willingness to reach as fair a solution as is likely in the circumstances. Instead, we are destined to have, for a very long time, the labeling of one side to this controversy as "sore losers" and the other side as "thieves."

II.

The interventions by the United States Supreme Court that we did see were, by and large, unfortunate, leaving many people in this country disturbed both about the legitimacy of the election of George W. Bush and about the good faith of the Supreme Court. There will long remain doubts about the propriety of what the United States Supreme Court did, which was essentially different from what the Florida courts were *trying* to do by supervising (as state courts often do) the implementation of state laws and the operations of state ad-ministrative agencies.

Some of you will recall that I have spoken twice before to this MENSA chapter. On both occasions, the United States Supreme Court was discussed. First, there was my critique of a book by two journal-ists, *The Brethren*, which presumed to expose the inner life of the Supreme Court to public view. My critique argued that the Supreme Court was not substantially "political," making it inappropriate for those journalists to investigate it as they had done, which was un-comfortably close to how members of the Congress and of the exec-utive are treated by the press.[22]

My second visit with you anticipated this visit, because it too had the Supreme Court involving itself with a Florida controversy. That visit had me discussing the propriety of a local government at-tempting to regulate animal sacrifices conducted in a more or less public way (at least in their consequences) by a religious sect. In that case, as in all too many other cases, the Supreme Court exhib-ited an ahistorical, and hence distorted, notion of what "the free ex-ercise of religion" shield protects in this country. We are left to won-der, by the court's intervention in *Bush v. Gore*, about its reading of the "equal protection of the laws" language in the Fourteenth Amendment.[23]

Particularly disturbing for many people was the order by the United States Supreme Court stopping the manual recount in Florida, especially when this was followed up a few days later by the ruling that there was not enough time to recount the votes, votes that might well have been counted by then (one way or another) if the court had not stopped the count. Such manual counting has evidently been resorted to from time to time in Florida; it certainly is resorted to in many other states, and it seems to be believed by competent observers to be usually more accurate, if done conscientiously, than machine counting. I note in passing that the "deadline" that the court seemed to be concerned about was far more flexible than a bare majority of the court purported to believe it was.[24]

The court's conduct here was made even worse by Justice Scalia's statement justifying the stopping of the manual recount pending the final arguments in and decision by the Supreme Court. It was a remarkably impolitic statement by a Justice, permitting some observers to believe that out-and-out political partisanship had moved at least this justice.[25] One consequence of the Scalia statement is that it makes highly unlikely any elevation of Justice Scalia to the chief justiceship, something that had been predicted earlier.

The resentment I have referred to is recorded in (among many other places) a front-page story in *USA Today*:

Six weeks after an uneasy U.S. Supreme Court cleared the way for Republican George W. Bush to become President, the scars left on the nation's highest court by the Florida court are evident.

The court's nine justices, uncomfortable with their role in such a high-stakes political contest, have remained tense with one another since the 5–4 ruling that shattered many Americans' image of the court as an institution above the partisan politicking that goes on across the street in Congress.

The Court has been slow to get back into its routine caseload, and justices have been meeting with each other and their staffs to try to ease any lingering bitterness and to boost morale. The justices' clerks, the ambitious worker bees behind the court's white marble edifice, nevertheless are nursing grudges.

Meanwhile, the Court has been bombarded with thousands of letters from angry Americans, some of whom have sent in their voter registration cards suggesting that going to the polls in November was a waste

of time. "For shame!" one letter said. Many letters to the justices have
been sarcastic, others more menacing. . . .

[Justice] Sandra Day O'Connor has told people close to her that in her
two decades on the court, she has never seen such anger over a case.
O'Connor, more than any other justice, has seemed disturbed by the
public wrath directed at the Court.[26]

One critical problem here can be traced back to the impression left by
Republican partisans in the Florida maneuverings that they believed
that a manual recount of the votes there was likely to show Albert
Gore the winner. Or, as a couple of informed conservatives have ad-
mitted to me, it is highly likely that more of the voters who went to
the polls in Florida intended to vote for Albert Gore than intended to
vote for George Bush in the November 7th election. How such intentions may be properly divined is, of course, a critical issue here.

A full-page advertisement in the *New York Times*, entitled "544 Law
Professors Say," put thus the complaints of critics of the Supreme Court:

> *By Stopping the Vote Count in Florida,*
> *The U.S. Supreme Court Used Its Power*
> *To Act as Political Partisans,*
> *Not Judges of a Court of Law*

We are Professors of Law at 120 American law schools, from every part
of our country, of different political beliefs. But we all agree that when
a bare majority of the U.S. Supreme Court halted the recount of ballots
under Florida law, the five justices were acting as political proponents
for candidate Bush, not as judges.

> *It is Not the Job of a Federal Court*
> *to Stop Votes From Being Counted*

By stopping the recount in the middle, the five justices acted to suppress the facts. Justice Scalia argued that the justices had to interfere
even before the Supreme Court heard the Bush team's arguments because the recount might "cast a cloud upon what Bush claims to be the
legitimacy of his election." In other words, the conservative justices
moved to avoid the "threat" that Americans might learn that in the recount, Gore got more votes than Bush. This is presumably "irreparable"
harm because if the recount proceeded and the truth once became
known, it would never again be possible to completely obscure the
facts. But it is not the job of the courts to polish the image of legitimacy

of the Bush presidency by preventing disturbing facts from being confirmed. Suppressing the facts to make the Bush government seem more legitimate is the job of propagandists, not judges.

> *By taking power from the voters, the Supreme Court has tarnished its own legitimacy. As teachers whose lives have been dedicated to the rule of law, we protest.*[27]

This, I suspect, will be the dominant opinion among intellectuals in this country, and probably abroad as well, about what happened in the 2000 election. This protest is grounded in a moral judgment that cannot help but remind us of the critiques made again and again both of the Clinton Administration by its opponents the last few years and of the abortion cases for many more years. It is a judgment that will likely be reinforced by the story that comes to be accepted, after exhaustive investigations are conducted into what "really happened" in the Florida voting. It would be salutary, of course, if the most persuasive recounting assures us that Mr. Bush won after all.

III.

One consequence of this controversy has been the dramatization of the Electoral College, leading many to question its modern usefulness. This is the system of voting provided in the Constitution for presidential electors, state by state, who in turn vote for the president. Each State is allocated as many electors as it has members in the Senate and in the House of Representatives. (The District of Columbia now has three electors.) There are 538 such electors altogether, with the winner being the candidate who gets the majority of them (at least 270).

All of the votes of each state are almost always allocated to the candidate who receives the most votes in that state. (The "most votes" need not be a majority of the votes cast in that state, but rather the most that any candidate got in that state.) Provision is also made in the Constitution for what happens, in Congress, in the event that no candidate gets a majority of the Electoral College votes. (There have been two occasions [following upon the 1800 and 1824 elections] when the House of Representatives had to choose the president and one other occasion [following upon the 1876 election] when an extra-constitutional remedy was conjured up.)

The term "Electoral College" is not used in the Constitution itself. But this institution has been called thus from very early in its history, and it is the name given to it in the Confederate Constitution of 1861 (which is modeled, for the most part, upon the United States Constitution of 1787).[28]

It is not generally appreciated that the Electoral College system was not the source of the problems confronted by us in November-December 2000, but rather the closeness of the vote in Florida. That closeness exposed problems in the modes of voting and of counting in that state.

IV.

The Electoral College system, far from being the cause of the difficulties in Florida, was responsible for containing the national problem this time around. Thus, the difficulties faced in Florida could have been encountered in several other states as well if the national popular vote, rather than the Electoral College vote, had been decisive.

It seems to be the case that there was no serious question in any of the other states as to who had won there. But if the precise count of the popular vote in all states mattered, which would be the case if the overall popular vote decided the contest, then substantial pockets of votes in various states (including how absentee ballots were dealt with) might have had to be recounted all over the country.

That is, the Electoral College system took "out of play," so to speak, almost all of the rest of the states, and this quite early in the process. The "puncture" was in the Florida compartment in the electoral ship of state; all other compartments in that ship were properly, and quite easily, sealed off.

The way that the Electoral College system works means, among other things, that safe, however narrow, margins state by state are transformed into a solid, easily recognizable majority, nationwide. There is about this transformation something of a "noble illusion," an illusion that it is very much in the service of legitimacy and continuity for us to accept. Critics of this system do not seem to recognize that any other reliable and workable system would also have to depend upon convenient assumptions and unexamined "facts."

The remarkable success of the Electoral College system, across two centuries, should caution critics who make much of flaws that have always been apparent to thoughtful supporters of that system.

V.

But there is a "flaw" in the Electoral College system that elicits a recurring concern, a "flaw" pointed up for many by the most recent election. That which is very much the concern of some is the "troubling" (however rarely seen) possibility that the winner of the popular vote nationwide may lose in the Electoral College.

This is what happened in 1888. It is, assuming that Albert Gore did lose in 2000, what happened this last time around. The 1824 election is murky here, since some states' electors were chosen at that time by state legislatures, not by a vote at large in those states.

It has long been obvious to some, but it nevertheless remains difficult to argue publicly, that any discrepancy between the Electoral College vote and the popular vote should not matter *much* if it was *not* understood at the outset of the voting that the overall numbers were all that mattered. If the overall popular vote had been recognized all along as decisive, then efforts would have been made to "pile on" in the states where candidates clearly had safe leads.[29]

VI.

If the Electoral College system is to be replaced (rather than reformed), a constitutional amendment would be required. What should it be replaced by? A nationwide popular vote seems to be the principal alternative advocated by the most prominent critics of the present Electoral College system. This proposal is usually qualified, however, by the suggestion that there be a run-off election if no candidate gets at least 40 percent of the total popular vote.

The political questions to be taken into account here can be daunting. Should not the replacement system one proposes take into account the likely campaigning that would result? How would political advertising strategies change? Would fraud be more likely, or at least more important? As things stand now, fraudulent voting in any particular state may not matter nationally if it is not enough to change the outcome in *that* state. But if the voting is nationwide, then any fraud anywhere can be advantageous in the final compilation.

Among the other consequences to be considered is what the effect on the political influence of minorities is apt to be once their votes are added to the national total rather than possibly providing the margin of victory in any particular state. (This is an odd state of affairs,

considering how some critics of the Electoral College system condemn it as "racist" and "elitist" in its origins.) Clues to the possible
consequences of changes here may be found upon considering what
the effects, both good and bad, were of the shift to the popular election of Senators in the early twentieth century.

One thing can safely be predicted about the abolition of the Electoral College system, and that is that it is hard to anticipate fully the
accommodations to and the consequences of whatever system re-
places it. But if there is no such abolition, there is still the need to explain to people at large, again and again, why the popular vote does
not really matter *in these circumstances*. One means of explaining
this is by recourse to sports illustrations. We all know that the total
points scored for a championship series of games do not matter as
much as total contests won. It is remembered, for example, that the
Pirates won the 1960 World Series 4–3, while the Yankees outscored
them by a ratio of about 2 to 1. Or, to use political examples, which it
may be more salutary to do considering our excessive appetite for
sports: The party that dominates the House of Representatives may
have had fewer voters supporting all of its House members than supported all of the House members of the other party. (The same is often true in the Senate, of course.)

It is well to return to the political perspective here for another reason, which may be decisive. Whatever the defects of the Electoral
College system, it is believed by informed observers to be virtually impossible to secure a constitutional amendment with respect to it because of the opposition of the small states. This critical fact, it can be
said, should be at the heart of any sensible discussion of this matter.

The smaller states, it is argued, would tend to be neglected in presidential elections if there were not the Electoral College system. If an
election is apt to be close, in the Electoral College vote, then the
smaller states get extra attention. After all, 100 of the 538 votes in the
Electoral College are provided pursuant to the Senate ratio, thereby
expanding the influence of the smaller states in the overall count.

A curious fact must be noticed here: The smaller states are seen to
prefer the Electoral College system, even as some complain that the
largest states dominate Electoral College calculations. Does not this
somewhat contradictory set of assessments suggest that things may
be properly balanced here, after all? A further restraining factor here
can be the recognition that the Constitution itself, which is widely re-

garded as a marvelous creation, was drafted pursuant to a system that provided one vote for each state in the Constitutional Convention.

The advocates of reform here, when confronted by the solid opposition by the smaller states to abolition of the Electoral College, can be usefully reminded of other reforms that would be even more salutary among us but that have little if any hope of success. I refer to such reforms as the abolition of broadcast and cable television in this country, the elimination of lotteries and other legalized gambling, the suppression of alcohol, tobacco, and narcotic addictions, and a dramatic reduction in our dependence upon the automobile.[30]

VII.

Of course, practical-minded advocates of reform are likely to look to changes that do not depend upon Constitutional amendments. An assessment of such changes can help us appraise the system we do have—and are likely to continue to have for some time.

One concern reformers sometimes have is with the so-called "faithless elector," the elector who does not vote for the presidential candidate that he had been pledged to vote for. Congress, by the use of appropriate incentives for the states, could probably eliminate this "problem." But it should be recognized that this has never really been much of a problem, with fewer than a dozen such electors (out of almost 20,000) since 1824.

Some would-be reformers believe Congress should be urged to press, again with appropriate incentives for the states, for the establishment in each state of the arrangement now found in Maine and Nebraska: electoral votes are allocated there by congressional districts, along with two votes for the statewide winner. With this system, too, there can be a difference between presidential electoral votes and the national popular vote, but that would be even less likely than it is now. It might be difficult, however, to persuade the larger states to reduce their supposed considerable influence thus.

One effect of this "reform," moreover, would be to move us closer to a parliamentary system, and perhaps also to a system of proportional representation, with little or no effective separation of powers in the national government. A comparison with various European governments, which have not been as successful as the American government over "the long run," is in order here. Also in order would be a consideration of the problem already noticed with respect to reliance upon a national popular vote for president. Would fraud be more likely, since each district counts? Would federal supervision of voting "have" to be instituted, as would be likely also with any system of national popular voting? And would drastic federal control over absentee ballots be required? As matters stand now, the national government has very little control of the voting that is conducted, which reduces thereby the power of incumbency.

Even if no reforms are made in how a state's votes are allocated, there are likely to be seen, in the coming decade, changes encouraged by Congress in the uses of voting equipment, in the modes of recounts, and in the registration of voters. For, it can be emphasized, the inadequacies revealed last year in the Florida system can readily be found in other states as well.

VIII.

We should step back now by asking, What is it that we really want? This question should help us consider properly all that we have touched upon here.

What *do* we want? Do we not want someone clearly chosen, according to a recognized arrangement that has a plausible rationale? The plausible rationale for the Electoral College system includes a respect for the principle of federalism, even as it discourages the modern tendency to rely upon thoughtless, if not even demagogic, plebiscites.

When I say "a plausible rationale" I am suggesting that the rhetorical aspects of these matters should be appreciated. Related to the rhetorical here is the poetic, the telling of a likely story in order to justify our institutions and how they have worked.

It usually does not matter much, after all, who *is* chosen president, once a choice is clearly made pursuant to the established rules—and provided that there has been a winnowing process, within the principal political parties, a process that has eliminated the more questionable aspirants for the presidency.[31]

It is only prudent to recognize that, no matter what system is used, chance will very much affect who is chosen. Mr. Gore, for example, would likely have won easily in 2000 but for the accidentally exposed

Monica Lewinsky scandal and Mr. Clinton's subsequent trials. And if Mr. Clinton had resigned (as I believed then he should have done), upon having had his deliberate deceptions exposed in 1998, Mr. Gore probably would have won reelection two years later. (Mr. Clinton is, in critical respects, our Charles Stewart Parnell.) Another deception that we are aware of, but to which we have turned a blind eye, is that last-minute change of "residency" from Texas to Wyoming which permitted a talented man to *appear* eligible for the vice presidency.[32]

The misconduct of Mr. Clinton permitted Mr. Bush to insist again and again that he would restore morality and dignity to the White House. One suspects, however, that if the mass media had subjected Governor Bush's past in 1999–2000 to the kind of scrutiny that Governor Clinton's past was subjected in 1991–1992, Mr. Bush would not have been as able as Mr. Clinton was to survive as a viable candidate. (Consider, for example, how much was made about whether Mr. Clinton had ever smoked marijuana. And consider, also, how much was made of *his* disinclination to serve in a war that evidently repelled him.[33])

We know, however, what the mass media are like—and so we can expect that efforts will now be made to dredge up conduct across decades designed to reveal the president as anything but a moral exemplar. One critical element likely to be exposed in the soul of Mr. Bush, I venture to predict, is that which permitted him to be as receptive as he, as governor, obviously was to the epidemic of executions in his "native" Texas. Governor Clinton's record here was also highly questionable.[34]

Conservative partisans, especially those in the mass media, have not provided models of self-restraint in dealing with more or less personal matters during the Clinton years, despite the considerable toleration for Mr. Reagan and *his* past that had been exhibited the preceding decade by liberal partisans. Mr. Bush, it can be said, has benefitted thus far from the reaction to the trauma of the Clinton years, just as Mr. Reagan benefitted, especially after the serious Iran/Contra irregularities were exposed, from the reaction to the trauma of the Nixon years.[35]

IX.

We should not try to make too much of Mr. Bush. Is it not likely that most of what "he" does now will be done by the cadre of fairly experienced men and women who have been recruited to run the government? This is likely to be seen in any modern administration that manages to get through our complicated and volatile electoral process and into office.

We should notice, as we prepare to close this examination of the ever-recurring Electoral College issue, that the original intentions of the Framers for that system are largely irrelevant today. Such intentions may be useful for understanding and using other parts of the Constitution, but that is far less so here. A critical consideration in 1787 had been the belief that presidential candidates, in the years then immediately ahead (once the country got past George Washington), were not apt to be as well known to ordinary voters as their own presidential electors, local political men who could be expected to know more than ordinary voters about worthy men elsewhere.[36]

Now, of course, the ordinary voter is apt to know far more about the principal presidential candidates nationwide than about the list of electors being selected in his state. Voters today usually do not even know the names of the electors chosen in their own state. Indeed, one way of describing what the United States Supreme Court did in December 2000 is to say that it presumed to act, in effect, as the Electoral College was originally intended to act. Still another way of putting all this is to say that our most recent election was really decided by the drawing of lots, but in a far more contentious and unsettling manner than an immediate and open recourse to lots would have been once it became evident that the Year 2000 presidential election was, and would remain, essentially a draw.

The federalism factor, which may have been of some importance for the Framers in devising the Electoral College system, continues to be important. Another factor of importance, but not one that the Framers made much if anything of, is that the Electoral College system usually gives us a clear winner easily and fairly soon after the election day voting is done. Still another factor is that the system does tend to discourage third parties. The Framers were themselves suspicious, it seems, of *any* political parties, but would they not have tended to prefer that political parties (if depended upon) be kept to two or three, with such large parties tending *not* to be monolithic?

Chance, I have argued, has been critical in providing us with the Electoral College system that we do have—or in providing us with the workings of a system significantly different from what had been anticipated. That system is obviously not sacrosanct, but the well-established, if it works reasonably well, should be respected, if not even cherished, especially if it is hardly likely to be changed soon. (The same can be said about other institutions, such as trial by jury, which too has various accidental features about it. Consider, as well, the equality of the votes of states in the Senate, whatever their sizes, the difficulties of which the emergence of national political parties has moderated.)

Statesmanship, in these matters, recognizes how much we are always apt to be governed by fortune, even as prudent efforts are employed to make proper use of the opportunities, including the steadying institutions, that we happen to have inherited.

C. A SAD CASE: THE SUPREME
COURT AND A PRESIDENTIAL ELECTION[37]

I.

I have long argued that it is very difficult, if not impossible, in constitutional adjudication to separate political judgment from constitutional reasoning. This means, among other things, that judicial review of acts of Congress tends to be a questionable exercise, aside from the obvious failure of the Constitution itself to provide for such a practice.[38]

The most notorious case in this country's history of an improper mixing of politics and constitutional adjudication is *Dred Scott v. Sandford*.[39] A majority of the United States Supreme Court evidently believed, on that occasion, that it could settle by judicial edict the great political issue of the future of slavery in the United States. In order to try to do so, the court had to repudiate, in effect, not only the Missouri Compromise of 1820 but also the Northwest Ordinance of 1787. In doing what it did, that court attempted to take away from Congress its comprehensive control over the future of slavery in the territories of the United States.[40]

It is probably generally agreed that it is a serious mistake for the Supreme Court to allow itself to seem to be divided along partisan political lines. This failing may be seen during the next decade as an effort is made by some members of the court to deny to Congress what it will have, one way or another—a comprehensive control over the economy of this country.[41]

II.

Partisanship affects, of course, how momentous issues are spoken of. We can see this when we watch a controversy from the sidelines. Consider, for example, the response we typically hear to the shootings in our public schools in recent years.

The typical conservative response was heard from the attorney general of the United States after the recent El Cajon, California, rampage. He said that violent entertainment aimed at youngsters contributes to an "ethic of violence," and he urged the media to help steer young people to a safer path.[42]

The typical liberal response, on the other hand, places much greater emphasis upon doing something to reduce markedly the availability of guns in this country.[43]

There is obviously something sensible about each of these responses. The limitations of each response should also be recognized. That is, if the souls of our citizens are in good shape, the proliferation of guns may not matter as much as it seems to matter now. And if guns are not easily available, erratic conduct is *apt* to be limited in its consequences. (Of course, machetes can be used in horrible ways, as can rental trucks full of ordinary fertilizer.[44])

A proper discussion of the issues here can be impeded by the misconceptions of many liberals as to what the First Amendment provides for and by the misconceptions of some conservatives as to what the Second Amendment provides for.[45]

III.

Consider, also, the arguments we typically hear when the issue of abortion is raised. The typical pro-choice advocate stands for the dignity and power of women. The typical pro-life advocate stands for the humanity and rights of the fetus.[46]

It is hardly likely that these two positions will be reconciled. They seem to be as far apart now as they were a quarter-century ago when *Roe v. Wade*[47] was decided. This is in marked contrast, and for good reason, to what the responses to and the status of *Brown v. Board of Education*[48] were after *its* first quarter-century.

The abortion controversy, like those relating to the status of slavery and those relating to the curbing of violence, seems to be better suited to a political than to a judicial solution. A political solution would have made much more of the exceptions to a general ban on abortions, exceptions that would have enlisted the at-least-tacit support of virtually all of the country. If the life of the mother is at risk, an abortion can be seen as trading one life for another. If the fetus is severely damaged, an abortion can be seen as saving a child from a miserable life. If the pregnancy is the result of rape or incest, an abortion can be seen as releasing the female from something involuntarily imposed upon her.

Even the pro-choice advocate can be led to wonder whether reliance upon the courts has been as good for her cause as it had once seemed, changing as it did the political alignments in this country. On the other hand, even the pro-life advocate can be led to recognize that the law, whether politically imposed or judicially developed, will have little to say once "safe" and inexpensive medication becomes available for self-induced abortions.[49]

IV.

Partisanship, with its unfortunate effects on judicial interventions, may be seen also in the way that the last presidential election was handled, particularly in Florida.

My own credentials here are suggested by three letters of mine to editors published in recent years, the first two in the *New York Times*. The first of these letters suggested that the vice president of the United States should be routinely chosen by means of a presidential nomination which the Congress would be asked to accept (just as is provided for now by the Twenty-fifth Amendment whenever there is a vacancy in the office of vice president). This proposal is designed to encourage a more deliberate decision here in which the Congress joins.[50]

The second of my letters, after the president confessed two years ago that he had grievously misled everyone about his personal conduct, suggested that he should simply resign, permitting us to get on with serious politics.[51]

My third letter, which was published in Chicago-area newspapers as well as elsewhere, was distributed three days after the November 7 election day. That letter, of November 10, 2000, asked whether it would not be prudent for the two major candidates to announce an immediate recourse by them to the drawing of lots to settle this matter.[52]

It seemed to me highly likely then, as I indicated in my letter, that no matter how the election was decided, it would be regarded by at least a significant minority as illegitimate. It also seemed to me that either candidate was as much "the choice of the people" as the other, and that we had in effect a draw.

Thus, it seemed to me then that it makes sense, in such circumstances, to set partisanship aside and do what would be generally seen as obviously patriotic and hence good for the country.

I have never gotten much support for this position, partly because of the partisanship that is difficult to forgo.[53]

V.

Partisanship was seen in how various issues were developed and argued in Florida. It could also be seen in how positions could be shifted dramatically as the circumstances changed.

One got the impression that each side would say just about anything to get past *this* obstacle, leaving other obstacles to be worried about later. For example, what should the status of technicalities be? Each side said *No* to technicalities in some circumstances, and *Yes* in other circumstances. This could be seen in the arguments about what constituted a properly marked ballot; and it could be seen in the arguments about what constituted a properly secured absentee ballot.[54]

The observer of all this was not encouraged to believe that statesmanship governed any of the principal players as each side maneuvered for the next advantage in the intense contest being played out during the month after election day. In short, much of what was said on all sides to this controversy was rather dubious.

VI.

The partisan infection that disfigured so many of the arguments we heard in November carried over, unfortunately, into the pronouncements of the United States Supreme Court in December.

The questionableness of how that court disposed of this matter was anticipated by what Justice Scalia said in justifying the stopping of the manual recount in Florida pending the court's determination of the issues. Critical to his approach, it might seem, was the assumption that no reliable recount of the Florida ballots could ever become known if the then-official recount were aborted.[55]

Among the dubious features of the court's pronouncements in December—pronouncements so dubious that they may have little precedential value—were its assumptions about electoral-votes deadlines, about equal protection, and about the interventions theretofore of the Florida Supreme Court. Far more time was still available than the court recognized. Equal protection concerns were rather contrived, considering the wide variety of voting practices in Florida. And what the Florida Supreme Court did in supervising quasi-administrative processes is done, and indeed has to be done, all the time by state courts.[56]

It should have been obvious to the United States Supreme Court that a political, not a judicial, solution was called for in this controversy. Or rather, it should have been apparent that it would be virtually impossible for the court not to appear to be making a political determination in these circumstances, especially since the interference with the state processes was implemented by those judges on the Supreme Court who usually make the most of states' rights.[57]

The Supreme Court, to put the best face on what it did in December, simply panicked. And thus it permitted critics to bring to bear against this court what was said by one of the dissenters in the 1973 abortion cases, that the decree of the court had been "an exercise of raw judicial power."[58]

It would have been far better to have allowed the state government people to proceed as best they could, subject always to the final political judgment of the Republican-controlled Congress of the United States.[59]

VII.

The Republican operatives, astute as they were in dealing with public opinion and with the courts last November and December, did allow the impression to develop that they were afraid of what a complete count of votes in Florida would show. But we can hope that the final count—that is, that which comes to be generally believed, when the dust settles—we, as citizens, can properly hope (as I have publicly hoped for several months now) that the final count will show Governor Bush the winner in Florida after all, whatever questions remain about whether a significant number of voters were effectively disenfranchised in that state.

A more serious problem than whether Governor Bush was "truly" the winner is how would-be conservatives conducted themselves. A healthy conservatism, which very much depends upon respect for property and hence for the rule of law, should discourage cynicism in these matters. A harbinger of things to come was the peculiar way in which the longstanding constitutional requirements relating to the state inhabitancy of candidates for president and vice president were casually circumvented last summer.[60] Also peculiar is the way that conservatives have come to tolerate deliberate avoidance of dangerous military service by leaders who nevertheless advocated or at least supported the wars that they personally managed to avoid.[61] In short, conservatives cannot expect to continue to possess and to enjoy the considerable part of the wealth of the country that they do, and which they have in some sense earned, if it should come to seem that they are not willing to share the burdens and respect the limitations that others are obliged to take seriously.

Be all this as it may, what we had in the Year 2000 election, after all, was a resort to the drawing of lots in settling upon a president—but a drawing of lots in an unsatisfactory way. A high-minded resolution of the controversy, in the interest of domestic tranquility, would have been something to hold up as a model of statesmanship. An apparent power play, especially if it compromises the reputation of the highest court in the land, is quite another model. It may take some time to sort out who the true winners and the true losers were last year. Perhaps all of us can be winners if the proper lessons are learned from our Year 2000 exercise.[62]

CONCLUSION

It is salutary, despite a worldwide interest both in presidential contests and in presidents, to caution ourselves against making too much of the American presidency.

We should be reminded, from time to time, of the subordinate place, in principle, of the president in our Constitutional system. This subordination is reflected in what has been said in this essay about the ultimate control of presidential elections vested in the Congress.

The understandable, however regrettable, elevation of the presidency may be seen in the practice, for some sixty years now, of our undertaking prolonged hostilities abroad without a formal declaration of war by the Congress. War and the fear of war "naturally" strengthen the presidency, or at least shield it from intended restraints.[63]

Political partisanship tends to cloud our judgement in these matters. Thus a fellow-panelist at the 2001 American Political Science Annual Convention (in San Francisco) lamented the lack of sufficient outrage in the public at large upon the exposure in 1998 of our president's moral defects. It was lamented that the Framers of the Constitution had not provided more effective means for handling such misconduct.

I responded that the president should probably have resigned in September 1998,[64] not because of his lamentable personal misconduct but rather because of his deliberate recourse to systematic deception upon happening to be charged with such misconduct. But, I added, most of those who are extremely outraged at the lack of sufficient public outrage with respect to *that* matter do not seem to be troubled at all by the judicial exercise of an electoral duty which does seem (and for good reason) to have been left by the Constitution to the Congress. This questionable intervention by the United States Supreme Court in a presidential election, I ventured to suggest, would probably have troubled the Framers far more than moral lapses by men in high places, regrettable as those lapses in personal conduct (and exposure of such lapses) may be.

Prudence is called for in determining which misconduct is the most serious in any particular epoch. For example, I have asked, was not the well-intentioned Iran/Contra usurpation far more serious an offense against constitutional proprieties than the self-serving Watergate criminality two decade earlier?

In any event, one does have to be prudent and hence cautious in determining how one's partisanship affects one's reading of evidence, of history, and of the Constitution itself.[65]

NOTES

1. *The Acts of the Apostles*, 1: 15–26. There remains some dispute as to whether Luke was indeed the principal author of *Acts*. See, on the Bible, George Anastaplo, "Law & Literature and the Bible: Explorations," 23 *Oklahoma City University Law Review* 515 (1998).

2. Other examinations by me of prudence and the Constitution are listed in the following bibliographies: "George Anastaplo: An Autobiographical Bibliography (1947–2001)," 20 *Northern Illinois University Law Review* 581–710 (2000); "George Anastaplo, Tables of Contents for His Books and Published Collections (1950–2001)," 39 *Brandeis Law Journal* 219–87 (2000–2001).

3. This talk was given to a Faculty Workshop, Loyola University School of Law, Chicago, Illinois, November 21, 2000. This was preceded by my letter of November 10, 2000, which is referred to in this November 2000 talk and is quoted in its entirety in the January 2001 talk set forth in Part B of this chapter.

4. The case for the Electoral College arrangement is suggested in my 1989 commentary on the Constitution. Also noticed there are the principal arguments usually made against the retention of the Electoral College arrangement. See George Anastaplo, *The Constitution of 1787: A Commentary* (Baltimore: Johns Hopkins University Press, 1989), 100–8, 314–35. The way the Electoral College system works is described in Sections III–V of Part B of this chapter.

5. The principal developments in the United States Supreme Court came after this talk (November 21, 2000) was given. See, for a sampling of materials available on this month-long controversy, Samuel Issacharoff, Pamela S. Karlan, and Richard H. Pildes, ed., *When Elections Go Bad: The Law of Democracy and the Presidential Election of 2000* (New York: Foundation Press, 2001). See, also, the Symposium, 68 *University of Chicago Law Review* 613 (2001); note 27 of this chapter.

6. See Section VII of Part A of this chapter.

7. Conservatives do need to be reminded of how much their property always depends upon reliable government, just as liberals need to be reminded of how much the liberties they cherish usually depend upon secure property. See, for example, my letter to the editor of October 9, 2000 ("On Personal Success and the Community"):

Dick Cheney, upon being reminded during the October 3rd Vice-Presidential debate that he is far better off financially than he was eight years ago, responded, "And I can tell you . . . that the government had absolutely nothing to do with it." "Absolutely nothing?" It has been pointed out since then that Mr. Cheney would probably not have the fortune he has so quickly made in "the private sector" without the contacts in the American and foreign governments that he developed during his years on the federal payroll.

Even more significant, however, is Mr. Cheney's failure to acknowledge (whatever he may truly believe) how much the success any of us may enjoy depends upon conditions, guidance, and support provided by the community, in large part through its various governments. Certainly, many of us can see how much better off we are than our equally-talented and equally-hardworking forebears were in the countries they came from. Our form of government and its operations have encouraged and helped empower us, something that the first great leader of Mr. Cheney's Republican Party recognized again and again.

Then there is the vital assumption, by all of us who may insist that we have "made it on our own," that our government will expend considerable blood and treasure to help us retain what we have gained. Much is to be said, of course, for appreciating free enterprise and individual initiative, but surely not at the expense of forgetting how much is owed by everyone in this country, and especially by the most fortunate among us, to the organized efforts and repeated sacrifices of the entire community.

See *Chicago Tribune*, October 20, 2000, sec. l, p. 24. See, also, the text at note 60 of this chapter.

8. See, for example, the text at note 54 of this chapter.

9. See, for example, Robin Toner, "Counting the Votes," *New York Times*, November 17, 2000, p. A1 (National Edition).

10. This was heard, for example, in 1960, when Richard M. Nixon was defeated by John F. Kennedy. See George Anastaplo, *Human Being and Citizen: Essays on Virtue, Freedom, and the Common Good* (Chicago: Swallow Press, 1975), 3. See, also, the text at note 35 of this chapter.

11. See "Men and Laws: America's Constitutional Crisis Requires a Political Solution," *The Times*, London, November 11, 2000, p. 29. See, on a political solution, note 24 and the text at note 59 of this chapter.

12. This letter is provided in its entirety in the text at note 21 of this chapter. It has been published in several newspapers. And it was called to the attention of several political leaders in Illinois at the time.

13. Concerns have been expressed, of course, about whether some Justices of the United States Supreme Court permitted themselves to appear to take on the original prerogatives of the Electoral College. See, on political maneuvering and the Supreme Court, David A. Kaplan, "The Accidental President," *Newsweek*, September 17, 2001, p. 28.

14. See, for example, Rick Pearson, "Democrats win lottery for remap [of Illinois legislative districts]," *Chicago Tribune*, September 6, 2001, sec. 1. p. 1.

15. See, for example, the text at note 1 of this chapter. What would be thought if it should now be learned that the United States Supreme Court had itself used lots to determine which side would prevail in its final ruling?

16. *Chicago Sun-Times*, November 15, 2000, p. 1.

17. See, for example, Plato, *Republic*, Book I.

18. *Congressional Record*, vol. 146, p. S11494, November 1, 2000.

19. As it is now, the power of incumbency tends to be limited to a state race here and there. See, for example, Julian Borger, "Jeb Bush blamed for unfair election [in Florida]," *Guardian Weekly*, London, June 14–20, 2001, p. 6.

20. This talk was given at a MENSA of Illinois meeting, Chicago, Illinois, January 27, 2001.

21. This letter was first published in the *Chicago Daily Law Bulletin*, November 13, 2000, p. 2, and thereafter in the *Chicago Tribune*, November 15, 2000, sec. 1, p. 20, in the *Hickory* [North Carolina] *Daily Record*, p. 10A; and in the *Chicago Sun-Times*, November 20, 2000, November 15, 2000, p. 32 (in an enigmatic form). See note 12, above.

22. See, for my review of Bob Woodward and Scott Armstrong, *The Brethren: Inside the Supreme Court* (1975), 1983 *Duke Law Journal* 1045 (1983). See, also, George Anastaplo, *The American Moralist: On Law, Ethics, and Government* (Athens: Ohio University Press, 1992), 275.

23. See *Bush v. Gore*, 531 U.S. 98 (2000). Instructive here is a letter from James A. Baker III, who is identified as "a former Secretary of State, [who] led George W. Bush's team in the 2000 presidential election dispute":

> You have once again described Bush v. Gore as a 5-to-4 decision ("In Year of Florida Vote, Supreme Court Also Did Much Other Work," news article, July 2, [2001]), a point that is accurate but also incomplete.
>
> It is sad to see you clearly imply—both in the text of the article and in the accompanying chart of major rulings—that the court decided unconstitutionality on a 5-to-4 vote.
>
> In fact, the 5-to-4 vote dealt with the remedy and whether there was time to fix the process. The court's holding that the lack of uniform standards for the recount violated the 14th Amendment guarantee of equal protection was decided on a 7-to-2 vote, with one of two Democrats joining six of seven Republicans.

New York Times, July 7, 2001, p. A24 (National Edition). Mr. Baker's understanding of the significance of the 7-to-2 vote can be questioned, but not his indication that he "naturally" (?) assigns political affiliations to members of the United States Supreme Court. See note 26, below.

See for my MENSA talk on animal sacrifices, Anastaplo, "Law & Literature and the Christian Heritage: Explorations," 40 *Brandeis Law Journal*, Part 23 (2000–2001).

24. I, along with others, indicated this to inquiring reporters. See, for example, Shailagh Murray, "Deadline to Set Electors Comes Under Debate," *Wall Street Journal*, December 1, 2000, p. A16. See, also, note 59 of this chapter.

25. Justice Scalia's concurring opinion, of December 9, 2000, included these observations: "One of the principal issues in the appeal we have accepted is precisely whether the votes that have been ordered to be counted are, under a reasonable interpretation of Florida law, 'legally cast vote[s].' The counting of votes that are of questionable legality does in my view threaten irreparable harm to petitioner Bush, and to the country, by casting a cloud upon what he claims to be the legitimacy of his election. Count first, and rule upon legality afterwards, is not a recipe for producing election re-

sults that have the public acceptance democratic stability requires." See the text at note 27 and at note 55 of this chapter. The court's final decision was announced on December 12, 2001. See, also, note 57 of this chapter.

26. Joan Biscupic, " Election still splits Court," *USA Today,* January 22, 2001, p. 1. See, also, "Impeach the Supremes," *The Nation,* August 20/27, 2001, p. 4; Roger Ebert, "GOP won by planting seeds of deception," *Chicago Sun-Times,* December 14, 2000, p. 7; Ronald Dworkin, "A Badly Flawed Election," *New York Review of Books,* January 11, 2001. Compare Michael W. McConnell, "A Muddled Ruling," *Wall Street Journal,* December 14, 2000, p. A26 (which seems to support the Baker positions noticed in note 22, above); Don Erler, "A Brief Look at the Judiciary vs. Legislature Question," *Ft. Worth Star-Telegram,* January 4, 2001, p. 13B.

27. *New York Times,* January 13, 2001, p. A7 (National Edition). See, also, note 25, above. See, on this advertisement, Richard A. Posner, *Breaking the Deadlock: The 2000 Election, the Constitution, and the Court* (Princeton: Princeton University Press, 2001), 211. See, for Judge Posner's vigorous criticism of the law professors who have commented on *Bush v. Gore,* Posner, *Breaking the Deadlock,* 198–220. See, for a vigorous criticism of Judge Posner's pragmatism, David Tell, "*Bush v. Gore,* Again," *The Weekly Standard,* September 3, 2001, p. 37. See, also, George Anastaplo, "Critique of Richard A. Posner on Law and Literature," 23 *Loyola University of Chicago Law Journal* 199 (1992). Judge Posner's use of the term "deadlock" suggests, at least to me, that drawing lots would have been a more sensible resolution here than judicial legerdemain.

28. See, for example, George Anastaplo, *The Amendments to the Constitution: A Commentary* (Baltimore: Johns Hopkins University Press, 1995), 361, 445. Also used in the Confederate Constitution is the term "federal," another term not used in the Constitution of 1787. See Anastaplo, The *Amendments,* 133, 344, 346, 430, 450.

29. I had occasion to comment on this situation in *The Constitution of 1787,* 100–7.

30. See, on the abolition of television, Anastaplo, *The American Moralist,* 245. See, also, note 53 of this chapter. See on our gambling craze, Anastaplo, "'Private' Gambling and Public Morality," *Congressional Record,* August 1, 1996, p. 59499 (abridged): also in Calvin M. Logue and Jean DeHart, eds., *Representative American Speeches* (New York: H. W. Wilson Co., 1997), 126–36. See, on the "war against drugs," Anastaplo, "Governmental Drug Testing and the Sense of Community," 11 *Nova Law Review* 295 (1987). See, on the tobacco-consumption problem, the following letter to the editor I submitted to the *New York Times,* April 3, 2000 (not published there):

Your correspondent (April 3, 2000) is right to remind us "that people who choose to use tobacco products are doing so with full knowledge of the consequences." He insists that smokers should not "be absolved of taking responsibility for their own actions." What should be said, then, about the "responsibility" for the "actions" of those who produce and market obviously harmful products, year after year, "with full knowledge of the consequences?" That is, should only those addicted to nicotine, and not those addicted to substantial profits, be expected to pay for the considerable damage done because of tobacco?

31. See, for example, George Anastaplo, "The Obscured Virtues of Smoke-Filled Rooms," *Chicago Tribune*, May 19, 1976, sec. 3, p. 4 (abridged); "Legal Education, Economics, and Law School Governance," 46 *South Dakota Law Review* 27, 236 (2001).

32. See the text at note 36 and at note 60 of this chapter. See, also, note 7, above. See, on the recommended resignation by Mr. Clinton, note 64, below.

33. And yet in 2000, Mr. Clinton's critics were quiet about the youthful intemperance of *their* presidential candidate, an intemperance evidently far more severe and perhaps more damaging physically than Mr. Clinton's had ever been. They were quiet as well about the successful avoidance of dangerous military service during the Vietnam War by *both* of their candidates, even though those men had evidently been willing to see other young men sent off to Vietnam. See note 61, below. This bears also upon our "natural" inclination to be highly selective in what we regard as an "outrage." See the Conclusion of this chapter.

34. Thus, Governor Clinton interrupted his campaign for the presidency in 1992 to return to Arkansas in order to get a convict executed. Questions have been raised both in Texas and in Arkansas, as elsewhere, about the mental capacity of some of those executed as well as about the caliber of the legal representation of those condemned to death.

35. Indeed, the Iran/Contra irregularities were far more serious, in their constitutional implications, than anything Mr. Nixon was condemned for, except perhaps the secret war against Cambodia. See the text at note 65 of this chapter.

36. That these electors would consider worthy men elsewhere was encouraged by the constitutional provision that one of an elector's two votes for President had to be for someone from a state other than his own. See the text at note 32 and at note 60 of this chapter.

37. This talk was given at the University of South Dakota Law School, Vermillion, South Dakota, April 5, 2001.

38. See, on "judicial review," William W. Crosskey, *Politics and the Constitution* (Chicago: University of Chicago Press, 1953), 1396–97; Anastaplo, *The Constitution of 1787*, 335.

39. 60 U.S. 393 (1857). See, on *Dred Scott*, George Anastaplo, *Abraham Lincoln: A Constitutional Biography* (Lanham, Md.: Rowman & Littlefield, 1999), 363.

40. See, on the Northwest Ordinance, Anastaplo, *Abraham Lincoln*, 39.

41. See, for example, George Anastaplo, "'McCarthyism,' the Cold War, and Their Aftermath," 43 *South Dakota Law Review* 103, 138-56 (1998). See, also, note 57 in this chapter.

42. See Ben Fox, "Teen was targeting vice principal in rampage, cops say," *Chicago Tribune*, March 24, 2001, sec. 1, p. 6. See, on proper restrictions upon violent talk and bizarre speculations, George Anastaplo, "Lessons for the Student of Law: The Oklahoma Lectures," 20 *Oklahoma City University Law Review* 19, 187, 198 (1995).

43. See, on proper restrictions on guns in this country, Anastaplo, *The American Moralist*, 367–74.

44. And now, of course, there are also hijacked airliners to contend with. However important legal and military measures may be in dealing with such atrocities, proper education and moral training are even more important (to which the law and a proper use of force can contribute). Consider, for example, the prescription for thoughtful Muslim leaders suggested in the following letter to the editor I prepared in September 2001:

> Among the innocent victims of the monstrous attacks last week on the World Trade Center and the Pentagon are the multitudes of decent Muslims worldwide who must endure the shame, for years to come, of the shocking abuse of American hospitality by their demented co-religionists, the kind of hospitality that Islam and its Prophet have always cherished. Is it not the duty of prudent Muslims everywhere to remind their peoples of what is truly noble in their great tradition?

See *Chicago Tribune*, September 21, 2001, sec. 1, p. 26; *University of Chicago Maroon*, October 2, 2001, p. 8 (expanded). See, on Islam, George Anastaplo, *But Not Philosophy: Seven Introductions to Non-Western Thought* (Lanham, Md.: Lexington Books, 2001), 175–224, 371–72; Bernard Lewis, "The Roots of Muslim Rage," *The Atlantic Monthly*, September 1990. See, also, Anastaplo, "Iraq Is a Prison and We Are Bombing Merely the Inmates," *Hickory* [North Carolina] *Daily Record*, November 27, 1998, p. A4.

45. See Anastaplo, *The Amendments to the Constitution*, 47f, 59f.

46. See, for example, Anastaplo, *Human Being and Citizen*, 46; Anastaplo, *The American Moralist*, 399.

47. 410 U.S. 113 (1973).

48. 347 U.S. 483 (1954).

49. See, for example, George Anastaplo, "Law & Literature and the Christian Heritage: Explorations," 40 B*randeis Law Journal*, 192, 476–84 (2001–2002) (that is, "safe" for the woman, not for the fetus).

50. See *New York Times*, September 20, 1992, sec. 4, p. 16 (National Edition). See, also, *Chicago Tribune*, August 8, 2000, sec. 1, p. 14.

51. See *New York Times*, September 11, 1998, p. A26 (abridged). (National Edition). See, also, *Chicago Daily Law Bulletin*, September 10, 1998, p. 2; *Hickory* [North Carolina] *Daily Record*, September 11, 1998, p. A-4.

52. See the text at note 21 of this chapter. See, on deadlocks and their proper resolution, note 27, above.

53. But then, I have never gotten much support for my proposal that broadcast television be abolished. See note 30, above. I scale down my objectives in the following letter to the editor of July 13, 2001:

> As we grow older, we naturally scale down our expectations. Thirty years ago I began campaigning for the abolition of broadcast television in this country. The campaign itself, I believed, could help us recognize how corrupting television, with its intense promotion of self-indulgence, has been in our community.
>
> Now I settle for much more modest goals. One such is the suppression of bicycle riding on city sidewalks by adults when pedestrians are present. This is an atrocity we see more and more of these days. Cyclists who are afraid to ride in the streets feel entitled to shift the risk to pedestrians who have no reason to expect a vehicle to race by them at close quarters.
>
> Such bikes ought to be impounded on the spot by the police, leaving it to their owners to explain to judges why they "had" to endanger pedestrians as they did. A campaign against this atrocity can not only contribute to the public safety but can also remind us of the duties we all owe to the community.

See *Chicago Tribune*, July 17, 2001, sec. 1, p. 14 (abridged); *Hyde Park Herald*, Chicago, Illinois, August 1, 2001, p. 4. (I identified myself as a "Frequent Cyclist.")

54. See the text at note 9 of this chapter.

55. See the text at note 25, above. See, also, note 25 of this chapter.

56. However suspicious conservatives can be about "judicial activism," they should be and are even more suspicious of administrative and quasi-administrative agencies which are not subject to judicial (as well as to legislative) supervision. See note 62 of this chapter.

57. See, on Justice Scalia, George Anastaplo, "*In re Antonin Scalia*," *Perspectives on Political Science*, vol. 28, p. 22 (1999). See, on Justice Thomas, note 41 of this chapter.

58. 410 U.S., at 222 (Justice White, dissenting).

59. See, for example, Thomas N. Neale, "Election of the President and Vice President by Congress: Contingent Election," Congressional Research Service, The Library of Congress, August 10, 1999. See, also, Lewis Deschler, ed., *Deschler's Precedents of the United States House of Representatives* (94th Congress, 2d Session, House Document No. 94–661), vol. 3, pp. 1–25. I am contributing a paper on this subject to a symposium which is to be published, in 2002, by the *Loyola University of Chicago Law Journal*. See the text at note 24 of this chapter.

60. See the text at notes 32 and 36 of this chapter. See, on the need for conservatives (if only in their own self-interest) to be scrupulous about respecting the rules and acknowledging the importance of community, note 7, above.

61. Consider, for example, my October 26, 2000 letter to the editor on this subject:

> It is curious to hear these days, in the wake of the *USS Cole* bombing, patriotic warnings from candidates about the inadequacy of the most powerful military establishment in history. How much more relaxed we are otherwise expected to be about patriotism is suggested by the fact that a more or less conservative party can nominate for President and Vice-President two candidates who are known to have supported American involvement in the dubious Vietnam War even while they, as young men, made determined (and successful) efforts to avoid having to serve in a war that they were quite willing to have less privileged young men drafted for. All this is an especially curious pattern of conduct on the part of candidates who now insist that they are very much concerned not only about our military preparedness but also about the moral character of our leaders.

See *Chicago Sun-Times*, November 1, 2000, p. 50; note 33, above. See, also, Samuel Taylor, Letter to the Editor, *Chicago Tribune*, October 12, 2001, sec. 1, p. 26. One passionate conservative replied to my letter thus: "This is an *ad hominen* rant. There is more than enough moral weakness to go around; there is good reason to worry about military preparedness." Certainly, there can be found reasons "to worry about military preparedness," even while one's country is the most powerful nation in the history of the earth, if one is temperamentally determined to worry about such matters. The September 2001 attacks on the World Trade Center and the Pentagon were not due to a lack of conventional military preparedness on our part. Such attacks are far more likely to be launched by the weak than by the strong. See note 30, above. See, also, note 65 of this chapter.

62. Justice Stevens's dissenting opinion in *Bush v. Gore* concluded thus (531 U.S. at 128–29):

> What must underlie petitioners' entire federal assault on the Florida election procedures is an unstated lack of confidence in the impartiality and capacity of the state judges who would make the critical decisions if the vote count were to proceed. Otherwise, their position is wholly without merit. The endorsement of that position by the majority of this Court can only lend credence to the most cynical appraisal of the work of judges throughout the land. It is confidence in the men and women who administer the judicial system that is the true backbone of the rule of law. Time will one day heal the wound to that confidence that will be inflicted by today's decision. One thing, however, is certain. Although we may never know with complete certainty the identity of the winner of this year's Presidential election, the identity of

the loser is perfectly clear. It is the Nation's confidence in the judge as an Impartial guardian of the rule of law.

63. See, on the control of Presidential elections by Congress, note 59, above. See, also, Anastaplo, *The Constitution of 1787*, 94–99.

Consider, on the power to declare war, the following letter to the editor prepared by me in October 2001:

> The national administration, as part of its response to the monstrous illegalities of September 11, has spoken often of going to war in or against one or more countries harboring terrorists. Attacks have been launched against Afghan targets. Now we hear talk about Iraqi targets. There still seems to be time, in the present circumstances, to have Congress consider a declaration of war against any country to be attacked by us. Such a declaration, preceded by a proper debate in Congress, would help clarify the current situation and focus everyone's attention on what is to be done, why, and how. It would be healthy to see, through such salutary self-discipline, a reaffirmation in this country of the constitutional proprieties and the rule of law.

See *Chicago Daily Law Bulletin*, October 9, 2001, p. 2; *New York Times*, October 13, 2001, p. A22 (National Edition) (edited); *Chicago Sun-Times*, October 16, 2001, p. 34. See, on declarations of war, Anastaplo, *The Constitution of 1787*, 333.

64. See, for my letters to the editor on this subject, *Chicago Daily Law Bulletin*, September 10, 1998, p. 2; *New York Times*, September 11, 1998, p. A26 (abridged) (National Edition); *Hickory* (North Carolina) *Daily Record*, September 11, 1998, p. A4; *Chicago Sun-Times*, September 13, 1998, p. 38A.

65. See, on Watergate and Iran/Contra, Anastaplo, *The Constitution of 1787*, pp. 32–33, 312 n. 41, 317–19 n. 85. See, also, note 35, above.

As for both the temptations and the restraints of partisanship: one can imagine how fierce the condemnations of the president in office would have been (at the hands of right-leaning critics) if the terrorist atrocities of September 11, 2001, had taken place before January 20, 2001. Thus, it seems, partisanship can, in some circumstances, make one more moderate and hence more prudent than one might otherwise be? See note 61, above.

Index

About the Contributors

George Anastaplo is professor of law at Loyola University of Chicago, lecturer in the liberal arts at the University of Chicago, and professor emeritus of political science and of philosophy, Dominican University. A prolific author, his most recent books are *The Thinker as Artist: From Homer to Plato and Aristotle; Abraham Lincoln: A Constitutional Biography; Liberty, Equality, and Modern Constitutionalism;* and *But Not Philosophy: Seven Introductions to Non-Western Thought.*

Ronald Beiner is professor of political science at the University of Toronto. He is the author of *Political Judgment* (1983) and editor of *Hannah Arendt's Lectures on Kant's Political Philosophy* (1982). His other books include: *What's the Matter with Liberalism?* (1992); *Theorizing Citizenship* (edited, 1995); *Philosophy in a Time of Lost Spirit: Essays on Contemporary Theory* (1997); *Theorizing Nationalism* (edited, 1999); and *Judgment, Imagination, and Politics: Themes from Kant and Arendt* (coedited, 2001).

Kenneth L. Deutsch is professor of political science at SUNY Geneseo. He has published six books: *Political Obligation and Civil Disobedience; Constitutional Rights; Modern Indian Political Thought; The Crisis of Liberal Democracy: A Straussian Perspective; Leo Strauss: Political Philosopher and Jewish Thinker;* and *Leo Strauss, the Straussians and the American Regime.* Currently he is preparing an introduction to political philosophy text.

Ethan Fishman is professor of political science at the University of South Alabama. His research deals with the application of classic Western ideals to contemporary American politics. Among his publications are: *"Likely Stories": Essays on Political Philosophy and Contemporary American Literature* (1989); *Public Policy and the Public Good* (1991); *The Prudential Presidency: An Aristotelian Approach to Presidential Leadership* (2000); and *George Washington: Foundation of Presidential Leadership and Character* (coedited with Mark J. Rozell and William D. Pederson, 2001).

Joseph R. Fornieri is assistant professor of political science at the Rochester Institute of Technology. He has completed two books on Abraham Lincoln's politics and leadership: an edited version of Lincoln's speeches and writings, and a study of reason and revelation in Lincoln's political thought entitled *Lincoln's Biblical Republicanism.*

Francis Fukuyama is Bernard Schwartz Professor of International Political Economy at the Paul H. Nitze School of Advanced International Studies of Johns Hopkins University. Previously he was a member of the Policy Planning Staff of the U.S. Department of State and a member of the U.S. delegation to the Egyptian-Israeli talks on Palestinian autonomy. His publications include: *The End of History and the Last Man* (1992); *Trust: The Social Virtues and the Creation of Prosperity* (1995); and *The Great Disruption: Human Nature and the Reconstitution of Social Order* (1999). Currently he is working on a book about the political consequences of biotechnology.

Gary D. Glenn is Presidential Teaching Professor of Political Science at Northern Illinois University. He has published on Xenophon's politics, religion and the Constitution, "limited government" in modern political philosophy, teaching political philosophy, and the relation of Catholicism and the American regime in such journals as the *Review of Politics,* the *Journal of Politics, History of European Ideas,* the *Catholic Social Science Review,* the *American Journal of Jurisprudence,* and *Perspectives in Political Science.*

Carnes Lord is professor of strategy at the Center for Naval Warfare Studies, U.S. Naval War College. He has taught international studies and political theory at the University of Virginia and the Fletcher

School of Law and Diplomacy, and has held senior positions in the federal government, most recently as assistant to the vice president for national security affairs. His publications include: a translation of Aristotle's *Politics* (1984); *The Presidency and the Management of National Security* (1988); and *Essays on the Foundations of Aristotelian Political Science* (coedited with David O'Connor, 1991).

Wynne Walker Moskop is associate professor of political science and American studies at Saint Louis University, where she teaches courses in political thought. Her research interests are leadership theory, gender and race in political community, and American political thought and culture. She has published articles and reviews on these topics in *Political Psychology, American Studies,* the *American Political Science Review,* the *Journal of Politics, Quarterly Journal of Ideology, Values and Public Life* (eds. Magill and Hoff), and the *International Encyclopedia of Public Policy and Administration.*

Richard S. Ruderman is associate professor of political science at the University of North Texas. He has written on Aristotle's understanding of prudence, democratic statesmanship, Homer's *Odyssey,* and the roles of parents and the state in education. His articles have appeared in the *American Political Science Review,* the *American Journal of Politics,* the *Review of Politics,* and *Social Research Quarterly.*

Peter J. Stanlis is Distinguished Professor of Humanities, Emeritus, at Rockford College. He also has served on the National Council for the Humanities. His publications on Edmund Burke include twenty-six articles as well as the books: *Edmund Burke and the Natural Law* (1958); *Edmund Burke: A Bibliography of Secondary Studies to 1982* (coauthored with Clara I. Gandy, 1983); and *Edmund Burke: The Enlightenment and Revolution* (1991). For thirteen years he edited *The Burke Newsletter* and *Studies in Burke and His Time.*